# Beyond Brick
## and Bone

# Antoinette M. Schippers

# Beyond Brick and Bone

## A True Ghost Story

**Book One of the
Gatekeeper Series**

Parkhurst Brothers Publishers
MARION, MICHIGAN

**www.parkhurstbrothers.com**

Consumers may order Parkhurst Brothers books from their favorite online or bricks-and-mortar booksellers, expecting prompt delivery. Parkhurst Brothers books are distributed to the trade through the Chicago Distribution Center. Trade and library orders may be placed through Ingram Book Company, Baker & Taylor, Follett Library Resources and other book industry wholesalers. To order from Chicago Distribution Center, phone 1-800-621-2736 or fax to 800-621-8476. Copies of this and other Parkhurst Brothers Publishers titles are available to organizations and corporations for purchase in quantity by contacting Special Sales Department at our home office location, listed on our web site. Manuscript submission guidelines for this publishing company are available at our web site.

Printed in the United States of America
First Edition, 2020
Printing history: 2020    2021    2022 12 11 10 9 8 7 6 5 4 3 2 1

ISBN: Trade Paperback        978-1-62491-150-7
ISBN: e-book                 978-1-62491-149-1

Parkhurst Brothers Publishers believes that the free and open exchange of ideas is essential for the maintenance of our freedoms. We support the First Amendment of the United States Constitution and encourage citizens to study all sides of public policy questions, making up their own minds.

Cover art and design by                          Rachael Davis
Interior design by                               Linda D. Parkhurst, PhD
Proofread by                                     Bill and Barbara Paddack
Acquired for Parkhurst Brothers Publishers
And edited by:                                   Ted Parkhurst

022020

*I dedicate this book to all those who have gone before us, ancestors, family, friends, and those who remain hidden in the shadows. May their lives be remembered, and their stories forever be told.*

# ACKNOWLEDGEMENTS

MANY THANKS TO MY PARENTS AND SIBLINGS with whom I lived and shared the experiences depicted in this book. Thanks also to my husband David, and children Rachael, Zak, Arra, and Ezra who believe me and encouraged me to chronicle this tale. I want to especially thank Arra who told me that this was my story, not just my ghost stories. Her suggestion opened the door to allow the spirits to speak, also Rachael whose poetic contributions and insights helped the full tale emerge. Thanks to Ted and Linda Parkhurst for taking on the task of helping me clarify and craft my words. Mostly, however, I thank the spirits of my childhood who relentlessly forced me to open my mind's eye to see them, and to tell their story, and my own.

# CONTENTS

# FOREWORD

I AWOKE SUDDENLY AND COMPLETELY IN THE WEE HOURS OF THE NIGHT. My sister, asleep in the bed next to me, breathed softly. The solitary light in the room came through a window from the streetlight out front. It cast long shadows across the floor and the bed. I remained perfectly still listening for the sound of someone else awake, hoping to hear a television, or my parents talking softly. I heard nothing. The house lay sleeping. Mostly sleeping. My heart began to beat faster. Moving only my eyes so as to not draw attention to myself, I noticed the carved brass handle on the closet door begin to turn. I held my breath, watching, frozen, unable to move. I was three years old.

The person we become—the way we see the world, and our place in it—is largely shaped by our first experiences. My earliest childhood memories include family, holidays, birthdays, maybe a favorite toy, but my clearest, most vivid memories coalesce around the multiple spirits with whom we shared my childhood home. I learned early on to recognize where the proverbial veil thins, and the things that sometimes slip back and forth through it.

This is something that did not go away for me. I liken it to a color or a smell. Once you've experienced a particular smell or color, you recognize it. If you've never encountered the smell of roses for example you won't recognize the aroma. How could a blind person, someone who has never seen color, be expected to identify magenta even if they are surrounded by it. Seeing spirits came to me as naturally as knowing the color blue. If you've never experienced different dimensions, or the beings who dwell there, you will not recognize them anywhere. If you have, however, the way I did, these "paranormal" things become just another part of the natural world. Knowing their presence, interacting with them, and acknowledging their nature became a part of me from early childhood.

In the pages ahead I will tell you how this came about. I will tell you stories of things that happened day after day, night after night, and year after year. While the stories might seem terrifying at times, as a small child they were just normal occurrences. Though they often made me uncomfortable, startled, or perhaps even frightened, these occurrences simply made up the fabric of my everyday life. These are the events that shaped the way I see the world, the way I see myself. These stories describe a world I know all too well. A world that exists deep in shadow but became clearly visible to me long ago, persisting to this day.

# Part 1

# A House of Spirits

## Origination

(ᴇ-ˌri-jᴇ-ˈnā-shᴇn—*noun* origin, begin, arise)

# Chapter 1
# Engenderment

(en-**jen**-der-mint—*verb*: to be produced or caused; come into existence)

GRANDCHILDREN SPLASHED AND SQUEALED in the inflated kiddie pool in the side yard. I moved my chair a little closer to a large jumble of cedar trees to take advantage of the last bit of available shade as the sun rose higher and higher on a hot July day. I had volunteered to keep watch over my grandchildren as they cooled off in the shallow pool. Beads of sweat gathered at my temples as I sipped a tall glass of ice water.

"Let's go play on the swings!" One of the five-year-old twins suggested enthusiastically.

Without hesitation, all four children clambered off to the backyard. I listened as they called dibs on swings and other playthings. With my lifeguard duties on hold I took a long drink of the cool, refreshing water and decided to enjoy a few precious moments of quiet.

Turning my attention to the cedars I noticed the varied tints and shades of green in the leaves, darker toward the branch but lighter near the edges, providing evidence of new growth. While most people respond "green", when asked the color of trees, I describe an abundance of varied hues, tints and tones that make up that "green."

Inhaling deeply, I shifted my focus to the scent of the cedars. I love that fragrance, and how it grows more pungent and aromatic on hot, humid summer days. Rising to return to the house, I paused to enjoy the aroma.

As I lingered, buzzing sounds grew more pronounced from inside the thick foliage. Before long several distinct pitches indicated the presence of a bumblebee along with several other smaller flying insects that occupied the space just beyond the fingers of the cedars.

An unseen bird called from the upper branches, then with a flutter of wings, flew off. Dry leaves rustled below as something skittered over roots and ground debris. I stood listening closely, enjoying the sounds, when a patrol of honeybees flew past disappearing into the dark depths of a world teeming with life just beyond my view.

Standing in the hot summer sun, I reflected on a multitude of hidden worlds just beyond immediate perception. I recalled frequently witnessing things both seen and unseen by allowing my attention to stray to the often-hidden so very nearby. Sometimes those hidden worlds brought wonder, even delight, but other times what existed just out of sight brought terror and menace.

⌒

I grew up in the middle of the twentieth century as the third child in an Irish Catholic family of ten. My brothers, sisters, and I were the fourth generation of my father's family to live in a two-story Victorian house on the northwest side of Chicago. It belonged to my great-grandmother whose own mother had bought it for her and her new husband as a wedding present in the late 1800s.

By the time I came along, ninety-year-old Great-Grandma Lyons could no longer manage the house, and so had been moved to a rest home in Wisconsin close to her eldest daughter, Theresa. Then my parents, along with their two toddlers, (eleven months apart), and myself moved in. I was only a few months old. Our rental payment covered the cost of my great-grandmother's care at the rest home. It was the only home I knew for all of my young childhood.

My father's mother, Angela Marie, had been born in, and grew up in "our" house. When we moved in Grandma Angela lived next door with her unmarried brother, Uncle Jack. Angela's mother had built the small brick house for her and her two little boys, Dave, and his younger brother Jerry in the early 1940's, they moved in after her marriage to my grandfather dissolved in a cauldron of alcohol and anger.

Angela Marie—my father's mother—was born in 1905 in an upstairs room of the house in the Portage Park neighborhood of Chicago. Angela spent her childhood navigating a growing and quickly changing city in the dawn of a new century surrounded by her extended Irish Catholic family. She was the second child, born five years after her sister Teresa, to be followed by three younger brothers.

Angela's mother raised her to be a proper lady, though she preferred to run and play with her brothers. She learned quickly that as a girl, certain expectations needed to be met. Her life lay ahead of her like beads on the rosary that she prayed sincerely and dutifully every evening. She asked the Blessed Virgin Mary for grace to fulfill the life that God Almighty had in store for her.

When she met David, her future husband, she was first struck by his stature. Side by side he stood noticeably taller and lankier than her father and brothers. A thick head of dark hair that he wore slicked back from his face accentuating his dark brow. His bright blue eyes were ablaze with vignettes of hope-filled days in a promising future. His easy smile and sharp wit were icing on the proverbial cake. She enjoyed his company and felt proud to be seen with such a handsome and attentive young man. Her parents, on the other hand, were not so sure about this fellow who was not, after all, Irish. Over time, however, his charming nature and quick humor warmed them to him.

Angela knew what to expect from a wedding. She and her mother visited the seamstress to measure for her dress. They planned the food and drinks. They talked about flowers and guests. She knew that she and her fiancé would have to meet with the parish priest for Pre-Cana counseling. At the meeting, she listened closely to the priest as he reminded her that she would be expected to perform all her wifely duties. She knew how to cook and keep a house, so she happily agreed to the only wifely duties within her experience. David and Angela promised to raise their children in the church and always remain devout. The priest blessed them and said a prayer that they would have many children. She smiled shyly at her soon-to-be-husband, unsure of just how that would happen, but stilled her trepidation knowing that the Blessed Mother would keep and protect her in all things. She knew children came from God but had little or no understanding of just how God administered the wonders of procreation.

~

Angela and David married in their parish church, then celebrated with family and friends in the house in which she grew up. They left the party to begin their new life as a married couple. On the honeymoon, when her husband suggested she get fully undressed, Angela turned crimson with shock and embarrassment. Her mother had embroidered a lovely white nightgown for her, and she intended to dress in that, buttoning it all the way up to her chin. She also intended to wear pretty new bloomers under it since she knew she would have to now share a bed with her new husband. She did not see anything funny as he laughed out loud when he saw her after she told him he could come into the room.

He came to her nearly naked with liquor on his breath. His large, rough hands found places no one—not even she—had ever touched. She pulled away from him and clung to her nightgown, pulling it tightly around her.

"*Stop it!*" she shouted, "*What do you think you are doing.*"

He looked stunned. She *had* agreed to perform her wifely duties. Still, seeing her fear, he softened.

"It's okay, dear wife," he said. "There is no hurry."

He leaned in and kissed her long on her mouth. The taste made her stomach turn. She realized that he noticed her repulsion. Clutching a half-empty bottle of whiskey, he sat in a chair across the room as Angela quickly leapt into bed—pulling the quilts up tightly to her chin.

Thus began a marriage that lasted just over ten years. Though two sons came of it, Angela hated when he touched her. She performed her wifely duties rarely and with her eyes shut tight and her clothes still on her body. Not once in all those tumultuous years did Angela allow her husband to see her *naked.*

Throughout their volatile marriage, my grandfather drank more and more, which brought with it a meanness that he often turned on his little boys. One Sunday afternoon, in a drunken rage, he made his sons, age four and six, watch as he burned their beloved stuffed bear, Michael Doll Bernice, in the backyard burn barrel. For good measure, he tossed in any other toys he deemed "not manly enough." Davy— later my father—and his younger brother stood holding hands as they watched in silent horror as their father stumbled back toward the house screaming in slurred speech for his wife while flames consumed their beloved stuffed bear.

My Grandma Angela pushed her husband further and further away until at last she pushed him entirely from the home. Her brothers, two Chicago police officers who lived with their widowed mother in their large, Victorian house, made sure that Angela and her two little boys were cared for and safe in the little brick bungalow in the side yard. When my grandfather left, my father's uncles told him that he, as the big brother, was now the man in the family. Since they replaced his own father and became his male role models growing up, my father took this to heart and hid all grief and weakness throughout his entire life.

Angela refused to give her estranged husband a divorce because she knew the church forbade it. She took great comfort in her church and dedicated her life to becoming an exemplary Catholic. She believed that the greatest thing she could do for the church was to raise a priest. My father, Davy, had a quick mind and a very pious disposition as a youngster. She made sure her sons both served as altar boys but took special care to connect her eldest to the parish priests. They spent many hours with him, sharing theological books and essays. Before puberty, my father decided he had "the vocation."

Grandma Angela took great pride in telling the other parish ladies that her boy, Dave, planned to become a priest. He passed the entrance exams and began studying at Quigley Seminary as a very young adolescent. He lived at home because his mother needed him, but studied throughout high school with the Jesuits, taking his initial vows after several years of study. Then he met a girl.

⌒

Young Dave was friends with the girl's cousins, Clarence and Ann Marie, who introduced them at a party one weekend. Dave and the girl, Jackie, struck up a conversation. After several hours it seemed as though no time had passed, and they realized that all the other guests had left. They laughed and parted without plans, but both hoped to meet again at another party.

Young Dave—who would become my father—and Jackie, who would become my mother—were smitten.

Jackie asked her cousin, Ann Marie, for more information about the intriguing, handsome young man, Dave. Ann Marie told her that he attended the seminary, studying to be a priest. Jackie knew that this should render him off-limits, but something about him took up residence in her thoughts. Constantly.

Jackie talked about Dave all week with her girlfriends at Saint Scholastica Catholic Girls High School. She told them about the way he made her feel as he looked into her eyes while discussing everything from ancient history and Shakespeare to politics and religion. Her friends listened, giggled, and called her Mrs. David Schippers. She left off the part about him attending seminary. The next weekend Jackie called Ann Marie hoping for another opportunity to see Dave.

Dave found himself unable to shake feelings that troubled him. He thought about Jackie from morning to night, finding himself picturing her beautiful green eyes, and sparkling smile. Lying in his bed in the room he shared with his younger brother, Dave imagined how soft her curly hair would feel in his fingers, how her lips might taste. As his body responded to thoughts of her, Dave quickly reached for his rosary. He had dedicated himself to the Church. He knew he needed to put lustful thoughts out of his head, but when he finished his prayers, and kissed the crucifix, he again imagined Jackie's lips. The next weekend, Dave called Clarence, hoping—longing—for another opportunity to see Jackie.

As Jackie descended the basement stairs to the rec room where her cousins and friends gathered, she scanned the room for Dave as nonchalantly as possible. Her heart jumped and her face flushed as she spotted him standing at the back of the room with a group of other boys. Then he saw her. Their eyes locked and involuntarily they headed straight for each other. She knew at that moment that her friends' teasing may not have been too far off the mark.

They left the others behind and went out back to sit on the back stoop where they talked for hours. Dave told Jackie that he attended the seminary, but then he reached for her hand.

"I'm not a priest yet," he told her. Then, looking down at their hands, he said, "Maybe I never will be a priest."

At the sound of those words, Jackie felt overcome with joy. She believed that she could love Dave for the rest of her life but felt guilty and sinful for desiring him. She feared that perhaps their love would rob the church of a wonderful priest.

At the end of the evening, Ann Marie offered to drive them both home. She dropped Dave off first. Jackie wanted more than anything for him to kiss her good night, but instead he took her hand as if to shake it, smiling sheepishly.

"I will call you," he said, turning to almost skip up the sidewalk to his front door.

As soon as they drove off, Ann Marie barraged Jackie with questions.

"Well looks like The Church will have to do with one less priest!" She laughed.

The next day Jackie went to confession. She spoke to the priest about how guilty she felt falling in love with a seminarian. The priest asked if the young man felt the same. She told him that she believed he did. The priest told her that no one knows God's plan, and that perhaps their love would result in the birth of a dozen priests. He told her that she should not feel guilty but promise to raise their family grounded in The Church. This gave her peace of mind.

Dave called Jackie and asked her out on the next weekend. On their first official date, Dave and Jackie went to the movies and saw the brand-new Disney feature film, "Cinderella." They held hands throughout the entire picture. Afterwards they walked along Milwaukee Avenue. Still-hand-in-hand, repeating the little mutterings of the mice from the movie, they stared into each other's eyes. Out of this conversation grew the pet names by which they knew each other until their dying days. That night, Dave walked Jackie to the door and kissed her. She wrapped her arms around his neck and kissed him deeply.

Jackie and Dave courted one another with passion and vigor. Jackie invited him to escort her to her senior prom. Angela became extremely suspicious of this woman who had designs on her son, the soon-to-be priest. She saw not only her status in the community, but a sure ticket to Heaven, dissolving before her eyes.

Dave remained at Quigley for another year while Jackie worked as a typist in her father's factory. They grew more and more entwined until at last Dave realized that he could never choose a life without Jackie. He withdrew from the seminary and took a job.

When they told my grandmother, Angela, that they wanted to get married, she grew livid! She couldn't fathom that my father, her son, could fall into the clutches of such a woman. She refused to speak my mother's name and referred to her as "That Woman" for many years until the end of her life when my mother cared for her so kindly.

Jackie and Dave married in April and had a reception at Jackie's home. They left the next day to drive to Wisconsin to stay with family friends for their honeymoon. In the car, in an attempt to disguise the fact that they had just married, Jackie didn't sit up against Dave. At every gas station and diner, however, someone congratulated them. Finding this hilarious, they agreed that they would have to downplay their affection for one another if they wanted to look like old married people.

When they returned, they rented a small apartment not too far from their parents and began their life together. The next year, their family began to grow.

When my great-grandmother's house became available, my parents still lived in their cramped second floor apartment. I had just been born, and a new baby along with a one-year-old and two-year-old filled the space to overflowing. Reluctantly, my mother agreed to move into the spacious family home next door to her resentful and bitter mother-in-law.

As a very little girl, my immediate world consisted of my house, Grandma's adjoining yard with her small, brick house, and all the relatives who visited. By the age of two, I had become fully conversational, much to the amazement and entertainment of my grownup relatives. I remember them positioning me on Grandma's dining room table to recite a bawdy poem beginning," Adam was the first man that ever was invented...."

They would laugh and applaud tiny me performing amazing feats of language beyond what one would expect from a chubby toddler. I loved the attention.

Our family grew by a baby a year. We scraped by, sacrificing so my father could attend law school at night while working full time at the phone company. He often came home tired—and sometimes volatile.

Mommy tended all the household tasks. She was a whirlwind, sweeping, mopping, dusting, planning and preparing meals, bathing, dressing, and raising a rapidly expanding brood. When I picture my mother as a young woman, I only see her pregnant with a baby on her hip and a skillet or mop in her hand. The demands of a young and growing family along with the stress of limited resources drove my parents to frequent, raucous arguments that often resulted in Daddy breaking a dish, vase, or a wooden chair.

One evening I clearly recall how Daddy flew into a rage. Quickly jumping out of harm's way, I realized I had left my favorite plastic toy horse on the couch. My eyes began to fill with tears as he picked it up ready to fling it at the living room wall.

"Daddy!" I pleaded.

His eyes met mine. He dropped the treasured toy onto the cushion, picked up a tumbler from the coffee table and launched that instead. As he stormed from the room, I snatched my horse from the couch and ran, clutching it to my chest, into the kitchen and the safety of my mother.

I learned very early on to monitor my parents' verbal sparring, watchful for any sign of trouble in order to get out of the way of danger before it spun out of control. I learned to read my parents' moods and to never test my mother's patience lest she swoop me up for a painful, harsh and humiliating lickin'. As a middle child, I paid close attention to the emotional temperature of my family in order to avoid attracting any trouble.

I vividly remember one morning when I was about two years old playing with little cars on the front room floor while my parents argued far off in the kitchen. I tried to tune them out, while remaining aware enough to move quickly if their fight spilled into the front room.

Davy, my rambunctious three-year-old big brother, ran a loop through the front room, into the hall, through the dining room then back around again growling loud engine noises. As he ran, he stretched out his hand to touch every surface or person he passed.

Kate, the oldest sister, sat on the couch comforting a baby doll in her arms—shushing, and telling it not to worry, that she would take good care of her. At four, Kate seemed nearly grown-up compared to two-year-old me. The way she lorded over us, ordering my brother and me about, demonstrated that she probably felt grown-up herself.

I observed the two of them for a time, then returned to playing with small toy cars and tiny plastic army guys that I pretended were a family. I tried stuffing them into the cars so they could ride to Grammie Ethel and Gramps' house.

While focusing on the little blue metal car stuffed with green plastic guys that I rolled back and forth on the ancient threadbare rug, I suddenly heard a clear, deep voice say my name right next to my ear. Startled, I turned quickly in its direction to find *nobody there.*

Neither Kate nor Davy gave any sign that they heard someone speak. My parents' voices had quieted, indicating that their argument had ended, so I turned my attention back to my toys. Seconds later the same voice spoke more menacingly. This time I could feel its breath in my ear. My whole little body shuddered with the chill of it. Still it seemed that no one else heard or felt that voice.

Though uncomfortable, and feeling vulnerable, I accepted the voice as part of the natural world that I was still discovering. This was my first experience of witnessing something reach out from a hidden world that others didn't notice. Just like the world beyond the cedar leaves. It was my first conscious encounter with a parallel spirit-world.

# Chapter 2
# Concealed

(kuh n-**seeld**—*verb*: to hide; withdraw or remove from observation;
cover or keep from sight)

BY THE TIME I WAS THREE YEARS OLD, voices from just beyond my view
became a regular occurrence. Soon, other things began making themselves known to not just me, but to my siblings as well. I learned that
sometimes things could happen nearby, that I, myself, could not see, but
that someone else clearly could. This was the case on an early summer
evening when I was four years old.

After a long and full day of playing in the backyard dirt, alley, and
under the front porch, we heeded our mother's call to come in and
wash our hands and faces for supper. Kate, Davy, Annie, and I cleaned
up leaving a muddy mess in the bathroom sink, on the washcloth, and
the hand towel. We sat down at the table with the baby nearby in a
well-worn wooden highchair. We never hesitated to devour whatever
my exhausted mother put on our plates. Fortunately for her, one of
our favorite treats consisted of cold green beans right out of the can.
I remember her spooning them in heaps onto our plates along with a
small piece of meat and mounds of rice with gravy made from adding
water and garlic salt to the pan drippings. We knew never to ask for
seconds of meat, but we could always eat as much rice or green beans
as we liked. When we needed more gravy, my mother would add salt,
garlic, and more water to the cast iron skillet and stir furiously on high
heat creating a diluted brown au jus.

My mother sat at the table with us, but rarely fixed a plate for herself. Instead she fed the baby, while nibbling off the baby's plate. My father attended night school after working a full shift at the phone company, so he never joined us for the evening meal, but ate his supper from his lap in the front room long after we had gone to bed. Even on weekends when he was home, he maintained this pattern to "not upset his system". I had no idea what that meant but knew that it would be a very bad thing if it happened.

Lively conversation, laughter, teasing, and sometimes a fracas or two ensued at suppertime. None of us needed prodding to join The Clean Plate Club but happily gobbled up every morsel. After supper we helped in the kitchen, clearing the table while my mother stored leftovers on a dish towel-covered plate for my father. We took turns washing, drying, and putting away the dishes. Then we could play until my mother cleaned up, put pajamas on the baby, and settled her down in her crib in the upstairs room.

On one particular night, my mother seemed especially exhausted. I knew this because she told us that it would be a bubble bath night. Bubble bath nights meant that all of us got in the tub at the same time. We all clamored upstairs to the master bedroom which all the children shared together. My parents took the small room at the end of the hall as their own. In the larger, L- shaped, "master" bedroom at the front of the house, they lined up three twin beds and a crib.

We stepped out of our dirty clothes and shoes, getting right down to our skin as my mother turned on the bathwater and gave it two good squirts of dish soap. We all watched with anticipation as the water poured in and the bubbles began to rise in the tub.

Somehow my big sister Kate never seemed to get dirty. She could even eat spaghetti without getting a morsel on her fingers, face, or even her blouse. It always amazed me to watch her eat and not drop a single bite. She never even appeared dirty after playing outside. On the hottest days her face might look sweaty, but it was never grimy like mine or my other siblings'. She always looked cleaner than the rest of us, knew more than us, and pretty much lorded over her younger siblings in every single thing. Kate was absolutely, without question, the epitome of a big sister.

"Mommy!" She asked, "Do I *really* have to get in the tub with *them?*"

I stood naked and exposed with my big brother, Dave, and little sister, Annie with filthy hands, face and feet. The only parts of our bodies that were not grime-covered were the parts hidden throughout the day by shirts and shorts.

My mother began to laugh as she carefully considered my big sister Kate, standing haughtily with her hands on her hips.

"No. Of course not. Just make sure your dirty laundry gets in the hamper before you put on your pajamas."

The way my sister, only two years older, questioned our mother's orders, and actually got rewarded with a reasonable response, seemed nothing short of a miracle. I couldn't wait to grow older like her, but right now a warm bubble bath with suds well over the tub rim awaited!

I climbed gleefully into the warm soapy water. My brother Davy splashed as he leapt in next to me. My mother lifted little Annie in beside us, and the bath-time play ensued. As we made bubble beards and hats, Mommy knelt beside the tub cracking up at our antics. "I really don't want to see the color of this water when you kids get out," she laughed, rinsing soap from our hair.

We played happily while the water cooled, and the dirt and grime soaked away. Mommy pulled the plug, then lifted little Annie from the tub into a waiting towel. She scrubbed Annie's little body dry, and—with a gentle pat on her behind—sent her off to clean pajamas on the bed. Next, she reached for me.

As the water sank lower, suds circled the drain. I watched my brother's expression change to melancholy as he tenderly held handfuls of soap bubbles safely clear of the drain. Tearfully, he asked Mommy if the bubbles would die and go away forever as they disappeared down the drain. My towel drying ended abruptly as Mommy turned to console him. "Oh Davy, you have such a gentle heart." she said as she embraced him, tears filling his eyes. "The bubbles don't die and go away. They go down the drain to see all their other bubble friends."

Davy seemed comforted by this image. I, on the other hand, knew for a fact that all things do indeed die.... But I also knew that not all things go away. Sometimes things die, and never go away.

We pulled on our pajamas and climbed into the twin beds that lined the wall, dormitory style. Kate had her own bed closest to the front window and the bathroom door. Davy also had his own bed next to the hallway door and the closet. Annie and I shared the middle twin. This was just fine with me. I had no desire to sleep alone in a bed in that noisy house. The baby crib stood across the room on the wall shared with the hallway.

The sun still stood high in the summer sky as my mother tucked us in and kissed us goodnight. Though she felt more than ready for *us* to go to bed, we, of course, had a different idea.

When she left the room, we listened for her footsteps on the staircase as she headed back downstairs to finish her seemingly endless chores before my father came home. We waited a few minutes to make sure she had gone well out of earshot, then began laughing and playing. I leapt from my bed to Davy's and back amid my big sister's admonishments to keep it down lest Mommy hear us and come up to give us all a lickin'.

We tried to keep it down, but sleep was clearly not imminent. As we giggled and jumped from bed to bed, little Annie suddenly became agitated. She fixed her deep eyes on the corner of the room between the front window and the bathroom door and began to cry.

"Go get Mommy." She cried softly.

"What did you do to Annie?" Kate scolded me, "Did you jump on her or something?"

"No!" I protested, "I didn't touch her."

Annie's eyes never left the corner of the room. We all became very still, and a slight panic began to rise in my chest. I looked where she stared and saw nothing, but I knew that didn't mean a thing. We had all seen things that weren't there.... All the time. We gathered on Annie's and my bed.

"Stop it." Kate said, grabbing her by the shoulders, "What's wrong? You're scaring us."

"Go get Mommy! Go get Mommy!" She cried more forcefully, with unblinking eyes.

"MOMMY! MOMMY!" We all shouted at once. Annie grew more and more agitated, beginning to hyperventilate.

"Okay ... together ... One. Two. Three ... MOMMY!"

We heard nothing from downstairs. She couldn't hear us.

"Louder!" Kate instructed.

"ONE. TWO. THREE. "**MOMMY!**"

Still no answer. We all looked at the door to the hallway frantically waiting to see The Slinky Lady, a familiar presence, glide past the door so we would know it was safe to go get our mother. We watched for what seemed like forever, but she never appeared. By this time, we had all grown terrified, panicked, and in tears.

"I'll go get Mommy." brother Dave said as he leapt from the safety of the pile of us huddled half on top of one another on the bed.

He flew from the room and ran screaming for my mother. Flying around the corner of the railing he raced down the eighteen stairs in seconds. Together, he and Mommy came sprinting into the room to find us all terrified—every one of us staring where Annie's unflinching gaze directed.

"Oh dear, what's going on?" Mommy approached the bed as all of us began to sob and cling to her in terror.

"Annie? What's wrong? Are you sick?" Mommy sat down on the bed. We all attached ourselves to her body as she gently picked up Annie. When she lifted her into her lap, Annie craned her neck to continue her unbroken gaze at the corner of the room.

Never changing her fixation Annie sobbed, "Mommy, there's a man in the corner. Tell him to go away. There's a man in the corner!"

We all looked into that corner. The light poured in from the front window, and from the bathroom adjacent. I saw no man but had no doubt whatsoever that she did.

"There's nobody in the corner." My mother said. "You were probably dreaming."

"He's there!" She screamed, pointing.

"Where? There's nobody there!" My mother replied. "Look. I'll show you." She set Annie back on the bed as her horrified gaze remained fixed unflinchingly on the corner of the room.

My mother bravely walked to the corner and flailed her arms from side to side. "See? There's nothing here."

Suddenly Annie let out a penetrating shriek and leapt from the bed. She ran, screaming like a banshee, past Mommy into the bathroom.

"What in the name of God are you doing?" Mommy's concern grew as Annie ran to the linen closet at the head of the bathtub.

We all rushed after them to the bathroom door to watch two-year-old Annie pull towels, sheets, and washcloths from the linen closet, and fling them over her head.

"Stop that right now!" Mommy tried to pull Annie out of the torrent of clean linens. "What is wrong with you? Have you gone crazy?"

"He's in here!" Annie shouted frantically. "He's in here! I'm going to find him and show you! He's in here!"

"Stop this. Stop right this minute." Mommy picked Annie up and carried her back to bed. She made us all climb back into our own beds and tucked us in for a second time that night. She sat on the bed with Annie and me for a long time, until we fell at last to sleep.

The next day, we couldn't wait to tell our father how Annie went crazy trying to find the man in the bathroom linen closet. Dad, chuckling, assured us that it must have been none other than the leprechaun that had troubled our family ever since our Great Grandma Annie Murphy tricked him into a wish, and out of his shillelagh. This story made perfect sense to our young minds and comforted us. For many years we talked about the time Annie saw the leprechaun run into the linen closet.

Though Annie was the only one who saw the man in the corner *that* night, there were things that we *all* saw, together, night after night. Every night.

# Chapter 3

# Recurrence

(ri-ˈkɘr- ɛ n(t)s—*noun*: an act or instance of recurring, return to a
previous condition, habit, subject, etc.)

ONE NIGHT MY BIG SISTER, KATE, JOSTLED ME AWAKE in the bed I shared
with my little sister. My big brother Davy, and sisters Annie and Colleen
breathed deeply as they slept nearby.

"I forgot to go to the bathroom before bed." Kate whispered,
"Will you watch for me?"

She shook her legs proving her dire need to go. The light burned
brightly in the bathroom, spilling into the hallway and bedroom. It
would take her only a few short steps to get from the bed to the bathroom, and yet I immediately agreed to be her lookout. My brothers,
sisters and I had an unspoken pact. We never, ever left each other alone
in that house, day or night, but especially at night.

"Okay I'm here," I replied rubbing my eyes, and sitting up as she
squeezed into the small bed next to Annie and me.

Though the temperature in the room felt normal I began to shiver
due to the late hour and having been suddenly woken from a deep
sleep. We huddled together silently, staring at the doorway toward the
empty hall.

Before long, the front edge of a woman appeared. At first, we
could see her face and the front of her body in silhouette. She appeared
illuminated by some strange other-worldly white light that seemed to
emanate from behind her. She manifested merely as an outline gliding
slowly and deliberately down the hallway from the stairs toward the

bathroom. We saw her take one step, then another, and another, never looking down, never looking from side to side, never breaking her stride. With each step the light seemed to spread out behind her, then catch up much like a popular toy at the time. *The Slinky Lady.*

Neither of us moved. We watched her walk past the bedroom door then disappear toward the bathroom at the end of the hall. The bathroom had two doors, one opened to the hallway and the other into the bedroom. Though we could see The Slinky Lady clearly in the hallway, we never saw her actually in the bathroom through the door to our bedroom no matter how tightly we would squint, or how hard we would try.

Shivering side-by-side we waited. Waited counting silently in our minds, *one one thousand, two one thousand, three one thousand ... eleven–twelve–thirteen one thousand....* Like clockwork, at fourteen her face began to appear again on the other side of the bedroom door, this time facing in the opposite direction toward the top of the stairs.

She wore a long white gown and her thick hair fell down her back. She seemed to be a small, slight woman who did not appear particularly frightening, though somehow, we knew better than to run into her in the hall or on the stairs. We did not know if she could see us, but we had no intention of drawing attention to ourselves in her presence. It just made more sense to all of us to keep quiet and stay out of her way.

After she glided out of view past the doorway heading back toward the stairs, we waited several seconds.

"Go!" I whispered just a little too loudly than I intended.

Kate leapt from the bed and sprinted to the bathroom. She wasted no time closing the door, as if she wanted privacy. She knew I didn't watch her but kept vigil with my eyes fixed on the door to the hallway, counting steadily.

Growing more and more nervous I continued counting under my breath ... *fifty-five one thousand, fifty-six ...* "Hurry!" I called out in the loudest whisper I could muster.

I heard the toilet flush, then my sister flew from the bathroom, jumping back into her own bed and under the covers just in the nick of time. As soon as she had jumped safely in bed, out of breath, with both our hearts beating just a little too fast, we pulled our covers up to our chins just in time to see The Slinky Lady appear again in the doorway. Though we really had no need to count out her disappearance and reappearance again we did. She appeared, disappeared, and reappeared again and again at the exact same interval, hour after hour, night after night, and year after year throughout my entire childhood.

Even in the summertime, when my mother put us to bed well before the sun set, The Slinky Lady still walked endlessly up and down, and back and forth. We knew she never stopped. We could feel it. We also knew that for some reason unknown to us we just usually couldn't actually *see* her with our eyes during the day, or else perhaps we simply didn't pay attention to her during the busy daily bustle. Even at those times, in the middle of the boisterously active days in a large family with many young children we never dared linger in her path.... Just in case.

〜

"HOLD THE RAILING AND WALK!" my father would yell from the living room every time he heard us on the stairs. We *always* held fast to the railing, but seldom walked down the eighteen stairs. Without knowing for sure that we would not run into The Slinky Lady, we took no chances wasting time with careful footsteps. My father's wrath actually seemed a much more predictable option than coming face to face unexpectedly with *her*.

As more babies joined the family and we got older, my sister Kate and I moved from the big room to a smaller one at the end of the hall. We shared not only the room but the bed as well. The room had two small windows facing the back alley close to the slanted ceiling where the eave came down, and another larger window close to the floor that faced our neighbor's house. It had an unsettling entryway that was actually a short alcove between the bedroom and the main upstairs hall with a door on both ends. The room also had a closet that it shared with the large front bedroom. It would have been a great place to slip through, if it was not so frightening.

Having a large family to tend, Mommy created a system of chores and expectations in which even the youngest of us participated. One of those chores involved putting away our own clean laundry.

At that time girls could only wear dresses to school, and every dress needed to be starched and ironed on the weekend. Even my brother needed dress clothes for school, so Mom had to iron his and my father's dress shirts and pants. With so many children, starching and ironing became an enormous, exhausting task for Mommy. She expected us to hang our school dresses in the closet as soon as she finished with them. If we neglected even a single item of clean clothing, so that it got wrinkled, she would mete out swift and severe punishment.

My sister and I had devised a ritual for hanging up our school dresses on Sunday evening. We always worked together, especially in the winter months when the sun set early. One of us would stand in front of the closet door to make certain it could not accidentally close, while the other quickly grabbed empty hangers. Then we slammed the closet door tightly shut. We put the dresses on the hangers. Next, we determined who would hold the door open, and who would hang. Hanging dresses meant stepping all the way into the dark closet, a truly terrifying prospect. For some odd reason that only my big sister knew, I usually seemed to lose the "Eeny-Meeny-Miney-Mo" to her, so hanging most often fell to me. She would pick up all the dresses on their hangers and instruct me to open the closet door. Taking a deep breath and steeling my resolve I would reach for the door handle.

"Stand there," I instructed with great seriousness, "Hand me one at a time, and don't move until I am all the way out."

Next, as quickly and carefully as possible, so none would fall off the hanger thereby prolonging the task, I hung up those dresses. With the last one safely hanging on the bar, I would jump back out of the closet. Together, we would slam the door, then turn and run as fast as we could, trying to outrun the other to the stairs. Sprinting down as quickly as possible to the never-ending sound of "HOLD THE RAILING AND WALK!" booming from my father in the front room.

One evening my mother handed me our dresses—instructing me to take them upstairs to hang them up. "Where's Kate?" I asked not intending to go upstairs or near that closet alone.

"She already took a pile up, now go ... scoot:"

Not seeing Kate in the front room with the others, and expecting to find her upstairs, I carried the dresses to our room. Our *empty* room. Frightened to find myself upstairs alone, I laid the dresses carefully on the bed and headed out of the room as fast as possible, foolishly not waiting to see if The Slinky Lady had passed.

Halfway down the stairs I saw my sister just inside the front room. I stopped to call to her. "Kate, come on, Mom wants us to hang up the dresses."

"I took up the stuff for the dresser. Mom said you should hang up the dresses."

"That's not fair!" I pleaded. "I'm not going into the closet alone. Come up and hold the door ... PLEASE!"

Thankfully, she took pity on me and started through the front room entryway towards the stairs. I began to turn to go back up ahead of her, but *before I could turn*, I let go of the railing for a split second only to feel two strong hands flat on my back pushing with such force that my feet left the stairs altogether. I flew toward a tall antique china cabinet at the bottom of the stairs, missing five or six stairs completely. I tumbled and crashed full-on into that china cabinet. It fell on top of me, the glass doors shattered, and all the fragile dishes and glassware displayed inside rained down upon me.

Kate stood frozen in the downstairs hall screaming uncontrollably at the top of her voice. My parents rushed past her, as she continued screaming. I lay in shock among the mass of shattered glass beneath the heavy cabinet.

"Don't move." My mother said urgently as she and my father

carefully lifted the cabinet off my small body. "Keep your eyes closed, there's glass everywhere."

I shut my eyes tightly as instructed but began to whimper.

"Davey pushed me! Davey pushed me!" I cried.

I believed that my older brother was the only one who could move quickly enough, and who had enough force to send me flying. But when I finally opened my eyes, I saw Davey standing wide-eyed in shocked silence behind Kate with the rest of my little sisters looking on from behind them.

"She just flew!" Kate screamed repeatedly amid sobs, "She just flew off the stairs into the china cabinet!"

My parents gingerly extricated me from that shattered mass of glass, and splintered wood. I didn't cry. I barely moved as my father's strong hands lifted the cabinet out of the way. My mother gently coaxed me up from the floor while asking, as she searched for blood or broken bones, if I was alright. She took me into the front room and sat me on her lap as she gingerly combed through my glass-laden hair, carefully removing many small shards from my skin and clothes. Later my mother took us upstairs to put us to bed. The dresses remained carefully arranged at the foot of our bed.

Kate still appeared distraught, and though without any serious injury, I remained extremely shaken as my mother tucked the bed covers securely around us.

"Davy pushed me down the stairs and he didn't even get punished," I implored.

"Davy was *not* on the stairs." Mom replied, "There was no one upstairs. You must've just lost your balance."

"No," I insisted, "I felt hands on my back! *Somebody* pushed me!"

"She didn't fall," Kate added, "She flew! She wouldn't jump off the stairs. I saw her back arch!"

"Shhhh," my mother spoke soothingly, "All's well, now just close your eyes."

Her expression, however, revealed a rare hint of concern as she stroked my hair. Neither my sister nor I said another word as my mother got up and hung up our dresses herself. Then she sat down again on the edge of our bed and with her strong hand lovingly stroked my back, softly humming "Doh Doh My Baby" as I drifted off to sleep.

The china cabinet disappeared that night along with all the broken glass and dishes. Though I survived without any major injury, we now all knew exactly what could happen if we met The Slinky Lady on the stairs. Though my parents referred to the incident as the time I fell down the stairs, my brothers, sisters, and I always spoke of it as the time I got pushed down the stairs. From that day forward we always held the railing tightly, but we never ever paused on the stairs, and we NEVER walked.

# Chapter 4

# Forlorn

(fɘr-'lȯrn–*adjective,* lonely and sad; forsaken. Expressive of hopelessness; despairing: bereft; destitute)

I AWOKE. The only visible light in the room came from the streetlight in front of our house. It shone indirectly through the window set close to the floor to the left. It fell across the length of the bed, barely illuminating the room. The slim shard of light from the window offered no real comfort. In fact, it only served to enhance the depth and blackness of the shadows.

Kate breathed softly next to me. We pressed our bodies firmly against one another in the middle of the full-sized bed. She lay on her side with her back to me, and I was on my back. Terrified, I remained perfectly still, listening and hoping to hear someone—anyone else who might still be awake. I prayed desperately to hear the sound of the television down in the front room, or my parents' voices talking softly in their own bed, but I heard only the sound of my sister's breathing. The house lay sleeping ... mostly sleeping ... except for me and whatever else watched or moved through that foreboding night.

My sisters, brothers, and I spent most of our waking hours making sure we never found ourselves alone anyplace in that house. Nighttime simply ramped up that urgency. At bedtime we even attempted to synchronize falling asleep. Kate and I would scoot as close to the center of the bed as possible, facing outward. We snuggled up to one another pressing our backs together. We always pulled our blankets, or a light sheet on hot nights, tightly over our shoulders, covering our necks and as much of our heads and faces as we could while still allowing an opening for breathing. We made certain to tuck our hands safely under the pillow or covers, leaving nothing exposed. Any bare skin left out would almost certainly be touched or tickled as we slept. Along with this nightly ritual, Kate and I also obsessed about closing the closet door tightly and securely.

"Did you close the door?" we asked each other night after night.

Taking turns, we hopped back out of bed to tug on the closet door handle directly opposite the foot of the bed making sure it held fast and couldn't accidentally swing open. After we each checked, sometimes more than once, we would begin to slow our breathing whispering, "Sleep ... sleep," until we drifted off listening to the fading whisper of the other.

On one particular night however, I found my unfortunate self wide awake and alone in the dark and sleeping house. Moving only my eyes in order to not draw any undue attention to myself, I attempted to use the tricks my mother had taught us to soothe myself back to sleep. Imagining my body as a bag of sand with a tiny hole in the top of my head I visualized the sand slowly draining from that tiny hole as I relaxed my toes, then my feet, then my legs, and hips. In a futile attempt to concentrate, I kept my eyes closed, but something in my brain kept telling me to open them and remain alert.

Upon opening my eyes for the umpteenth time, I noticed the ornately tooled, antique brass doorknob on the closet door begin to turn. My breath caught in my throat and my body stiffened, unable to move. Squinting to determine if my eyes mistook light for motion, or perhaps my mind played tricks on me as my mother often claimed, I fixed my gaze on the doorknob. Stealthily, carefully, I reached for my sister's hand hoping to secretly squeeze it to wake her, but with her back to me and her hands tucked deeply under her pillow, her hands remained out of reach. The comfort of her company was unavailable unless I dared to move enough to wake her. Any movement, I knew, might draw unwanted attention to me. I feared that eventuality so much that I remained as still as a corpse.

～

The sounds of my own blood rushing in my ears and my heart pulsing in my chest terrified me. My heartbeat was so loud that I feared that *it* might hear my heart, too. Perfectly still, I tried to calm myself. Experience had taught me that my best defense was to render myself invisible, knowing that If *it* thought I was sleeping, it might not trouble me. In that moment, what I hoped for more than anything else in the whole, wide world was for *it* to *not* to approach, nor even appear to me as I lay trembling silently in my bed.

With eyes squeezed, I stared through trembling eyelashes at the doorknob. It continued to turn. *It's turning too slow to be real,* I told myself in my mind. *It's my vivid imagination like Mommy always says. I am imagining things.*

Then the latch on the door clicked.

Instantly, I shifted my gaze away from the closet door toward the window and the light outside. I did not, under any circumstances, want to see what lurked inside that dark space beyond the closet door. My eyes followed the wall around the closet, purposefully avoiding looking at the door. Without moving an extra muscle in my body, I scanned from the window, to the ceiling, to the hallway, and then back to the window. On the third or fourth time around, I could no longer ignore the closet. Out of the corner of my eye, I noticed that the closet door was half opened. I turned and stared into it, riveted, terrified, and breathless.

Even before I actually saw him, I could sense him watching me. I tuned into that place just beyond perception where other things dwelt in that house. As his form became gradually clearer, I could not look away. For some inexplicable reason, I sensed no malevolence or imminent danger, and so I relaxed a little—trying to see him more clearly. The outline of his face grew sharper, then his body as well. He wrung his clasped hands desperately in front of him. The man stood about as tall as but thinner than my father. Watching him hesitate in the shadows just inside the closet, I noticed his strange clothing. I saw the puffy sleeves of a long shirt hemmed just above his knees—almost like a woman's nightgown. I saw pearl buttons down his front unlike anything my father, or any other grown-up man I knew, ever wore. Scanning his body from top to bottom I noticed that he began to fade at the knee. Had he had no legs—or perhaps invisible legs? Yet, he glided slightly forward toward me in the doorway. Instinctively, I pulled back away from him. Then I noticed the streetlight catch his eyes. From that moment I could not move. He captured my total focus with his dark, sad, eyes that seemed to speak directly to me.

Though I could not look away, my terror began to dissolve into grief, a new emotion in my young life. I had experienced sadness. I certainly knew fear, even terror. I understood anger and had witnessed rage. I knew many varied emotions, but I had never experienced what the man in the closet projected and made me feel—a hopeless, endless, abject misery of an unfathomable depth. I felt his immense agony and I pitied him with my whole heart and soul.

For the first time ever, awake alone in the house, I did not experience fear. Instead I experienced only the great sorrow of the man in the closet. Tears began to roll down my cheeks, filling my ears and wetting the pillow. I did not cry like I normally might have, with heaving breaths and sobs. Instead, silent tears of hopelessness fell from my body as my five-year-old heart ached along with his. I lay quite still, weeping for a long time, at last, mercifully drifting off to sleep.

⌣

Songbirds sang in the tree just outside my window and bright sunlight filled the room when I opened my eyes to the new day. I could feel Kate's warmth as she breathed heavily, still asleep next to me. The house was quiet, the rest of my family having not yet awakened. Relieved that the night and my ordeal had ended, I stretched, rubbed my eyes, and thought about the strange, disturbing vision from the night before.

I took comfort in the thought that what I had experienced in the night must have only been a dream, after all.

Turning over after a few minutes, I sat up just as my sister began to stir. To my great horror, the closet door stood about halfway open, exactly as I had seen it the night before. Blood froze in my veins as I realized that I had not dreamed it after all. It really happened. The sad, sad man *had* watched me through the open closet door in the night. I could not deny the reality that I had felt his grief along with him. I could not move.

Kate yawned deeply as she sat up in bed next to me. She noticed me staring at the closet and vehemently inquired, "Why did you open the closet door?"

"I didn't." I replied. "I didn't open it."

# Chapter 5
# Manumission

(man-yɛ-'mi-shɛn—*noun*: the act of manumitting; to release from slavery or servitude.)

AFTER THE FIRST TIME I SAW THE MAN IN THE CLOSET, I became a restless sleeper. I frequently found myself the only one awake in the wee hours of the night. It became unnerving to experience the unsettled spirits in our house alone in the dark. Sometimes I would see the dreadful, grief-stricken man in the closet. Sometimes I would watch The Slinky Lady glide up and down in the hallway and staircase. At other times I would sense or even see an old man in the corner. Sometimes some other unknown entity lurked near my bed. Even if I saw no one, I always knew something horrific, even dangerous, lay in wait somewhere in the shadows. I felt helpless and extremely vulnerable, unable to fall back to sleep in that silent, yet terribly "noisy" house.

One night after waking suddenly from a sound sleep, before I opened my eyes, I heard a soft whisper next to my ear.

"Don't open your eyes," it said. "You don't have to be afraid. I am here."

The voice sounded somehow familiar and quite comforting, though it belonged to no one I recognized. It made me feel secure and warm, not even remotely resembling the thing that often menacingly called my name, randomly sucking out my warmth and my energy at all hours, whether I was awake or asleep.

Every night before bed my brothers, sisters, and I would kneel down next to the bed and fold our small hands to say the bedtime prayer our mother taught us:

*Angel of God, my guardian dear,*

*To whom God's love commits thee here.*

*Ever this day be at my side*

*To like to guard, to rule and to guide.*

*Amen.*

Hearing this gentle voice speak to me so reassuringly made me think that, perhaps, my guardian angel had come just in time to protect me. I thought that if it was not my guardian angel whispering, at least I could tell it belonged to someone else who loved me very much. It didn't matter at that moment who showed up to help me. I knew without a doubt that someone had come to protect me, and I felt grateful indeed.

Next, without actually speaking words, she communicated to me that I did not have to stay awake alone in my bed.

Then close to my ear she whispered. "I'm here. Float up and come with me."

"Float up?" I pondered, but somehow, I knew exactly what she meant.

I lay very still willing my consciousness to rise up off the bed. I felt light and warm, but most of all safe, something I had never experienced after having woken up in the middle of the night in my childhood home.

"Take my hand. Come outside to play." She said.

My hand moved, though it was not actually my physical hand, it more resembled an illuminated image of my hand, my spirit hand. I reached out to take the gentle hand reaching for me. It felt sure and strong and conveyed a powerful love for me. She knew me, and I knew that above all else she would keep me safe.

"Open your eyes," she said.

Opening my eyes, I was surprised to find myself standing under the streetlight on the sidewalk in front of my house. I knew it was night-time and that it should be dark, but everything appeared lit in a strangely pleasant amber glow. I could see every minute detail absolutely clearly without a single shadow cast. Looking up and down the block from my front yard I began to worry. My mom and dad would have a fit if they caught me outside in the middle of the night!

"It's okay," she said as if reading my thoughts, "Don't worry, you are still asleep in bed."

Strangely this made perfect sense. I was dreaming, or at least some part of me was dreaming.

"You can float, you can fly." I heard her say, but I still did not turn to look at her, my guardian angel.

I took a step, then a jump, willing myself forward and upward. Gradually, I discovered that I could use my own breath much the way one blows a down feather to keep it afloat. I floated high above the streetlight, then up above the house. I could see the darkened window where I knew I lay sleeping. Though at first, I felt tempted to check, I decided to not look inside, but kept my attention focused on the marvelous new sensation of weightlessness and freedom.

I floated lightly back down to the ground. Then I tried a new motion. I found that I could bounce myself off the porch wall like a rubber ball. I flew up and over, I floated, flipped, and bounced gleefully without any sense of time passing. It all felt so gloriously fun, but most of all I was no longer on the inside of the house where *they* could touch me, scare me, or make me have feelings that were not my own. Safe ... I felt completely safe.

I never got winded or fatigued. I played, and played, and played. Before long the sun began to rise. I stood, now feeling alone, scrutinizing the house nervously, sensing the darkness and uncertainty just inside. Though I did not want to, I knew I had to go back into that house. Not sure exactly how to do that, I again began to worry.

"Take my hand." She whispered from behind me.

*She came back—or had she remained there with me all along?* I wondered.

I reached for her. I could tell that she was a grown-up by how I had to reach up to take her hand. I looked not up toward her, but only at my own small hand in hers—never feeling a need to see her face but enjoying the tender touch of her hand holding mine.

In an instant, I felt myself falling very quickly, and woke with a start. I sat up and looked around to find Kate, already awake and sitting up. I felt giddy and wonderful! I had never experienced a more restful night's sleep. I smiled knowing that I now had the secret ability to escape any night I chose. After that I decided to fly away every night I possibly could.

Whenever I awakened in the night, I followed what my guardian angel had taught me and quickly left that house. I played in the front or in the backyard. In winter I floated with snowflakes. I fell with rain drops in the spring. Before long I found I could go further, willing myself to the playground, to the woods, or the lake. I never ever stayed in the house, though. Every night I made a plan to get out of there as quickly as possible.

Before long, I stopped waiting to be awakened in the night. Instead of falling asleep normally I would close my eyes, completely relax, and will my consciousness outside. When I tried to tell my sister that I flew away every night she looked at me like I was crazy and called me a big liar. I tried to tell my mother and a few others, but soon learned to keep my nightly travels to myself.

Through the years I used this skill in multiple situations, not only to escape intrusive spirits, but to distance myself from pain, or just to move freely, unencumbered by a body that, after becoming ill as a youth, left me in pain and crippled for the rest of my life. It never seemed odd or unnatural to me, it was just something I could do, and so I did.

Sometimes I noticed others also moving around in that bodiless state. On more than one occasion I recognized individuals on the street, in awake life, that I had seen in my dream travels. At first, I avoided eye contact because it frightened me just a little, but later, when our eyes would meet, we would smile and nod in acknowledgment. I remember once, as an adult in New Orleans, I kept seeing the same man from my spirit travels in different places in Lafayette Park. He'd catch my eye and smile broadly. Then after moving on I would see him in a new location. Though startled, I soon came to the conclusion that the man I saw didn't actually have a physical body, but perhaps existed only in spirit form. Nothing surprises me in such a magical place as New Orleans—where its ghosts and spirits are openly celebrated.

One night in my early twenties as soon as I left my body, I felt myself pulled quickly in a direction I had not intended. There I saw my cousin Joey. He stood in a thick fog, seemingly confused and frightened. I could see nothing else, and could not tell exactly where we were, though it felt similar to a familiar Lake Michigan beach.

I approached him smiling. He relaxed and smiled back. Without uttering a word, I bade him to follow. We went to a forest, over the lake, and then a park. We flew over the city and basked in golden light. Soon I saw him crane his neck looking off into the distance. He turned back to me, grinned and quickly disappeared into space as if being sucked away by a powerful force. I did not understand what had happened and thought that he probably just woke up.

Later, I learned that his appendix had burst that night creating a life-threatening emergency. He rode to the hospital by ambulance. They rushed him into surgery where he nearly died on the table. The next time I saw him he told me that while he was "under" he dreamed about me. He started to tell me the rest of the dream, but I stopped him, and told him myself.

His eyes grew wide, "What? How do you know?" he implored.

"I was there," I said. "I travel in my dreams."

He had nothing else to say but looked at me quizzically and startled. I just smiled and changed the subject.

My fortieth year brought many positive changes in my life, including better health and spiritual awakenings. As a young teenager I had been misdiagnosed with a painful terminal illness and told I would not live beyond my thirties. When I learned the actual nature of my disability in my late thirties and received treatment, it felt like a reprieve. I now had endless possibilities ahead of me. The treatment also gave me greater mobility and significantly less pain. I still night-traveled, but not as much. Without having to escape from pain or fear, I could sleep normally at night. Life was good.

One night I dreamed an entire, extremely detailed day from my early childhood. I watched myself wake up in the morning and play with my brothers and sisters. I watched my mother, so young and beautiful, preparing food, and cleaning up. I heard our conversations. I watched myself eat dinner and help with the dishes. I watched us watch *Lassie* on the old TV. I woke smiling from that dream with morning still hours away. I decided to spirit-travel to my childhood home. I wanted to see if the spirits still dwelled there. I had no fear knowing that I could escape back to my body in an instant if things became dicey. I visualized the house as it had looked in my dream, when I was a child, though I expected to find myself at the present-day house. To my surprise I found myself instead standing in the streetlight in front of my child-hood home. Looking through the darkened windows, I silently slipped inside. I noticed the cluttered living room. I smiled at the drying clothes hanging on the backs of chairs and from the chandelier in the dining room. I had almost forgotten that, having no clothes dryer, my mother used to drape wet laundry around the house after we went to bed. I moved from room to room, noting every detail and lovingly looking at my sleeping childhood family. With great trepidation I entered the room where my sister and I slept. As I stood next to "my" bed I began to sense the other spirits in the house. I felt them moving closer. I wondered if they would see me there. I knew the man in the closet stood just behind the closed door, waiting, watching. My attention quickly shifted to my small self in the bed. She (I) began to stir and stretch with a slight groan. I sensed the man in the closet reaching for the doorknob, and saw it begin to turn. I leaned down close to the child's ear.

"Don't open your eyes," I said. "Don't be afraid. I am here."

# Chapter 6
# Lurking

(lɛrk-ing—*verb*: to lie or wait in concealment; remain in or around a place secretly or furtively; to exist unperceived or unsuspected.)

As OUR FAMILY GREW, my father's wages at the phone company needed to stretch further and further. He hated his job when it required him to go into the homes of delinquent customers and shut off their phones. If an old person or young family answered the door, Daddy would give them a few more days, marking on his work order that nobody was home. He felt extremely guilty and conflicted about this, but he did it anyway, telling us that sometimes doing the *right thing* may not look like the right thing to someone else. He told us that we had to use our own moral compass.

Daddy often spoke about how, when he attended the seminary, a favorite mentor priest had complimented his aptitude for the law and hoped he would study canon law—perhaps even working at the Vatican one day. Though he never regretted leaving the priesthood to become a husband and father, he still yearned to study law.

Mommy encouraged Daddy to pursue his dream and apply to law school. His mother and uncles, however, told him he was crazy to leave a good paying, steady job for "some pipe dream," especially since he had a young family to support. His mother, already disappointed in him for abandoning the priesthood for "that woman," strongly discouraged any "high falootin' notions," admonishing him to not act like he was better than everyone else. Grandma Angela pelted Daddy, saying, "If a steady job with decent wages is good enough for your 'copper' uncles, it's good enough for you!"

Mom, when they were alone, assured him that it was admirable to try to better himself, and that they could handle the challenge together.

Daddy's mood darkened as he struggled with the decision. While weighing his choices, Daddy grew more anxious. At times, he seemed angry at no one and everyone all at once. Mommy took the brunt of his irrational wrath, but it also sometimes spilled into our play. While all this happened, another kind of darkness enveloped our house. We had become familiar, if not comfortable, with The Slinky Lady, disembodied voices, and even the man in the closet, but now something else began to fill the dark spaces just beyond our discernment. Though unseen, it introduced a visceral caliginosity that kept us all on edge. I could sense its approach much like a noxious odor. The room would grow cold and it seemed that—even on the brightest sunlit days—the light in the room would dim. It wasn't always there. It came and went, but the threat of it, the promise of it filled every moment. I began to observe it work its hideous augury on my father, as I began to see him change before our eyes.

He could be a loving, winsome storyteller such as when we would all lie on the cool grass on summer nights in Grandma's backyard. We would position ourselves like spokes on a wheel with our heads touching. My father would point out the constellations as he masterfully recounted the Greek myths that the stars and planets represented. I developed a great love for mythology listening to the sound of my father's voice as I gazed in wonder at the vastness of the universe.

I remember being curious and asking about the fraying rope scapulars tied around his waist. He said that he received them when he took his first priestly vows. Part of those vows required him to read and say a series of prayers several times a day, including his rosary. He kept this vow his entire life—long past the fraying of his scapulars. I sometimes imagined my father as a priest whispering secret Latin words, wearing embroidered shiny robes while lifting the body of Christ high in his hands.

I would watch the faded bleeding heart of Jesus encased in plastic float in the water when we would all gather next to the bathtub for stories during his bath. He used to tell us about Erbert and Gerbert, two little boys who traveled through history on Halley's Comet's tail to explore amazing times and places in history.

Sometimes, as we listened enthralled at some climactic point in the story, he would stick his big toe into the dripping spigot causing the water to build up pressure. Then he would adjust his toe just right so that streams of water would squirt us right in the face. We would all squeal and laugh with delight.

At other times, he was overcome with a darkness, silently brooding, even volatile as if looking for a fight. We kept quiet and stayed out of his way when those moods manifested. Mommy told us he was under a lot of pressure. I understood this because—just like the squirting bath water—sometimes his rage seemed aimed directly at his children. When that happened, Mommy placed her own body between him and us, sparing my siblings and me from becoming his new target. It only took a quick look from her to make us scurry off as far from him as possible— usually next to the empty toy box in the back corner of our messy, toy-strewn playroom.

While we cowered from the loud, corporeal danger, a more ethereal one often pinned us down. When we cried in that hidden spot, it often wasn't due to the loud voices and crashing sounds from the other room, but instead from the oppressive shadowy thing that loomed over us. When I felt that presence begin to lift, I knew my parents' fight would soon be over. It was as if the thing fed off of anger and fear. The fight and our terror seemed to satiate it ... for the time being at least.

～

When my father finally made the decision to attend law school, our world changed abruptly. He no longer came home at suppertime. Instead, he became a night student at Loyola Law School. Mommy absorbed the extra work as our family grew to five children, all under five years old. Sometimes, she also seemed to absorb the effects of the hungry dark entity. I could track its shadow across her face, watching her mood change quickly. With her, it never lasted long, nor did it have the same violent effect as upon Daddy.

On Saturday mornings we would rise early to go to six o'clock Mass. The church was nearly empty, and the priest always kept his homily short. Daddy liked it this way. We partook in the required ritual without the vapid ramblings of the priest. I liked it this way as well. We didn't have to dress up as we did for Sunday Mass, but wore play clothes, though my mother, sisters, and I had to cover our heads with a lace chapel veil. I found it quite curious that boys and men had to take their hats off in church while women and girls were required to put them on. Though my grandmother told me it was sinful to question the church, I wondered, nonetheless.

After the service we dipped our fingers in the holy water, blessed ourselves, then piled into our dilapidated car, heading for the zoo, a forest preserve, or a park for a weekly adventure. Mommy always made salami or bologna and mustard sandwiches that she packed back into the Wonder Bread bag. We never knew where we would end up, but it was always someplace wonderful and free of cost.

My parents explained that these early morning adventures made it possible for us to have the place to ourselves. I learned from Daddy how desirable it was to avoid crowds. The mere presence of nearby picnickers agitated him so that he made us leave when other folks showed up, spoiling our pristine fun.

After the weekly outing, we headed home to clean the house. Each of us had designated Saturday chores assigned by Mommy. We tykes were not just picking up, but dusting baseboards, scrubbing floors, changing bed linens, finding a place for every toy in the playroom, clearing off the tops of tables, and even the credenza, and washing the multitude of finger smudges off of the door jambs and windows.

Daddy would play classical music at full volume on the record player as we all pitched in. I recall him on his hands and knees scraping old wax and grime from the linoleum kitchen floor with a butter knife before applying a new coat of wax. I remember Mommy—a scarf tied around her hair and wearing a stained apron—kneeling on the bathroom floor and dipping an old rag into a bucket of soapy water over and over again to scrub every inch of it, even behind the toilet and under the sink.

Though my little sister devised all manner of schemes to avoid the work, most of us dove in cheerily. We knew that "many hands make light work," as my mother often said. We also knew that after just a few hours the house would look and smell fresh and clean. Plus, we were rewarded by having the rest of the weekend to do as we pleased, which usually meant dashing outside to meet up with other neighborhood children to play until the streetlights came on.

For Daddy, it meant settling down to study his law books and write vast notes on his many yellow legal pads. Mommy made a beeline to the grocery if it was a payday week. On other weeks, she gifted herself a few minutes to relax on the couch while the baby napped. This never lasted long for Mommy; preparation for supper, a baby needing changing, or my father needing a cold beer often denied her any respite.

With such a large young family, the house was rarely clean past Sunday night, but it sure felt great for an interlude. We were assigned daily chores as well, but they were more maintenance than cleaning. Daddy only participated on Saturday morning since on weekdays he didn't get home until long after our bedtime.

The weekend ended with my father putting his books away after supper so we could all enjoy an evening together. I looked forward to this unless something unexpected happened. The unexpected did often intervene, and not only to the children.

# Chapter 7
# Disquiet

(dis-ˈkwī-ɘt—*verb*: to deprive of calmness, equanimity, or peace; disturb; make uneasy)

ALONE AT LAST AFTER ANOTHER SEEMINGLY ENDLESS WEEKDAY of washing, feeding, and cleaning up messes after a brood of young children, Mommy sat down on the living room couch to watch some TV. Every one of us kids finally had fallen asleep upstairs.

Mommy told herself that the laundry and dishes were as good as they were going to get after such a long weary day. Checking the time, she smiled knowing she could still catch most of *The Rifleman* on channel seven before having to heat up food for my father who would come home exhausted at about nine o'clock, after working all day then attending night school.

*He'll be tired,* she thought, *Good thing I have a nice supper for him.*

She never really considered her own day's work, how she had been pulled here and there since early morning wrangling five small active children. She didn't think about having to juggle all of the household chores on her own while her husband worked and went to school. She loved her husband and her family and had learned early-on that it was her duty to take care of them so Daddy could do the important things without worry. She tucked her feet up on the couch to fend off the evening chill, lit a cigarette, and settled into the show.

After only a few short minutes she thought she heard something upstairs. "Damn!" she thought, "Who's up now?"

Putting her cigarette in the ashtray on the end table, she got up to turn down the volume on the TV. The set stood on a metal stand against the wall shared with the front hall. Looking toward the stairs as she adjusted the volume, hearing more footsteps, she turned the volume off completely and walked to the bottom of the staircase. From there she could see the entire hallway upstairs. She stood completely still and listened for the sound of one of her kids moving about or calling for her. The only thing she could hear were heavy, steady footfalls that seemed to be moving toward the top of the stairs.

"Kate? Davey? Is that you?" she called aloud. No one answered. Her skin began to tingle, and the hairs on the back of her neck and arms stood on end.

She called to her children again by name, "Davey? Annie? Tiyi? Colleen? Kate?" Still she heard no reply, only continuing, distinct heavy footsteps coming toward the top of the stairs.

Placing her hand on the railing at the bottom of the stairs Mommy again called her children's names. Again no one responded. Then, to her horror, she felt the railing heave as if a heavy hand grasped the top of the railing for support preparing to descend the staircase. The ancient wood groaned slightly. Mommy pulled her hand quickly away in terror. She squinted her eyes, straining to see what she knew was there but could not see. The railing again groaned, and the top stair creaked. Then she both felt and heard it move to the next step. She listened, straining to see something, as slowly and deliberately the footsteps descended the stairs. The railing moved as the ancient staircase groaned and creaked with every invisible step.

My terrified mother somehow found the protective determination and courage to stand her ground knowing that whatever came toward her down those stairs stood between her and her children. She took a slight step backwards and put her hand on the front doorknob ready to run into the street screaming for help if she ever saw someone, anyone, anything. As the footsteps came closer and closer, she crossed herself and asked Jesus, Mary, Joseph and all the saints—including Saint Michael the Archangel—to protect her and her little children.

"Please God," she silently prayed, "Please sweet Jesus, if it's evil send it away."

Crossing herself again she prayed for fortitude, "If it's evil send it away, but if it's good please give me the grace to face it."

The footsteps gradually continued down the staircase, but when at last it reached the fourth step from the bottom it suddenly just stopped. Mommy stood with her senses piqued, staring at the hallway and stair-case with her hand on the front door for what seemed to her like an eternity.

She jumped nearly a foot as she felt the front doorknob turn in her hand. Seeing my father, she threw her arms around him. "I'm so glad you're home!" She exclaimed, holding him tightly. He smiled and kissed her.

"What a welcome!" he smiled, "Is everything okay?"

She decided not to trouble him with her own drama that evening. She smiled back shaking her head and taking his briefcase out of his hand.

"Just peachy!" she lied, trying to smile convincingly.

Still Mommy glanced one more time up the staircase and toward the children. Troubled, but relieved that he was home, she went to the kitchen and set about warming his meal as he headed down the hall to get out of his work clothes. While in the kitchen, hearing my father changing in the bedroom, she began to rationalize the strange events of the evening.

*I must have just heard squirrels on the roof,* she told herself.

Even lying next to her husband, she tossed and turned through the night, waking frequently to listen for someone upstairs.

The next night as Mommy settled down, once more waiting for my father's return, she began to sense that something was just not right. Intuition told her that she should check on the kids. She turned the television down and listened. Hearing nothing, she told herself that she should stop acting like a silly "scaredy cat" and just calm down. She turned the volume up just a little and returned to her spot on the couch. As soon as she took out a cigarette and before she could strike the match, she again heard the dreaded footsteps.

"Jesus H. Christ!" She muttered as she jumped up off the couch and shut off the television.

Walking on tiptoe, hoping beyond all hope that *it* would just go away, she went to her post. This time she did not even bother to call to the kids. She knew we would not answer. She waited at the bottom of the stairs watching and praying fervently.

"Dear God ... Dear God" she spoke under her breath.

She knew that what she heard coming towards her could not be squirrels on the roof. She knew that squirrels could never make that sound. She knew the distinct sound of footfalls on each step. One creaked, another groaned.

*Besides,* she thought, *what would make the railing heave the way it did?*

She stood there listening and watching until the footsteps stopped again at the fourth step from the bottom. Once more, after the footsteps stopped, she tried to rationalize.

*Branches rubbing against the side of the house, maybe?*

Still, she stood guard between the staircase and the front door until Daddy returned. Seeing his weary demeanor, she decided again to not trouble him.

In the following weeks, night after night Mommy silently endured this terrifying ritual. She continued to keep it to herself, trying over and over again to rationalize the sound. Then, one afternoon while visiting Grandma Angela next door, and who grew up in the house in which we now lived, she mentioned her nightly ordeal.

"You know," she said as nonchalantly as she could, "It's the craziest thing. Lately I've been hearing what sounds like heavy footsteps in the hallway upstairs, and on the stairs."

She shrugged it off with a slight smile so as not to seem totally crazy, all the time watching my grandmother's expression closely for any sign of skepticism or disapproval. "It's probably just squirrels on the roof, or branches hitting the house, or something. I guess I'm just a little nervous alone with the kids while Dave is at school late," She laughed nervously.

"Oh, don't worry about *that*," my grandmother said matter-of-factly, barely looking up from the death notices in her lap. "It's just Pa. He won't hurt you or the kids."

"What?!" Mommy tried to determine if my grandmother was pulling her leg, "Pa? Your father? You can't be serious. Pa's been dead for what ... twenty years?!"

"Well you know that, and I know that," my grandmother replied, "But I just don't think Pa knows that."

Pa was my grandmother's father who had lived and died in the house. My mother tried to control her fear and maintain her composure as my grandmother continued.

"We've all heard him, and some of us have even seen him."

Mommy tried to make sense of my grandmother's words as she went on.

"Teresa said that one day she was up in the master bedroom, sitting at the vanity as she put the finishing touches on her makeup when Pa just walked right in. Surprised, but feeling overjoyed at his presence, she turned and told him how great it made her feel to see him."

Mommy nervously fumbled for a cigarette as my grandmother continued, "Teresa asked him if he was alright. She said that he looked confused as he told her that he felt fine except that he kept wondering where she, her mother, sister, and brothers had gone. He told her that he kept calling and calling for them, but nobody answered."

Mommy listened silently. If she had not heard the footsteps herself, she would find it hard to not think that the old woman had completely gone around the bend.

My grandmother continued, "Teresa told him that everyone was doing just fine. She said he smiled and nodded in a sad, but satisfied way, then he turned and, without another word, left the room. When it finally hit her that she had just carried on a conversation with a ghost, she jumped up to follow him into the hall. Of course, he had completely vanished."

Seeing the alarm on Mommy's face, my grandmother tried to reassure her, "You don't have to be afraid of Pa. He's harmless. Just tell him you are Davy's wife and the children are his great grandchildren. Tell him that he's scaring you and ask him to please stop."

Mommy did not know what to think. Could the footsteps on the stairs really belong to her husband's dead grandfather? This seemed almost too much to fathom. She tried to dismiss it as just stories from a superstitious old woman. However, that very night, home alone with her sleeping children before my father returned from work and law school, Mommy again heard footsteps coming through the hallway. After what my grandmother had told her, she concluded that it sounded nothing at all like squirrels, or branches, or anything else of which she tried to convince herself. She knew for certain that what she heard could only be the sound of an old man walking laboriously down the hallway toward the top of the staircase.

She stood at the bottom, took a deep breath to steady her nerves, and crossed herself, again imploring all that is holy to protect her and her children. Then she spoke to him. She did not speak out loud fearing that he might actually answer her. She did not, in any way, want to have that happen. She did not want to see him or have a conversation with a ghost. She just wanted him to stop.

*Pa*, she thought, *I'm Jackie. I'm Davy's wife. Those children sleeping upstairs belong to your grandson Davy and me They are your great grandchildren. I'm alone while Davy is at law school. You are scaring me. Please stop. It's fine that you are here, Angela told me it was you. You can stay if you want, but please, please don't frighten the children or me anymore.*

The footsteps stopped before descending the stairs. She felt the atmosphere lighten, and her fear subside. She waited, listening for a long time. Though she knew he remained in the house, he had listened and heeded her plea. After that she never heard disembodied footsteps on the stairs again.

# Chapter 8
# **Blackout**

(blak- ˌaût–*noun:* the extinguishing or concealment of all visible lights)

EVENING CAME EARLY IN THE LATE AUTUMN in Chicago where I grew up. As the days grew shorter, darkness sometimes fell before suppertime. In the house where I spent my childhood, darkness often seemed to loom even more foreboding than in other places in the world, for everyone who lived there knew all too well that lurking behind doorways, around corners, or deep in the shadows, frightening things waited and watched.

My brothers, sisters, and I had an unspoken pact with one another that we would never leave the other alone at any time in that house. Of course, this rule did not apply if you and the sibling on whom you depended for company had experienced some kind of falling out. Such was the case with Annie and me on one late autumn evening.

After supper, when I was growing up, all the children would work together to clean up the kitchen and do the supper dishes. Mommy assigned each of us a specific kitchen chore—assignments that rotated weekly. The hands-down favorite chore for each of us was clearing the table. When you got to clear the table, it meant that you also got out of the kitchen first.

Each evening my family would gather in the front room to watch a few TV shows before bedtime. If you managed to finish your kitchen chore *first* it meant that you would also have first pick for a prime position to watch our favorite after dinner TV shows.

For that reason, the least favorite chores consisted of those that kept you in the kitchen after everyone else had completed their tasks and had already found a good spot in the front room. It meant that you probably had to sit on the floor, and maybe even miss the first part of the program. Worse than sitting on the floor, however, it also meant that you might find yourself alone, or nearly alone in the kitchen.

Sweeping the kitchen floor and putting away the dishes after someone else had washed, and yet another had dried them, always meant that you would be the last one in the kitchen. Mommy tended to the task of putting away leftovers if we had any, so she would often remain in the kitchen with the unlucky kids left to complete the kitchen clean up. However, if no leftovers remained—which happened more often than not—Mommy would leave the rest of the work to her children, and join my father sitting close together on the couch.

Located in the back of the house, the kitchen felt isolated and creepy. It was two full rooms away from the front room where the rest of the family gathered. One Sunday evening, when no leftovers needed storing, Mommy, Daddy, and all but Annie and I settled down in the front room to watch our favorite weekly TV show *Lassie.*

On this particularly unfortunate night it was my job to put the dishes away. I frantically climbed up and down a tall kitchen chair that I had pushed up to the cupboard. I worked as quickly as humanly possible, making sure I did not drop a single dish, glass, or pan. My younger sister, Annie, wore an angry expression, as she furiously swept the kitchen floor. I do not recall what transgression caused the rift, but we did not speak to one another. When everyone else had finished their chores only she and I remained. The race was on! The last one out of the kitchen had to turn off the lights!

Feeling discouraged as I considered the several large cooking pots and pans I still needed to put away, I saw Annie grab the dustpan just as I heard the *Lassie* theme music began to play on the old black and white TV. Everyone else sat in the front room—the full length of the house away from me.

"Wait for me?" I begged to no avail. "C'mon!" I pleaded "I still have all these pots and pans to put away. Wait just a minute for me, please! I'm almost done."

Without a word, my sister shot me a heartless glance and dumped the contents of the dustpan into the trash. After quickly stashing the broom by the back door and—without ever even looking back at me—Annie ran toward the front room.

My heart sank as I stood on the chair watching her speed through the darkened dining room toward the safety of *Lassie* and my family. I frowned at the remaining dishes on the counter, then, overwhelmed with self-pity, forced myself to hurry even faster.

I reached up, stretching to put a large bowl in its spot on an upper shelf in the kitchen cupboard. All at once I froze in place as I began to feel that all-too-familiar, terrifying chill invade the kitchen. Every hair on my body stood on end as if charged with static electricity. I shook it off and quickly climbed down, turning to the remaining dishes. Bravely, I pushed the growing terror back as I laboriously climbed back up onto that kitchen chair to put away the last of the dishes.

I tried to soothe myself under my breath, "It's okay, you're just panicking because nobody else is in here. You are almost done. It's okay. It's okay, just keep going and get out of here...."

Suddenly, without warning, everything went black as every light in the house went out! I stood there all alone—in the pitch dark, on a chair—unable to see a single thing, knowing my back was exposed to that terrifyingly-charged room. I dared not move a muscle, nor did I hardly even breathe. I listened for the familiar sounds of a kerfuffle from my family that normally occurred in surprising moments such as lights suddenly going out, (which happened quite often), but I could only hear the sound of *Lassie* continuing to play on the TV.

I felt as if I was completely alone in the whole wide world, and horrifyingly vulnerable. I blinked and squinted trying to force my eyes to adjust to the pitch blackness. Then I began to feel dank, foul-smelling frigid air on my cheek, and in my ear. I prayed it would not speak to me. I did not want to hear the sound of it. I could feel its long penetrating exhale increase as it moved closer and closer. I strongly sensed the power of whomever, or whatever—far too close, invading my space.

Mercifully, the breathing subsided, but then to my great horror, I felt long icy fingers touching me from behind. The fingers began at my heels. Then slowly—terribly slowly—they moved up the backs of my legs. I shuddered and tears welled up in my panicked eyes. I tried desperately to keep absolutely still as the otherworldly fingers reached my bottom, then moved up my back. They lingered on my neck, then reached the back of my head. I felt my hair lift up as that thing pulled any living warmth from my body. When it reached the top of my head and began to move down over my forehead toward my eyes and mouth, I could wait no longer.

"Mo-o-ommy." I called out in a hoarse, trembling whisper. I took a deep breath and then, mustering every ounce of courage, I found my full voice and shouted, "MOMMY!"

The icy fingers instantly stopped as if the sound of my tiny voice had somehow broken its spell. Then, from the front room, I heard my mother call back to me,

"It's okay darlin'. Hurry up and come in here. Just follow the light. The TV is still on."

Needing no more encouragement, I leapt from that chair flying like a fury through the dark kitchen and dining room. I never slowed down even as I crashed my hip into an out-of-place dining room chair. Reaching the front room, I saw my entire family huddled tightly together, half on top of one another on the couch facing the inexplicably-still-playing TV set. I leapt directly into Mommy's lap, jostling the baby who began to fuss, then squeezed in between my parents. Any sense of safety and relief quickly passed as we all noticed through the front windows that the lights in all the other houses on the block remained on. The blackout had only affected our house ... again.

"Why did the lights go out?" My brother asked.

"It's just old wiring I suppose," Mommy replied. "Maybe a fuse blew. There's a bunch of stuff plugged into that outlet."

She looked over at my father who sat nervously scanning the

darkened rooms. His knee bounced up and down furiously as he began to tremble with increasing intensity.

"Jesus Christ." He said shakily, "I guess I'd better go down to the basement and check the fuse box." Turning to my mother, he asked, "Do you know where I can find the damn flashlight?"

"In the dining room. Top drawer in the credenza," she replied, indicating the large ornate cabinet that came with the house.

My father did not look relieved in the slightest.

"Jesus Christ." He muttered again.

My brothers and sisters and I exchanged worried glances of disbelief and horror at the thought of Daddy making his way alone through the pitch darkness—armed only with a flashlight—to the most terrifying place in the house, perhaps in the whole world ... the basement.

I watched Daddy, still shaking, rise from the couch and gingerly make his way toward the dining room to look for the ever-elusive flashlight. No one spoke. None of us took his or her eyes off him.

I watched as my father fumbled in the deep, cluttered drawer, muttering cuss words loudly as he aggressively tossed things aside. Finding the flashlight at last, he shook it and pushed the switch. A dim beam of light emerged from the bulb. Cursing again he turned it off and shook it, smacking it hard on its back end. Again, he pushed the on switch. This time the light seemed a tad brighter.

"Jesus Christ. God in Heaven. Jesus, Mary and Joseph and all the saints ..." He muttered.

With extremely slow and deliberate steps, Daddy inched toward the basement door in the hallway located under the stairs, and out of our direct view. We all held our breath staring at the doorway beyond which he disappeared just as *Lassie* ran for help to rescue little Timmy, oblivious of the terror we now experienced. I secretly wished that we had a Lassie-dog of our own who could bravely go with my Daddy and protect him in the basement. I thought that Lassie would bark at anything that tried to touch me with icy fingers, and how she would never have left me alone in the kitchen to begin with. I glared at

Annie, who had abandoned me in the kitchen to face the darkness all alone, then looked back toward the arched doorway between the dining room and the hall where the weak flashlight beam blinked as my father searched for the basement door handle.

We listened for the sound of the basement door. I heard the click of the ancient latch, then the slow rising-pitched *squeeeak* as he slowly pulled the dreaded door open.

All of a sudden, just as quickly as they went out, every light in the house came back on. I heard the basement door slam shut, and watched my father, in a dead run, toss the flashlight on top of the credenza and fly back into the front room. He plopped down into his place on the couch, visibly shaking. His forehead glistening with beads of sweat, even though our drafty old house admitted cold autumn air in through every crack.

My very practical, and scientifically minded younger sister, who took pride in looking at all things critically, pointed to the lamp next to the TV.

"How come that light went out, but the TV stayed on?" she implored, "Aren't they both plugged into the same outlet? Aren't they on the same fuse? And besides, I don't think the TV tubes could actually keep the TV going for that long without an electrical source."

"Old wiring." Mommy said.

"Jesus Christ." My Daddy added.

# Chapter 9
# Terror

(**ter-ɛr**—*noun:* intense, sharp, overmastering fear)

WHILE MOST OLD HOUSES CAN EASILY LAY CLAIM TO A CREEPY BASEMENT, the basement in the house where I spent my childhood jerked that description up several notches from creepy to abjectly terrifying. Very little in my young life could entice my siblings or me into that basement. Even my parents spent as little time there as possible.

From time to time, however we would double dog dare each other to stand alone just inside the basement door that opened outside to the driveway as the others closed the door and counted. It was a contest to see who could bear to stay in that chilling domain alone the longest. We chanted the seconds: twenty ... twenty-five ... thirty ... OPEN THE DOOR! OPEN THE DOOR!

The trick was to close your eyes and not look behind you toward the furnace or the coal bin. The trick was to keep your hands on the wooden door trying in vain to maintain a connection with the outside, and the others there. The trick was to wait as far beyond that moment when the chill gripped your heart, and you sensed something creeping toward you as you possibly could, until, at the very last minute, before it touched you, you began banging on the door yelling "OPEN THE DOOR!"

We had an implied covenant with one another that the very second one yelled "OPEN THE DOOR" the others would fling it open, allowing the occupant to rush out into the sunlight and safety as the others slammed the door behind them. This morbid and frightening challenge frequently occupied us through weekends and long summer days. On those occasions, we spent hours on end *unsupervised* as was the norm for children in our neighborhood during the late 1950's, and early 1960's.

Many other children on the block spent the same feral hours roaming the neighborhood looking for fun and adventure. We often played with one boy who lived with his crazy Italian mother and grandmother at the end of the block. All the kids in the neighborhood generally played together, though we did sometimes take pleasure in playing "war" and battling kids from the next block. We learned early-on about "outsiders."

Jimmy, however, was one of us, though we did think he was kind of whiny and sometimes even a cry-baby, so from time to time we teased him for entertainment or set him up for practical jokes. Still, he loved us, and we played together all the time. We'd walk to the end of the block and stand outside his garden apartment shouting in a sing-song pattern, "Yo-o Jimmy! Can you come out and Play-ay?"

We could hear his mother yelling after him in Italian as he would come bouncing up his stairs. Then we'd run off to whatever adventure we had planned for the day. I recall with tremendous guilt one time when we went too far.

That afternoon we decided to take turns playing the "standing in the basement game." Some of us made it to ten, some even to thirty. Jimmy stood back watching our terrified faces as we emerged breathless before laughing uncontrollably to disperse the rush of adrenaline. After we had each taken at least two turns, we asked Jimmy if he wanted a go at it. He backed away from us appearing anxious and worried, shaking his head and telling us he did not want to go in the basement. We cajoled him, jostled him playfully toward the door, and called him a big chicken. My brother pinky-promised to open the door as soon as Jimmy shouted for us to open it. I noticed a hint of cruelty in a couple of my siblings' eyes and didn't know if I wanted to go along with this plan. Each of us knew what to expect in that basement. Each of us lived with the spirits in that house every day, but Jimmy was completely unprepared. I suspected that my brother and sister had something mean in mind. Even today, I regret not piping up to put a stop to what happened next.

Finally, Jimmy nervously agreed to accept the challenge. With great trepidation he walked down the few stairs to the basement floor. I remember his terrified eyes, and second guessing the plan as my sister slammed the door hard. Instantly he began to beg to let him out. The rule was to open the door immediately, but instead my siblings held it closed, laughing cruelly. Jimmy screamed and yelled. He pounded on the door and bawled, then he began to whimper pitifully.

"Let me out! Let me out! Mama! Mama!" he begged.

Then he fell silent. That was more than enough for me.

"Open the door," I screamed. "Open the goddamn door!"

I pushed my sister and brother aside. My sister fell hard on her behind as I pulled the door open to find Jimmy in a trembling heap on the basement floor with his eyes closed and his arms wrapped tightly around himself. He was rocking back and forth, as if to comfort himself. I felt like a warrior as I furiously leapt down those steps into the basement with balled up fists ready to fight anything or anyone that got in my way.

"C'mon Jimmy. It's okay." I said gently as I tried to pull him to his feet. "It's okay. Come on outside."

When he looked up at me, his expression expressed such terror and betrayal that it broke my heart. I apologized to Jimmy and shot penetrating angry glares at my siblings as they laughed, mocking Jimmy's innocence.

"I want to go home." he stammered in tears. "I just want to go home."

Before my brother or sister could even think of mocking him further, I shot them another look and said, "Don't you dare, or I'll tell Mommy."

They stood silently as Jimmy and I walked away from the basement door.

"It's okay," I said to poor Jimmy. "Don't go home yet. Let's play next door in my grandma's yard. We can climb the cherry tree if she doesn't catch us."

I never ever took part in anything as remotely cruel as that again in my life ... and I never will. I often wonder what the priest thought in confession when I told him how my siblings and I tortured my poor defenseless friend by making him go into our basement. He didn't respond right away, but soon just blessed me and told me to say three Hail Marys, and three Our Fathers.

～

In those days we had a big old, noisy used washing machine in the middle of the basement, but we had no clothes dryer. In the spring, summer, or warmer autumn weather, my mother would carry the damp clothes to hang on the clothesline in my grandmother's backyard next door. She would exit the back basement door where a solitary window illuminated the few stairs that led to the outside[. In the winter, however, she would have to bring the clothes back up the long, rickety, stairs into the house where she would hang the damp laundry from every chair back, light fixture, lamp, and door frame. Sometimes when Mommy did laundry, we children would sit at the top of the basement stairs, keeping the door open for her, and watching as my mother quickly and expertly loaded and unloaded that machine from seemingly endless baskets of laundry.

"Okay, I'm coming up," She would call out. "Open the door and get out of the way."

Lugging those heavy baskets of damp laundry up the treacherous open basement stairs took considerable effort and concentration. One missed footfall could mean disaster for all of us. She panted, struggling with the heavy load past the abandoned coal bin, over the threshold, and into the bright light and warmth of the dining room. Thrusting the basket up and onto the dining room table, Mommy would catch her breath and instruct us to shut the door tight and remember to latch it. Heaven forbid one of the littler kids might open that door to those dangerous stairs.

"Who's been messing with the bricks again?" She would scold as she shook each item of laundry, smoothing out damp wrinkles as best she could. "The whole house is going to fall down around us if you kids keep pulling the bricks out of the foundation."

"Not me" Each one of us eagerly assured her.

"Well *somebody* is pulling those bricks out. There were three on the basement floor. Your father is going to have a fit if he sees that again."

As we each looked accusingly to one another I thought, *Fat chance Daddy is going to ever see that. He avoids that part of the basement like the plague.*

The only place in the basement Daddy ever went was the tool bench against the back wall, located under a bank of windows. He never actually worked there, but that's where he stored his tools. Even in the dead of winter, if he needed a hammer or wrench, Daddy would exit the back door off the kitchen—in any weather—rain, snow, or hail, he would walk down the treacherous outside stairs and follow the path around the side of the house to use that basement door.

We knew better than to touch or move any of his tools. He knew exactly where to find each one. If we moved a tool and he had to spend any extra time in the basement looking for it, there would be hell to pay! My father's rage came and went often unexpectedly. We would never in a million years do something sure to bring it on. Yet, from time to time, tools did go missing, only to be found on the washing machine, or in the coal bin, behind the ancient furnace, or even under the basement stairs to the house. No manner of denial could convince him that we hadn't been playing in the basement with his tools. Screaming and cursing, he would yell at Mommy as if *she* deserved all the blame.

"AND they've been pulling down the brick wall again!" He would turn his rage in our direction. "Leave the GODDAMNED WALL

ALONE!!!!! And stay the *hell* away from my tools!"

We all knew better than to bring attention to ourselves by pleading innocence, so we would stand silently waiting for him to calm down, hoping it would happen sooner rather than later. I remember trying to think of who to blame for the tools and the wall. When my father would leave the room, we would interrogate one-another.

"What's wrong with you?" My oldest sister would say accusingly, usually directing her scorn toward my older brother. "Why would you do that to Daddy?"

Then she would haughtily leave the room as if she was a grown up as well, and we were mere underlings. The rest of us would just raise our eyebrows, shake our heads and shrug our shoulders to prove we stood blameless.

On one occasion when my mother was busily hanging laundry in the dining room, she asked me to go down into the basement to get a book of matches she had left on top of the washer. My throat tightened as I begged her to ask Davy. He never seemed afraid and took on all manner of frightening tasks willingly. Davy, however had gone outside with the rest of the big kids. Only the baby played nearby. I was my mother's only option.

"Don't worry." she said knowingly. "I'm right here hanging up these clothes. It will take you all of thirty seconds. Please help me."

How could I say no? The day, though cold, was bright and sunny. The green plastic radio played pop songs as my hard-working, and heavily pregnant mother labored to keep a growing brood clean and fed. I took a deep breath to steel my resolve, told myself I had nothing to fear, and went to the basement door. Turning back to my mother before opening it I asked, "Are you sure they're on the washing machine? I'm not going to have to search around, am I?"

"Right there." she assured me, "I just couldn't carry them in the wet laundry basket, and there's no pocket in my stretch pants."

Opening the door, I looked down the long narrow stairs built against the wall to the old coal bin.

"Years ago, everyone heated with coal," my grandmother had told me. "The coal wagon would come up the street, and folks would go out to buy however many shovel-fulls they could afford. Then the coal man would shovel it right through the chute into the coal bin. His hands and face always appeared black from the coal dust. Sometimes your father and Uncle Jerry would follow the coal wagon picking up big chunks of coal that fell from the wagon. They'd yell after the coal man that he dropped some, and the coal man always told them to keep it because they were so honest."

Looking into the dim basement, I imagined my father and his brother as very honest little boys. Though many years ago the old coal furnace had been converted to an oil-burning one, coal dust still clung to the walls and floor of the ever-empty coal bin. My mother warned us against "getting into" that coal dust for the terrible mess it could make.

"Are you going or not?" My mother's voice brought me back from my imagining. I stepped down three stairs and bent to look across the expanse of the basement, past the hulking furnace, toward the washer. There I clearly saw her book of matches right where my mother promised. Sighing deeply and holding on for dear life, I scampered down the rest of the basement stairs. The very moment my feet hit the roughly-poured concrete floor, I knew I was not alone. I could feel a chill beyond that of the unheated basement. The same familiar chill that made every hair on my body rise, made my stomach flutter, and my heart jump. Though the washing machine and the matches lay only feet away I could not move. I did not look from side to side, because I knew in the very core of my being that something lurked just to my left.

My heart beat faster as I began to hear a scraping sound. Slowly, slowly ... *Scrape. Stop. Scrape. Stop.* I tried to figure out just what could possibly make that sound when I suddenly heard a loud *Plop.* Startled, I jumped and quickly turned to look to my left where, to my horror, I saw one of the foundation bricks on the floor. I did not wait for what might happen next as again I heard the scraping. I could see another brick slowly pushing itself slightly outward, uneven with the rest of the wall.

Leaving the matches on the washing machine, I turned and sprinted three stairs at a time back up. Slamming the door shut, and with my eyes bulging in terror, I quickly latched the basement door.

My mother, never looking up from the laundry, asked, "Did you get the matches?"

"They weren't there." I lied. "I'm going out to play."

Though I knew I had committed a sin by lying to my mother, I hoped that God would understand the extreme circumstances and forgive me. As I ran to get dressed in my outdoor gear, I wished I could have been as honest as my father and Uncle Jerry, but even more, I wished that those goddamn bricks would just stay put.

# Chapter 10
# Empyreal

(em-'pir- ē-ɛl–*adjective*: pertaining to the highest heaven in the
cosmology of the ancients; pertaining to the sky; celestial; formed of
pure fire or light)

I LOVED GOING TO GRAMMIE ETHEL'S, (she was my mother's mother). Her
house in the suburbs was a respite from the chaos and volatility of my
own home. Her place seemed so fancy and perfectly ordered, and I
always felt safe there.

Daddy's mother was old and crippled with arthritis which made
her very impatient with children. Grammie Ethel, in contrast, appeared
elegant and beautiful. She never had a hair out of place, and always
wore red lipstick and large clip-on earrings.

When we went to her house for supper once a week on Wednes-
days, we would find an ever-filled candy bowl on her coffee table. We
could eat as much as we wanted—even before supper! When it was time
to get ready to go home, she would whisper in our ears, telling us to put
a handful in our coat pocket as we left.

Grammie and Gramps also had a cabin on a lake up north in
Wisconsin. My mother would pack cold fried chicken, buttered bread,
and fruit, along with a glass milk jug filled with water for the drive. We
would pile in the car, leaving well before dawn for the nine-hour drive
Up North for vacation. Then my brothers, sisters, and I would spend a
few weeks by the lake with my parents and grandparents. This way we
escaped the oppressive summer heat in the city. For me, their two-room
cabin perched atop a hill overlooking a beautiful, clear lake in the

north woods of Wisconsin also became a respite from the oppressive nonhuman beings who lurked just out of sight in our house in the city.

When I was five years old, my siblings and I traveled with Gramps to spend a couple of weeks Up North by the lake. That year, we went without my parents who remained in the city for the birth of another baby, my brother Tommy. Grammie Ethel and Gramps slept in a small room set off from the rest of the living area by a wall that only went part way up to the peak of the ceiling. There were small single beds laid out along the side wall under a bank of windows near the door. The children slept in a bunkhouse just a few short yards from the main cabin. The buildings were connected by a wooden sidewalk. It seemed like such a great adventure to sleep in sleeping bags on the bunkhouse's salvaged WWII bunk beds with Aunt Judy and Uncle Jeff, my mother's much younger siblings.

Up North was a feast for my senses. I loved the smell of jack pines and sand in the hot summer sun. I could only hear the sounds of birds and other forest creatures. If I heard my name, I could be sure it was Grammie Ethel or another family member, not some ghostly thing calling me from a place I couldn't see. Grammie Ethel never yelled at us, and Gramps only became cross if we didn't roll up our sleeping bags at the foot of our bunks each morning.

He would warn us that deadly spiders and wood ticks could crawl into any unrolled sleeping bag and wait for a hapless victim to climb in at night. He would also never tolerate for us to leave fishing tackle or water toys on the pier to become booby traps for the next unsuspecting fisherman or swimmer. We lived in swimsuits or comfy play clothes and didn't put our shoes on our feet unless we went on a trip to town. As far as I was concerned, it was the most wonderful place on earth.

One morning I awoke before the others. Daylight barely poked above the horizon, and a thick fog lay over the entire forest and clung to the surface of the lake. I climbed out of my sleeping bag into the chilly morning as quietly as I could. Shivering, I put my feet onto the cold wooden floor of the bunkhouse, pulled on my jeans and T-shirt, and rolled up my sleeping bag. Then, I tiptoed through the door to sprint across the cool wooden planks of the sidewalk, damp with heavy morning dew. I scurried to the main cabin, enticed by the mouth-watering aroma of fresh coffee and bacon.

The screen door squeaked and slammed as I burst inside. I saw Gramps, sitting in his usual place at the head of the long wooden table. He sat before a large cup of steaming coffee that he slowly stirred with a silver teaspoon he had filled with a dollop of butter. He would dip the spoonful of butter in sugar and then stir slowly as it melted into the dark liquid. My grandmother turned from the stove. She always appeared fresh and tidy in her brightly colored apron. Even at this early hour she wore lipstick and earrings. Her neatly coiffed hair stood in stark contrast to my own ragged and wild mass of tangles.

"Oh look!" she exclaimed, "It's our little early bird. Climb up next to Gramps and I'll get you a cup of something warm to drink."

I pulled myself up on the tall ladder-backed chair and let my grandfather pull it in close to the table. My chin barely rose above the tabletop, and my small legs swung freely off the edge of the woven jute seat. My grandmother brought a cup filled with coffee, warm cream, and sugar. She placed it on a matching saucer before me on the table. I leaned over to smell its delightful aroma. Thanking her, I strained up as tall as I could and began sipping my coffee. As I sipped, I gazed absently through the large picture window to watch the mist swirl over the obscured lake.

"It looks like ladies dancing." I said to no one in particular.

"It's a fairy mist." Grammie replied from the kitchen. "Look closely and you can see them. If you listen, you might even be able to hear them sing."

"I can't hear anything." I replied.

"Well you won't hear them from inside the cabin. Why don't you finish your café au lait and take a little walk out to the point? You might hear them there—away from everybody"

My eyes grew wide at the thought of walking out into the misty woods alone. I had never been allowed to do that before. Excitement quickly overtook my trepidation as I gulped down the last of my warm, sweet drink. I noticed my grandfather's raised eyebrows as he looked at my grandmother with surprise.

"Really?" he said, "Fairies?"

"Never mind." My grandmother replied as we walked to the small front stoop. "Stay on the path until you find the special sitting tree. Sit very quietly and you might hear them."

Butterflies fluttered in my belly at the thought of venturing into the wilderness alone in the early dawn. It felt more like excitement than like the terror I felt anytime I was alone, even briefly, at home.

"Remember," She went on, "Do NOT go into the water without a grown-up! Right?"

I nodded. Of course, I knew to never put so much as a toe in the lake without adult supervision. We all knew that children who did not follow this rule drowned all the time. I started down the sandy path toward the point as my grandmother watched smiling. I turned around a time or two to make sure she kept watching and saw her waving me on.

Though only a short distance, the mist and my small stature caused the cabin to soon vanish behind me. For a moment anxiety almost took hold, and I nearly turned back more than once, but the allure of fairies gave me courage. The cool moist sand stuck to my bare feet as, bravely, I ventured on.

Only a few yards from the water's edge, I found the sitting tree. Long ago, local Native Americans had tied the young pine sapling down to signal the direction of a hunting trail. It grew upward a couple of feet from the ground, turned at a right angle for another couple of feet, then grew straight toward the misty sky. I pulled myself up on the horizontal section of the trunk to sit and listen for the fairy music that my grandmother had promised.

At first, I only heard birds singing their morning symphony and flying insects who buzzed annoyingly around my face. Sitting as still as my little self would allow, I strained to hear more. The place that drew my attention was just beyond my visible range, so I watched attentively, much as I did when watching for The Slinky Lady.

At first it sounded like a far-off, sustained chord, very faint and thin. Soon the birds fell silent as the harmonic tones increased. I squinted into the mist, and to my delight saw enormous wispy creatures—beautiful swirling beings—swirling fluidly with the music. I watched transfixed until one after another they turned their lovely faces toward me. I could feel and hear them calling my name, beckoning to me to join them in their ethereal dance. Unlike the voices in my house, these did not threaten or frighten me. Their melodic and soothing voices warmed me—a feeling much like the one I had experienced with my guardian angel. Maybe they were fairies. Maybe angels. It didn't matter to me at all, I just wanted to join them.

Though my body remained on the Sitting Tree, it felt like I flew from my perch to join the dancing fairies above the lake. It felt so familiar and easy. All I had to do was exactly what my guardian angel had taught me. My consciousness lifted up, rose into the mist, and swayed with the music, swirling side-by-side with the fairies my grand-mother anticipated. I danced euphorically, weightless and unencum-bered by fears or preconceptions. I was as beautiful and magical as the fairy-beings themselves.

All at once, I laid down beneath the dancing spirits, my conscious-ness stretching out over the surface of the lake. Without my body limiting my field of vision, I saw every wave, from shore to shore, all at once. I saw the sky, the mist, the shoreline, and the forest simultane-ously without having to turn my head to look around. It felt as if my consciousness spread out and floated on the wholeness of the lake. At first. I floated only on the surface, then it seemed that I actually became the lake itself. In my chest and belly, I felt the fish wiggle and the underwater foliage sway with currents. Behind my eyeballs, every living thing in the lake swam and skittered. My insides were waves and depths, undulating as the lake's gentle waves rose and fell on the shore.

Above me I could see the spirit dancers and hear their music in tones that I had never heard before in my life. I felt totally calm, serene, and euphoric.

The sun rose higher casting a vivid golden hue on the swirling mist. I watched in amazement as it began to dissipate above me. Suddenly I remembered my grandmother's warning to stay out of the lake. At the thought of returning to her dripping wet, panic set in. With a loud rushing in my ears, I felt my body jerk back to physical reality, where I sat, perched and dry on the Sitting Tree. The mists had vanished, and with it the spirit folk and their amazing and mystical music.

I hopped down from the Sitting Tree and ran full speed ahead back to the cabin. My grandfather's booming laughter rang out as my bare feet leapt onto the wooden walkway, then swiftly scampered up the stairs and back to my family, and familiar reality at last. Breathless, I burst through the screen door to find a noisy brood of siblings talking excitedly with my grandfather about the day ahead as they ate their breakfast and drank their own café au lait.

"Where were *you*?" they all seemed to ask at once.

I didn't know how to answer. I didn't really have a clue where I had gone.

"Never mind ..."

My grandmother rescued me by putting her arm around my shoulders ushering me toward my place at the table. She leaned in with a conspiratorial wink as she set a plate of thick-cut bacon, homemade buttered biscuits, and scrambled eggs in front of me.

She never asked, and we never really spoke of that morning again, but I knew she knew that I knew, and that would just have to do for now. Many years would pass before the forest spirits or fairies made their way back into my life, but the gate had opened, and for the first time I realized that I had a key.

# Chapter 11

# Tormented

(tòr- ,ment- ɛd–*adjective:* to be afflicted with severe usually persistent or recurrent distress of body or mind)

WHILE MY SIBLINGS AND I ENJOYED OUR VACATION Up North at the lake, our Daddy and Mommy remained in Chicago for the birth of their sixth child. My mother felt like an expert by this time, but my father never escaped the anxiety and worry that took place in the smoke-filled, cold, green Naugahyde, and stainless steel "Father's Waiting Room" at the hospital.

Daddy knew everything was completely out of his control. He had no idea what happened behind those large swinging doors, but he knew it involved blood, medical instruments, and risk. It made his stomach turn. He resented having to sit with other nervous fathers, especially those who took it upon themselves to strike up a conversation. He could be charming in most public situations, but never enjoyed it.

The other expectant father in the room asked him if this was his first.

"Number six." he replied trying to end the conversation by returning to the pages of his law book.

"SIX!" The stranger exclaimed.

"Wow! Your wife must be a real sex kitten. You must never sleep!"

He hated everything about hospitals, but this he hated most. Indignant and embarrassed, my father shot the crass stranger a dirty look, and didn't even dignify him with an answer, but simply returned to study his book. The chastened stranger stood up and began pacing near the door until another poor hapless father-to-be arrived with whom he could banter.

Daddy studied fervently every chance he got in order to pass the bar exam. He had to prove the priest wrong who told him that he would never make it if he tried to go to law school at night while working a full-time job, and at the same time raising an ever-expanding family. Daddy had already graduated with high honors in the spring, but the last hurdle still lay before him. Not one to settle for squeaking by, he intended to ace the exam for prompt admission to the bar.

After a couple of hours, a portly nun, dressed in a white habit with a large winged veil, arrived at the door. Hearing her call his last name, my father jumped up.

"It's a boy." she said, "Mother and son are doing just fine. I will come get you after your wife has time to get prettied up, and you can meet your son. Congratulations." she said flatly as she turned and disappeared through the heavy doors.

The crass stranger stood up and slapped my father on the back.

"A boy!" he said, "Congratulations, do you have a cigar?"

My father, approving even less of this ill-mannered fool, shook his head smiling uncomfortably. Though he did indeed have a pocketful of cigars, he decided to wait and share them with his uncles back at their pub.

*Another son!* he thought smiling as he sat back in the uncomfortable chair. He had four daughters and one son who already carried his father's and his name. He looked down at the text in his lap.

*I'm going to name him after the patron saint of lawyers*, he thought, *A tribute like this to Saint Thomas More couldn't hurt as I prepare for the bar.*

Soon the same nun appeared again in the doorway. The other two men jumped to their feet in anticipation, then slumped back into their chairs when she summoned Daddy to follow her.

Daddy smiled broadly as he entered the ward where Mommy sat propped up in bed. She looked tired but beautiful in the new lacy bed coat that her mother had bought for her for her laying-in. She wore makeup and lipstick, and her hair had been brushed back, making her curls shine. Her green eyes sparkled with pride as she indicated the tiny red-faced bundle in her arms.

"Meet your new son." She said.

He kissed her gently on the lips. Then, with tears in his eyes, Daddy spoke to his new son.

"Well hello there little guy. Hi there, Thomas More."

"Tommy." my mother said approvingly. "It's a good name. It's a very good name."

Soon the charge nurse burst in, and—without smiling—took little Tommy from my mother's arms.

"I'll take the baby to the nursery," she said, "Your wife needs to get some rest so it's time for you to move along. You can see your baby in the nursery in a few minutes. Now, no dawdling."

She walked briskly away with Tommy in her arms. Daddy stroked Mommy's hair, and—calling her by her pet name—kissed her again. Vowing to return the next day, Saturday, to visit, he promised to bring her some flowers to brighten up the sterile maternity ward where she would stay for at least five days.

From the hospital he went directly to his uncle's pub. Though it was after 10 p.m., the place still bustled with regulars, Mrs. O'Brien and Harry the Hat, plus a chorus of the sundry neighborhood rabble.

His Uncle Gerry, laughing, shouted out a loud "Hoy! Hoy! It's the new father! What is it, another girl?"

Everyone turned to watch my father enter with a fistful of cigars.

"It's Thomas More!" my father stated proudly as he passed out cigars to his uncles and the others in the room. Cheers rang out as Uncle Gerry lined up shots of whiskey and glasses of cold beer to celebrate Daddy's great accomplishment—a new son.

Daddy—weary from waiting room tedium—sat and laughed, and drank until the time came to shoo out the patrons and close the pub. When he stood up from the barstool, he teetered from the effects of the alcohol.

"Let Jack drive you home." Uncle Joe ordered. You shouldn't get behind a wheel tonight.

After a lame protest, Daddy relinquished the car keys to Uncle Jack who was only slightly less inebriated. My father rolled down his window to breathe the summer night air. Leaning against the door he nodded off in the front seat for the fifteen-minute ride home. He awoke as Jack turned off the engine and tossed the keys into his lap.

"Go on," slurred Uncle Jack, "Get inside and sleep it off."

Then Jack stumbled across the front yard to his own house next door. My father sat in the passenger seat trying to keep everything around him from spinning Then he looked up at the house. He had left no lights on when he drove Jackie to the hospital early that morning, racing against the clock to get her there in time. Now the empty house loomed gray and foreboding in the streetlight with pitch blackness within.

Daddy looked at the front door, then at the darkened windows open slightly to let summer air in. He reached for the car door handle and began to pull, but something stopped him. He felt instantly sober as terror rushed through his veins. The hair on his neck and arms rose in warning that something terrible awaited him inside that dark and dread-filled house. He pulled the car door shut tightly, pushed down the lock button, and rolled up the window leaving just a crack open. Shifting his gaze quickly from window to window, looking for some-thing, though he knew not what, he slumped down low in the front seat, watched lightning bugs flash in the front windshield, and waited for first light.

Daddy awoke sweating profusely with a powerful hangover. In the overheated and rank car, the bright morning sun was blinding. Stretching his cramped and aching body as best he could, Daddy opened the car door and stood up.

His head swam in the hot late July heat. He still felt drunk from the night before. Realizing that he had not eaten a morsel the day before, he knew he had to go inside the house and get some breakfast.

He had to go in ... alone. He needed a bath and a shave, plus he needed to make a phone call Up North to tell his in-laws and kids about the birth of Thomas More. He knew his uncles at least would have spread the word to his side of the family.

*Okay,* Daddy steeled his resolve, thinking, *It's the middle of the day. You can go into your own house and take a bath, for Christ sakes*

He walked up the driveway and around back to enter through the kitchen door. The moment he crossed the threshold, the bright morning seemed to darken. Despite the sunlight and the oppressive July heat and humidity, the house felt cool and dim. He opened the icebox and rummaged through for packages of food wrapped in tin foil that Mommy had prepared for him. Though she left detailed notes on how to heat them up, he decided to just eat what was inside cold. He would go next door to his mother's house for a strong cup of coffee before he headed out again, but right now a cold beer sounded like just what he needed to quench his thirst, and perhaps abate his pounding head. He found an opener and popped the cap off of a long-neck bottle. He took a long drink of cold beer while watching the cap roll across the kitchen floor. Looking at the kitchen clock he saw it read 9:35.

As he took his first bite of a roast beef sandwich, he thought he heard someone walking in the dining room. He stopped chewing to listen more closely. The only sounds came from the neighborhood outside. He picked up the bottle of beer and raised it to his lips. Once again, he heard the unmistakable sound of footsteps walking through the dining room into the front room and toward the stairs.

He froze listening, then called, "Jack. Is that you?"

No one answered. He knew he should check to see if someone was in the house, but he was terrified. If it turned out that nobody—*no living body*—was there, it might actually be *something* he did not want to confront as the only living soul in that house. Instead he turned on the green plastic radio on the kitchen windowsill and turned it up full volume. He gulped down the rest of the beer and opened another, carrying it with him upstairs to the bathroom. He could still hear jazz playing from the kitchen as he plugged the bathtub drain and turned on the water. He purposely banged things around, creating his own racket in an attempt to drown out any telltale noises.

Daddy wet his shaving brush and lathered up his stubbly face, preparing to shave. His hands shook as he lifted the safety razor to his cheek. Looking in the medicine cabinet mirror over the sink, he scraped the sharp blade across his rough stubble. He kept the water running to rinse the razor after each stroke. Shaking the water from the razor he pressed it to his throat as he raised his eyes back to the mirror. He jumped, slicing the skin, thinking he saw a shadowy figure slip behind him.

Spinning around, he found nobody there. An icy chill ran down his back and warm blood ran down his neck. The sight of his own blood dripping onto his undershirt induced a crazy vision of the whole bathroom splashed with blood.

Cursing aloud, Daddy told himself to stop acting so jumpy and reached for a wad of toilet paper to blot the blood. He tore off a small piece and stuck it to the wound, then he opened the medicine cabinet to look for his styptic pencil. He decided to finish his shave in the tub—away from the mirror. Stripping down and listening to the running water, he climbed in and finished his shave. After scrubbing his face and body quickly, he climbed out of the tub. Wrapping a towel around his waist he hummed loudly making his way down the hall to his bedroom and fresh clothes.

As he reached the top of the stairs, he felt the unmistakable presence of something right behind him. He spun around, and suddenly felt it behind him on the other side. Turning again he felt that it taunted him staying always behind him out of sight.

"*Stop it!*" he shouted out loud.

But it did not stop. Daddy ran into his room and grabbed fresh clothes, all the time screaming for it to leave him alone. Buttoning his shirt, he sprinted down the stairs, stumbling and slipping down three or four steps on his backside. Shaking and out of breath, his fear surprisingly transformed into terrible grief. He felt devastated and hopeless. Sitting in the middle of the staircase on a hot July morning, with the kitchen radio blaring across the house, my father put his head in his hands and began to sob.

He couldn't tell just how long he sat there, but after a time the feeling just left. Daddy stood up, rubbed his wet eyes, brushed off the seat of his pants, and walked shakily back to the kitchen. He pitched the remains of his sandwich into the garbage can, grabbed his keys and wallet from the kitchen table, and departed through the back door.

His mother saw his red eyes and the cut on his neck when he walked through her side door looking for coffee.

"Jesus, Mary, and Joseph Davey!" she exclaimed You look like hell warmed over! That woman is going to be the death of you!"

"Jesus Ma," he mumbled, "Don't start in on me—I barely slept."

"Well," she went on, "You wouldn't have to deal with this if you were a priest ..."

"Ma!" he started to argue but, realizing the futility of it all just shook his head and gulped down the tepid coffee.

Dave missed Jackie's coffee, but he missed her company even more. He hated to be alone. Most of all he hated being alone in that oppressive house. He wondered whether he would survive the next four nights.

He stopped at the florist and splurged on a bouquet of roses, then drove to the hospital where he found Jackie in a sitting room wearing a brightly colored housecoat, smiling and looking rested and happy.

"Tommy's such a good baby," she reported, "He took the bottle so well, and I got to sleep through the whole night." Then looking closely at her haggard husband said, "You look like you haven't slept in a week! You didn't stay up all night studying, did you?"

Jackie playfully tousled his hair and snuggled herself against his body. He smiled boyishly and told her that he hadn't slept.

"I just can't sleep without you beside me." he said. "I miss you. When can you come home?"

"You know they won't let me leave for a few more days. You'll be alright. Just don't work ... or drink too hard. Did you talk to the kids?"

"Jesus Christ!" Dave had completely forgotten to call in his hurry to escape both the house and his mother's nagging.

"Well, that's okay," Jackie comforted him. "We can call collect from the pay phone. My dad said to call collect anyway so that everybody on the party line can secretly pick up to hear the good news first-hand." They both laughed.

Jackie had such an easy way of making him feel better no matter the situation. Even though he felt like a failure for not having enough money to afford a long-distance call. With his own family admonishing him for risking a good job at the phone company, his father and mother-in-law always encouraged and commended him for taking the risk to better himself. Though he knew they would not judge him he still felt the sting of guilt at not providing enough for his wife and children—and having to call collect.

Holding the receiver between their ears they had to shout louder and louder as the signal got weaker when one after another person that shared the party line Up North picked up to eavesdrop.

"A boy! Well how do you like that!" Gramps exclaimed, "Congratulations!"

"How are you feeling dear," Grammie Ethel asked my mother.

They motioned for all us children to gather by the phone to talk to our parents. We couldn't stay on the line for long because long distance calls cost lots of money, but we did have time to say and hear how much we loved and missed each other. Gramps let us talk a little longer to describe the fish we caught. I wanted to, but decided against, telling my mother about the fairies so as not to waste precious minutes on the phone.

After hanging up, my father began to feel melancholy again.

"I wish they were at Jerry's so I could go see them every night," he sighed.

"Seriously?" my mother replied, "They are having the time of their lives Up North, and this will give us a few days when I get home to relax before having to ..."

"I know," Dave said, "I'm just lonely in that empty house."

Just then the nun interrupted, "Your wife has to get rest so she can get her strength back. Visiting hours are over until this evening."

My father wrapped his arms around his wife's tiny body. He felt the softness where two days ago her huge belly came between them. He did not want to go, He wanted to stay with her where he felt safe and loved.

"I'll come back this evening." he said.

"You don't have to do that. Stay home where you can study in peace and quiet. I'll see you tomorrow."

They held their embrace kissing deeply until the sound of the nun clearing her throat broke in. Dave went to the nursery where he gazed at little round-faced Thomas More. He tapped on the glass, but a room full of crying newborns, and disapproving nurses made any connection with his new son impossible. He walked away.

When he got home, he saw that his brother Jerry and his wife Pat had come to spend Saturday afternoon at Angela and Jack's house. The ballgame played on the transistor radio in the yard. Jerry handed his brother a can of cold beer and shook his hand vigorously.

"A new son! How about that!"

Dave smiled happily. He and his brother had a special bond. He always loved spending time with him. They drank beer and had a game of catch in the yard. Every so often my father would glance up toward the dark windows of his house next door with dread. Sometimes it made him shudder.

They made a fire in the burn barrel and roasted a few hot dogs over the flame, as the sun began to sink in the sky. Before long Jerry and Pat had to head for home so they all went inside to say goodnight to their mother. Angela sat in her overstuffed chair next to the fireplace watching the tiny screen on the enormous television set across the room. Eyeing his own house through the window behind his mother's head, Daddy wanted to ask to sleep on her couch. He would have done so but for the fear of her or his brother thinking him less of a man.

"I'm going to stay out in the backyard for a while before going to bed." He said, "It's such a beautiful night and I think I'd like to look at the stars for a while."

"Don't drink too much Davey." His mother admonished.

Though everyone told him how much she bragged about him and his accomplishments, she rarely spoke a kind or supportive word directly to him. She didn't want him to get a big head, so she saw it as her duty to make sure he knew he wasn't any better than anyone else. She needn't have wasted her energy.

As Daddy headed out to the backyard, he again began to feel sad. He thought of Jackie and how lovingly she treated him. She frequently told him what a remarkable and beautiful man he was. She snuggled and hugged their children and him all the time. He tried to recall ever hugging his mother but could not think of even once. Her Irish upbringing and failed marriage left her cold-hearted and closed off. Suddenly he felt tremendous guilt thinking of his sainted mother that way. Her life had been difficult. Abandoned by her good-for-nothing husband to raise two young boys, she now suffered with the terrible pain of rheumatism. He had no business judging her, still he longed for the comfort of his wife and children, and he dreaded beyond reason having to go back into his house alone.

Dave settled into the scratchy green and white woven chaise lounge in the backyard. He listened to cars speeding up and down Montrose Avenue across the alley, beyond the row of flats that lined the busy street. He turned his gaze to the sky and began identifying constellations. He easily found Draco the dragon, Hercules and Scorpio, then noticed the giant red star Antares. The vastness and infinity of the heavens gave him comfort. He knew that God looked down from somewhere out there, and suddenly realized that two days had passed without him saying his prayers. He remembered that his prayer book lay in its place on the end table next to the couch in the front room inside his dreaded house.

"Jesus Christ!" he thought. "I'm not going in there tonight. No way."

But his duty to God and the church prevailed. He got up out of the lawn chair and walked silently through the back gate that joined his and his mother's houses. He walked up the stairs to the back porch clearly lit by the streetlight in the alley. His heart began to beat faster as he slowly made his way to the kitchen screen door. He opened it slightly and reached his hand around the door frame searching for the light switch. Flicking it on he opened the door and walked in. It remained cool even though the day had been a real corker. He thought to himself how well built these old houses were to stay cool even in summer, unlike the cardboard houses sprouting up in the sprawling suburbs just outside the city.

Dave felt his stomach growl as he remembered the tasty tin foil packets that Jackie had stored in the icebox.

"She takes care of me even though she just had a baby," he thought. "I am such a lucky man."

He found a hamburger smothered with caramelized onions. This he thought should be heated up, so he found the instructions on a legal pad on the table.

- *Preheat oven to 350.*

- *Put foil packet on a pie pan (Under the silverware drawer)*

- *Bake for 20-25 minutes until heated through*

- *I love you*

He turned the oven knob to "light" then opened the oven door, struck a match, and set it to the opening to light the oven. It came to life with a *whoosh*.

Dave splashed cool water on his face and washed his hands with a little dish soap in the kitchen sink. Then, turning toward the dark front of the house, decided to fetch his prayer book and sit for his evening prayers. He chose to not turn on the dining room light since the switch rested on the wall near the basement door, but instead aimed directly for the lamp on the end table not fifteen feet in front of him. The rooms did not appear completely dark due to the city lights entering through the bank of front windows. Just two or three steps into the dining room he felt a formidable rush speeding toward him from the front of the house. He saw nothing but felt as if something ran into him, pushing him backward into the kitchen. It passed right through him. In no uncertain terms something communicated to him to GET OUT.

He didn't stop to second-guess, but ran out the kitchen door, down the stairs and back into his mother's backyard. Standing there trembling with bulging eyes he contemplated the weight of what had just happened. He felt like a coward but knew he would not spend a single night alone in that house.

Noticing the light still on in his mother's house, Dave quietly entered the side door into the kitchen, hoping to grab a couple more beers without arousing his mother's curiosity.

"Davey? Is that you?" He heard her call from across the house, "What are you doing in there?"

Though he wanted to rush in and tell her what had happened and beg to sleep on the couch or even in the basement, he didn't but simply replied, "Just grabbing a couple more beers."

"You've had enough!" she screamed. "Get out and go home. You've got to take me to church in the morning and I don't want you hungover."

"G'night Ma." He said and slipped back outside into the yard between the two houses. He stood there a long time considering his options, then decided that he would sleep in the lawn chair under the cherry tree and hope that the dew wouldn't be too heavy. Making sure no one looked out windows or walked in the alley, he peed into the rocks next to the house and settled in for a long uncomfortable night in the yard.

He awoke early with birds calling loudly from the branches

overhead. Fortunately, nobody had seen him sleeping in the yard. His mother would think he had passed out and would scold him all day. Steeling his resolve, he went into his house to change into his suit for church. Dave grabbed the empty beer cans strewn next to the lawn chair and headed cautiously up the stairs to the back porch. He tossed them into the can on the porch and opened the kitchen door.

A blast of heat met him, and he realized he had left the oven on all night. The tin foil packet of dinner dripped onto the tabletop, spoiled after having sat all night in a hot kitchen.

Frantically, he shut off the oven, horrified by the image of his whole house burning down because of an inexplicable danger. He vowed to drink no alcohol that day, pushed fear behind himself, and went upstairs to freshen up and get ready for church. He felt ridiculous thinking of how he had worked himself up as he got dressed without incident.

Dave grabbed his rosary and prayer book and headed next door to help his mother get ready for church. The heat in the kitchen overwhelmed him. He retrieved the wire fan from the front room and positioned it in the back doorway to pull some of the heat out. The cloth-covered cord didn't quite reach the outlet, so he went into the dining room to search for an extension cord in the credenza drawers.

Though the morning temperatures reached near 80 degrees, he felt a chill with his back to the hallway and the basement door. Finding no extension cord, he abandoned his project and set the fan on the side of the sink so it could at least blow the hot air *toward* the back door if not directly through it.

After church my father dropped his mother back home and helped her make lunch. He ate a sandwich with sweet pickles and potato chips, and drank a cold beer abandoning his resolution not to drink.

"One beer," he thought, "was hardly drinking."

As soon as he finished eating, Dave drove to the hospital to spend the day with my mother. Visiting hours on Sundays lasted the whole day, so no sour old nun would make him leave. He and my mother walked to the nursery window together and spoke about little Tommy More.

"Look at that big head!" my mother exclaimed, "He's got a big brain in there ... a lot like yours, my brilliant husband."

She leaned against him and he put his arm around her. Glancing from side to side for a disapproving nun or priest, he pulled her close and kissed her for a long time.

"You've already been drinking?" she asked, "Are you doing okay?"

He thought it best to not tell her about almost burning the house down, or sleeping in the yard, and just laughed. "I had a beer with lunch at Ma's after church. Did you get communion today?" he asked changing the subject.

"Of course. The priest came around before we got up this morning. Don't worry about me. The priests and nuns are making sure there are no lost souls in their care. I can't wait to get to go home! I'm going stir crazy in here."

"You have no idea." my father added.

Storm clouds gathered in the western sky when Dave left the hospital early Sunday evening. Arriving home in broad daylight, my father nervously climbed the stairs, went into the bathroom and grabbed his toiletries. Next, he grabbed suits, shirts, underwear, socks— everything he would need for work over the next few days—and carried it all down to the kitchen. He set his toiletries next to the kitchen sink and hung his clothes over the back of a kitchen chair. Then he grabbed a bed sheet from the linen closet in the bathroom, and a pillow off the bed. He set those things on top of a box on the back porch. He made sure to tuck his prayer book, and rosary in his suit pocket, and piled his law books on the back-porch floor.

Then he strode next door and grabbed the chaise lounge lawn chair from his mother's backyard and set it up under the bank of windows on the back porch. He knew he would sleep safely out of the weather, but even more importantly safe from whatever terrorized him inside that house. If he got caught, he decided to just say he wanted to sleep on the porch to keep cool.

Many years prior, a large tree had fallen on the old back porch taking out the entire roof. Dave's uncles had demolished the rest of the old porch and attached this entirely new one. For some reason unknown to my father at the time, the porch felt safe and peaceful, as if it had nothing whatsoever to do with the rest of the unspeakably troubled house. Here my father camped out, entering the house only for a cold beer, or to heat up a tin foil meal to eat outside or on the porch. He remained there until the day my mother and new baby Tommy came home several days later.

My mother asked no questions when she noticed Dave's back porch camp. She knew all too well the effect the house seemed to have on her husband. She couldn't imagine how difficult it must have been for him while she lollygagged in the hospital after having a baby. She also couldn't fathom the thought of herself ever having to spend a week alone in the house.

# Chapter 12
# Escape

(i-'skāp–*verb*: to slip away from pursuit or peril; avoid capture, punishment, or any threatened evil.)

By the time we returned from Up North my baby brother Tommy and my parents had settled in. We learned that my father named him Thomas More after the patron saint of lawyers. He hoped this might curry special consideration at the culmination of his law studies, and the formidable exams that lay ahead. The incidents of unpredictable violent episodes from my father increased as the bar exam loomed. I watched my father closely for warning signs whenever I found myself in his presence. I took on the role of watcher so I could warn my brothers and sisters of danger, while also protecting myself.

I could feel the dark thing coming before I actually saw it. I would sense that familiar chill in the room. I also noticed a slight change in light, though nothing really physically changed. Then my father himself would change. It always started with the color of his face. We could clearly see it begin to happen. He would grow increasingly agitated, then flush, red, and eventually almost purplish. Next, he would begin to rub his forehead vigorously with tensed fingers. Soon he would start to scan the room displaying a terribly ferocious expression, with flat eyes that didn't seem to recognize us, or focus on anyone or anything. He'd clench his fists, lower his chin toward his chest, until a low growl began to emanate from deep in his throat. He would rise slowly and deliberately, with a terrifying ferocity, then begin biting his clenched fists. We would all try to scatter before his clenched fists slammed down on the end table, card table or any other surface nearby sending everything flying. He would stand there growling, then begin to roar loudly and unintelligibly in the most hideous way.

Though everyone who lived there experienced spirits daily, my father seemed to bear the full brunt of whatever dark entities shared our childhood home. Our young lives were certainly marked by considerable chaos, and even ghastly events from time to time. We frequently saw full-bodied apparitions lurking in closets or gliding down the stairway. We also often heard unexplained footsteps, unintelligible whispers, and disembodied voices calling our names from around corners, other rooms, and sometimes even right next to our ears. I frequently saw movement in my peripheral vision, often turning quickly only to find nothing there. I recall the hairs on my body standing on end as all warmth suddenly emptied from a room, sucking out even the light, leaving the room visibly darker. Then the chill would subside just as quickly as it came. I always felt on edge, never letting my guard down, even in sleep. I felt stressed and exhausted every minute of the day or night. Even so, watching the torture Daddy experienced made every other encounter seem almost trivial. It disturbed my sense of safety, but even so I never felt truly under attack the way Daddy did. He suffered countless attacks of what I can only describe as possession.

Daddy worked hard for his young family. He worked to feed five children under five years of age plus his wife and a brand-new baby. He had a day job with the phone company, then went to law school at night. In every spare minute he studied. Though a small office at the top of the stairs could have served as a quiet place for him to work, my father never stayed there alone for any length of time. Instead he and my mother set up the old wooden playpen in the middle of the front room, not to contain the baby or toddlers, but as a study spot for my father. They placed a card table and folding chair in the middle of it. My father sat inside that playpen writing and reading case law in the middle of the busiest room in the house.

The playpen, they told us, kept our curious, sticky, little, dirty hands from his papers, pens, and other "Daddy things." We never questioned why he didn't use the desk upstairs. Not a single one of us ever wanted to be alone in a room anyplace in that house either. My father worked like this for hours amid all manner of family noise and distraction ... until he didn't.

His unexpected and often unprovoked rage could appear at any moment. Sometimes amid children bickering, sometimes in peace and quiet. I could not, for the life of me, figure out what brought it on, but it always hit like a tsunami.

"Get some air" My terrified mother shouted from the safety of the dining room, with us gathered watching in horror behind her. "Take a break and go outside."

Daddy would turn and glare, nearly unrecognizable, at my mother. He looked not at all like the father I adored, but like an extremely dangerous, wild animal about to pounce and eat us all alive.

Sometimes Mommy's interjections diffused the situation, and Daddy went into the yard where he instantly calmed down. Sometimes they didn't. At those times my mother would shout at us to run next door to Grandma's house to get my dad's Uncle Jack. Uncle Jack was a railroad cop. We saw him as the good guy who could protect us from our raging father. When Uncle Jack came, he invariably convinced Daddy to take a break and go next door for a cold beer. It always snapped my father from the grips of his—and our—torment. Together they left the house, and we, without a word, resumed our activity.

I remember how odd it seemed that Daddy's flushed face reverted to normal the minute he crossed the threshold to the porch. His entire demeanor changed; not slowly over time, but instantly. It seemed as if he didn't even remember that only moments before he stood ready to tear his wife and children to bits.

One Saturday afternoon, my father sat reading on the couch in the front room. Having completed his studies for the day, he seemed relaxed. We had just come in from a game of whiffle ball in Grandma's yard next door. My siblings and I sat on the floor playing nicely. Davy busily pushed toy cars around on the rug. Kate colored in a tattered coloring book staying carefully inside the lines. My little sister, Annie, played with blocks or Lincoln logs, and I played with my doll. One-year-old Colleen nibbled on saltines surrounded by a sea of soggy crumbs as she sat in the middle of the room among all her bigger siblings. Mommy tended a big pot of red beans for supper in the kitchen while the new baby, Tommy, slept in his bassinet.

Suddenly the temperature in the room dropped. I immediately looked to Daddy, knowing from experience what might happen next. I observed his color change, as I carefully began to move away from him, hoping to not attract his attention. I tried to warn my brothers and sisters of the impending danger. His foot began to bounce rapidly up and down, shaking his knee violently. His book remained opened, though it became exceedingly clear that he no longer read the text. I saw him grip the book tightly as if ready to rip it apart. His face contorted as he tucked his chin down close to his chest and began to growl.

Every one of us froze, staring. My other siblings also noticed the danger. We watched this creature that had been our father, laughing and pitching home runs only moments before, grip the base of a large, heavy lamp perched on an end table to his right.

Focusing an irrational rage on his small children on the floor before him, he began to lift the lamp. It shook in his hand and he appeared to struggle with it. I wasn't sure if he tried to hold it back, or raise it pushing against an unseen force that seemed to usurp his will. His muscles trembled with fatigue as he gripped the base of the heavy lamp.

In the midst of his growl it seemed his own voice struggled through.

"Get out." He growled.

I tried to recognize my father somewhere deep inside this monster that threatened us so imminently.

"Ge-e-et O-o-ut! He growled as he raised the weapon above his head.

I stared frozen, unable to move, unable to look away, unable to save myself. My brothers, sisters, and I sat like frozen ducks.

Suddenly and miraculously, our mother came running in from the kitchen wiping her hands with a dish towel. Seeing Daddy in this terrifying state and recognizing the very real danger he posed to every one of her children, she barked an order, "Run! Get out *now!*"

Daddy stood waving the enormous lamp in the air as if ready to bash in all our heads. The General (our mother), had given an order; we leapt to our feet. My big sister grabbed the squirming baby, and we scrambled toward the front door. My mother stood helplessly in the dining room with our ferocious father between her and us.

"Dave! Dave! Stop!" She screamed as he chased us toward the door.

We bolted through the hallway, pulling the heavy wooden front door as if it were paper. We ran across the expanse of the porch and flew down the stairs heading to the safety of our grandmother's house next door. Our possessed father followed us out, roaring like a madman.

The others did not look back, but I stopped as soon as I crossed the driveway. I turned to look back at Daddy, hell-bent on murdering us all.

As he stepped out of the house, I watched his body go limp. His hand just opened and dropped the lamp, which crashed into a million pieces on the porch floor. I saw him look around in the sunlight. He appeared confused, weakened. He dropped down onto the top step of the porch, put his head in his hands, and began to sob.

Uncle Jack came running past me shouting, "Get in the House. Go on. Get out of here."

Seeing my strong father so broken, I wanted to run to the safety of my grandmother. I really didn't want to stare at Daddy's shame and torment, but I couldn't move. I couldn't take my eyes off my weeping, defeated father.

Uncle Jack sat down on the step next to him. Mommy stood in the front door nervously wringing the dishcloth still in her hands, her expression, a cross between terror and pity. Uncle Jack put his arm around his nephew. I had never seen this before. The closest thing to physical contact I'd seen between them was a handshake or maybe a playful pat on the back. But this was new. Uncle Jack held my father tightly with both their heads down. They spoke, but I couldn't make out what they said.

Then through tears and snot, Daddy looked up and saw me watching. His shoulders heaved as he sobbed, "Jesus Christ. I'm so sorry. I'm so sorry. "

He looked in Uncle Jack's face. "What is wrong with me. What in God's name is wrong with me? I tried to stop, but it was just too strong! I tried to warn them. I tried to stop it."

Again, he dropped his face in his hands and wept. Mommy joined them on the top step and gestured for me to go to Grandma's. She sat down on the other side of my father and laid her arm around his shoulders.

I turned and ran into Grandma's front room where my brothers and sisters excitedly reported how my father tried to kill us all with the lamp.

My horrified grandmother hushed us, attempting distraction with the promise of a cookie. Before long, Mommy came in to gather us all up to go back home. As we walked out of Grandma's door, I noticed that both Daddy and Uncle Jack had vanished from the front porch.

I wondered if they had gone inside, but soon found out that they were not there either. My father did not come home that night. Though my curiosity was unbearable, I knew better than to ask my weary mother where he'd gone. My little sister who hadn't yet learned the "don't ask, don't tell" rule flat out asked where Daddy had gone.

"He's sleeping next door at Grandma's tonight," my mother explained. "He just really needs to get a good, peaceful night's sleep." We all nodded in both relief and understanding as we hugged our mother good night.

*Don't we all*, I thought, *Don't we all.*

# Chapter 13

# Serpent

(ser-pent—*noun*: a snake; a wily, treacherous, or malicious person)

My father graduated with honors from law school the same day Kate graduated from kindergarten. We all stood for photos with him in his cap and gown, and Kate in her construction-paper cap and collar from Mayfair Grammar School.

After passing the bar, my father got a job for the United States Justice Department. This meant that, although he worked long hours, he came home most evenings, spending more and more time with us. Far from a relaxing respite from the world, the house, or something in it, seemed to torment him more than ever.

He frequently lashed out at Mommy or at us children. We walked on eggshells to avoid triggering his wrath and made sure to do our chores on time at 5 o'clock so no toys cluttered the front room when Daddy got home. My mother warned us that he worked hard and needed time free from bickering or fighting on our part when he came home to relax. Though we ran to greet him at the door with hugs, kisses, and gleeful shouts of "Daddy's home!" every evening, we knew that we needed to give him time to change out of his business suit and into his comfortable clothes before "bothering" him with stories or questions. Based on Mommy's careful instruction, I realized early on that, though Daddy seemed strong, competent, and brilliant, he was also quite fragile. It was up to us to not set him off.

One evening every single one of us had followed my mother's directive meticulously so to not bother my father, and yet, when he went into his room to change his clothes something else set him off. Something alone in the room with him, behind the closed door, pushed him into a rage. Mommy rushed to him in the bedroom.

Over the sound of *Garfield Goose* on the old black and white TV set, we heard raised voices from my parent's room at the end of the downstairs hall. Their conversation grew louder and louder, and more heated by the minute.

"Turn up the TV," Kate ordered.

None of us wanted to hear it, and my oldest sister always tried to keep us both in line and protected. However, as the argument grew louder it began to bleed through, beyond the blaring television, into our evening. We all jumped to attention startled by the sound of a loud crash followed by my father's terrifyingly familiar growl.

"Dave! Dave!" My mother's voice grew panicked. "Dave!" She screamed.

Fearing the worst, and worrying about my mother's safety, along with perhaps a little bit of ghoulish curiosity to witness a big fight, we ran to the end of the hall. Through the partially open bedroom door I saw my father, face down on the floor in his underwear. His contorted and purple face invoked alarm in each of us. He sprawled across the floor with his back and neck arched so that I knew if his eyes focused, he could see us watching. I don't believe he did see us, however, since he gave no indication of awareness of his surroundings and said no words. He never acknowledged our presence, but instead began reaching out, one hand after the other, clawing at the hardwood floor with his fingernails, and dragging himself in our direction. His body writhed unnaturally. His face first lifted toward the ceiling, then lowered toward the floor, over and over again in a serpentine motion. I could barely breathe. I had seen my father in fits of anger and rage, but this did not even remotely resemble the Daddy I knew. This looked like something else altogether. He looked like an evil serpent or dragon—writhing and contorting toward us on the floor.

Mommy—both hands covering her mouth—stood frozen in terror

and disbelief next to the dresser, unable to look away from our father, who crawled on his belly in an unnatural way. He inched toward us, his children, as we cowered in the hall doorway. As he moved closer, we backed up, huddling together in the hallway, pressed against the basement door.

I heard his growl begin to form words, "*On my belly like a snake.*" emerged from deep in his throat sounding not at all like my father's voice. "*On my belly like a snake....*" This creature continued to drag our father's body fully into the hall next to the stairs.

When my mother finally saw us there, her maternal instincts kicked in. "Get out of the way" She screamed as our father slithered, growling and drooling, toward the stairs. In tears, she walked helplessly behind him muttering under her breath, "Dave. Dave. For the love of God, Dave."

We moved aside, standing together in the front room archway, out of his path, where we watched the entire disturbing spectacle.

When our father reached the bottom of the stairs, his body twisted, and he began to ascend. I noticed that his fingernails bled as he clawed at the first step. What happened next is a vision that haunts my nightmares to this very day. He began to drag his body up using only his fingernails and his teeth, growling ferociously "*On my belly like a snake.*"

He bit down hard into the edge of each of the eighteen oak stairs, leaving deep marks that remained embedded there forever. Tears began to fall from my eyes, and my brothers and sisters and I all began to sob uncontrollably. Mommy stood helplessly at the bottom of the stairs calling to him, as Daddy slithered toward the upstairs hall. I will never forget the terror in her eyes as she turned to give us one warning glance, then flew up the stairs after him. We all ran to the bottom of the stairs where we watched him continue his serpentine crawl into the hall toward the bathroom, the exact route that The Slinky Lady traversed day and night.

Both he and my mother disappeared out of sight upstairs into the bathroom. None of us children dared to run up to see the continuation of this nightmare. Sobbing, we exchanged glances, trying to think of what we should do when we heard Mommy scream, *"Help!!! Help!! Jesus Christ Dave! NO! Somebody HELP! Go get Uncle Jack! Hurry! Go get Uncle Jack! Oh, sweet Jesus, Dave STOP!"*

I had never heard Mommy sound like that. Sister Kate bolted out the front door like lightning as all but the littlest of us ran upstairs.

Mommy, screaming and in tears, had both arms wrapped around Dad's left arm, holding it with all her might. His muscles trembled with the struggle. My father was not left-handed. Through his clenched teeth he snarled, *"I do not deserve to live. I am nothing. I do not deserve to live!"*

Then for a moment his demeanor shifted, and he looked at my mother with terror in his eyes. His voice was pleading in his own recognizable voice. "Jackie! Please! Help me! Stop me. Stop this, I'm not strong enough. Jesus! God please help me." He begged.

Just as quickly, Dad morphed back into the previous demonstate, growling, spitting, and cursing at my mother—then looking over her shoulder to curse and spit at us. I saw a razor blade in the hand my mother restrained. He held out his right wrist preparing it for the assault.

We all began to sob, begging loudly, *"Daddy! Daddy! No! Please Daddy!"*

Suddenly Uncle Jack rushed past the tangle of terrified, blubbering children. He ran straight into the bathroom, and before my mother could say a word, he punched my father hard in the face with his storied right hook.

Our father crumbled to the floor as we stood trembling and weeping in disbelief. Shaking oddly, Daddy looked up at uncle Jack who, fist still clenched, stood over him ready to land another blow if needed. Daddy began to sob uncontrollably, and his color gradually returned to normal.

"Thank you. Oh Jackie ... Jack ... thank you. What is wrong with me? Jesus Christ. Mother of God. What in God's name is happening to me?" With all of us still watching from the hall Uncle Jack instructed my mother to get my father some whiskey.

This time nobody told us to leave. They were too occupied with my poor father. We children stood there staring as my mother returned with a large glass of whiskey. Daddy, who sat crumpled in a broken heap on the bathroom floor, poured the brown liquid down his throat as his uncle sat on the edge of the tub talking softly to him. After a minute, my mother just closed the bathroom door.

I looked into the eyes of my siblings. We were all crying, unsure of what to do next and trying to make sense of the scene we had just observed. Finally, Kate ordered us back downstairs. With my mother, father, and uncle Jack still in the bathroom, we all deferred to her authority and dutifully returned to the front room. *Garfield Goose* had long since concluded, so the six of us, aged seven to one, sat in stunned silence watching Fahey Flynn read the evening news.

After that night we never spoke about what happened. Neither sibling nor parent offered explanation or reassurance. When my mother returned to finish making supper, she barely made eye contact with us. I went into the kitchen to see if I could help. She stood at the stove opening cans of corned beef hash to fry and serve with cold canned green beans. Her voice choked as she thanked me, "Yes, darlin', will you please set the table?"

Even though setting the table fell to my brother that night, I didn't argue. I just grabbed a stack of plates. "I love you Mommy." I said, not knowing what other words of comfort I could possibly offer.

"I love you too." She replied, her arm around my shoulder. She looked sadly into my eyes and promised, "It will be okay. It will all be okay."

I smiled back at her but wondered who she was trying to convince me or herself. Neither of us believed a word of it for a minute.

# Chapter 14

# Reconstruction

(rē-kən-'strək-shən—*verb*: to construct again; rebuild; make over. To re-create in the mind from given or available information)

MY FATHER DID NOT COME HOME FOR A FEW DAYS after his 'breakdown" in the hall and bathroom. When he did, a strange hush fell over the house and all of us who lived there. No one ever spoke a word about what had happened. We were expected to just forget it and continue with each new day as if nothing ever happened.

I found this impossible. Every time I closed my eyes to sleep, I saw him, or what consumed him. Sometimes the very moment I opened my eyes I thought I could see his contorted face appear briefly in the dark close to mine. Sitting on the couch in the front room to watch TV, I had a full view of the archway with the hall and staircase behind it. My attention shifted involuntarily from the TV screen to the stairs, where I frequently envisioned a slithering monster ascending the stairs with bleeding claws. A shudder and nausea overcame me until I distracted myself in some way. The stairs still bore the scars from my father's teeth, much like the deep scars entrenched in my memory.

I recall one time running up the stairs in bare feet and feeling searing pain in the arch of my foot. Limping to the top of the stairs I sat on the floor to see what had stabbed me. A long sliver of ragged wood had embedded deeply in my foot. My mother had to dig it out with a needle and tweezers since it had broken into several smaller shards. I winced with each new assault on my tender skin. After removing every tiny bit, my mother painted on mercurochrome so it wouldn't get infected. The red stain made the injury appear much worse than it actually was. Though in reality it was only skin deep, the psychic injury went much deeper. I knew that slithering monster had gotten me again.

Nightmares in which I was chased by an enormous fearsome beast plagued my sleep. In the dream, the beast tried to devour me. In that dream, I ran shouting for my father to save me. When he appeared, however, he joined in the chase—his body moving as if he had no bones. I would wake in a cold sweat. Waking never brought much relief from my nightmares because, after all, I lived in a nightmare whether asleep or awake.

Sometimes, while sitting very still, distant, deep-throated, laughter would sound from somewhere just beyond my view. It was as if that dark thing took pleasure in my family's suffering. I began to withdraw into my imagination. It started with me imagining safe places I had visited such as Up North or Grammie Ethel's house, and then projecting my consciousness to those places, sometimes instead of sleeping, and even sometimes to avoid having to remain in a very unfriendly waking reality. My mother noticed.

"Penny for your thoughts," she would say as I sat motionless staring off into space. She would jostle me lovingly. Sometimes when she wasn't occupied with her endless chores, she would even sit down next to me. Forcing a smile, I would lean into her. The last thing my mother needed was to have to worry about me. She had enough to deal with holding the whole family together in the midst of entropy.

"Nothing, just thinking."

When she had time, she would attempt to engage me in conversation, but even with her right there next to me I could still see dark things moving out of the corner of my eye. I would have preferred to have my mind focused somewhere outside of that house than in it among the memories and spirits that plagued me. Even with Mommy right there beside me, I never felt safe.

My father changed as well. Before long large bottles of cheap whiskey and gin became staples in the house. The minute Daddy returned from work, Mommy made him a cocktail. He would gulp it down before changing out of his suit. After changing, he would go to the kitchen cupboard for a tumbler. Starting with a few ice cubes, he'd then pour it full of liquor. I distinctly recall the sound of the "glug, glug, glug" as he filled the aluminum tumbler to the brim. He would carry his drink to the couch where a pile of books and his eager children awaited him.

The time between the drink my mother made and about halfway through the one he made for himself was the sweet spot for us kids and my mother. He would listen as we told him details of our daily escapades. Then he told heroic tales of fighting the mob at the U.S. Attorney's office enhanced with descriptions of characters with names like Teets, Rocko, and The Tuna. Adventures that normally happened only in the movies were Daddy's workday life. We loved to hear him unspool the deceits of underworld characters.

When his eyes became watery and red, we knew that our precious time had come to an end. My mother usually noticed first and told us all to go play or watch TV, "Leave your father alone so he can relax." We knew better than to push our luck, begging for one more story or asking one too many questions.

My brothers and sisters would scatter, but I usually remained sitting silently on the far end of the couch. Daddy would pick up one of his books. He loved to read. I loved to read too. It provided yet another avenue to escape my troubled world, but more important to me it was also a connection that Dad and I shared.

I sat reading my own books as Daddy dove into tomes from great authors such as Belloc, Breasted, Chesterton, and Gibbon. As the evening went on and his tumbler of liquor waned, I made sure to observe him more closely. Sometimes his head would begin to nod. That meant that things would remain calm. Sometimes his leg would start to shake. When that happened, I knew that the time had come for me to make myself scarce, because invariably a loud, violent fight would follow. I would sometimes try to distract him by asking about Plato's

*Republic* or *The Decline and Fall of the Roman Empire*, and sometimes it worked ... for a while. But always after bedtime on those nights we could hear screaming and crashing from downstairs where my parents battled.

Some evenings Daddy would stumble through the front door, his eyes already watery and red. On those nights, Mommy would hustle us into the kitchen for supper, warning us that we should keep quiet because Daddy had had a very bad day. This meant, of course, that we were about to have a bad day as well.

My father used liquor the way I used reading and daydreaming. It dampened the frightening sounds that relentlessly stalked us in our home. It dulled the effects of entities who slipped back and forth between the world we could see and a world we could not. It sated the thing that seemed to hunger for our very souls, keeping it at bay for brief moments at least. No matter how much we tried to avoid it, however, the house somehow continued to spew its poison into our world. Liquor, while intended to dull his torment, soon began turning my father into another monster, in much the same way as the thing that consumed him, making him writhe like a serpent while torturing everyone who lived in that house.

Still, I loved my father. I longed for his approval and for a meaningful connection with him. Our shared love of ancient history, especially Egyptian history, provided that connection.

When I was born, my mother wanted to name me Antoinette Marie after her French speaking Creole great aunt. My father objected, saying that the nickname for Antoinette was Toni. He told her that Toni sounded like a tough girl standing on the street corner with a cigarette hanging out of her mouth. He told her that no daughter of his would ever be called Toni. My mother replied that they didn't have to call me Toni, that they could call me anything.

"Anything?" my father asked.

And so he gave me the nickname, "Tiyi," after the chief wife of Amenhotep III, King Tutankhamun's grandmother. My father, and the name he gave me, unsurprisingly led to a great interest in Ancient Egypt.

I had learned to read well before kindergarten by watching *Sing Along With Mitch* on TV. Mitch Miller directed a choir. The entire show consisted of him conducting that choir as they sang standards and popular songs. He encouraged the TV audience to sing along at home by "following the bouncing ball." The lyrics appeared at the bottom of the screen and a magical ball would bounce above the words so the audience could follow.

My folks loved that show. Because I loved to sing, we watched it together. I quickly realized that the ball bounced on the words the people sang and started recognizing words in other places. When my father would read to us from *A Bad Child's Book of Beasts* by Belloc, I would look closely at the pages anticipating the rhyme and thereby reading the text.

By the time I reached six years of age, I was a fluent reader. Daddy gave me anthropology books and history books intended for readers far beyond my years. Then we would discuss them. At the age of eight I read all volumes of *The Decline and Fall Of The Roman Empire* by Gibbon. Daddy explained things that I didn't understand, filling in cultural and historical context, but I largely held my own in our book discussions. This delighted him, and so in turn delighted me. When my other siblings were told to leave Dad alone, he would call me to him to talk about the books we shared. This relationship somehow seemed to shield me from his wrath when he lashed out from the effects of liquor or the oppressive forces that lurked in our house.

Soon I began to hyper focus on Egyptology. I read about the great dynasties, and learned about Hatshepsut who, though a "mere" woman, actually became a Pharaoh. We studied the pyramids and Egyptian mythology. We visited The Field Museum, spending hours in the Egyptian collection. Hieroglyphics fascinated me, and I longed to learn to read it.

Though we lived in chaos and volatility much of the time, I also remember many amazing things our parents did for us. They took us on outings—just one of us at a time. With six children and one on the way, everything else in our lives happened in a large group. This made our occasional one-on-one dates even more special.

One Saturday, my father and I went to The Oriental Institute at The University of Chicago. It was heaven on earth for hopeful future Egyptologist me! Without having to accommodate impatient siblings, Dad and I took as much time as we wanted, reading every word of explanation at every exhibit. After several hours in the exhibits, Dad told me that I could choose one thing from the gift shop. I knew exactly what I wanted and headed straight for the books. I searched through all the titles looking for a beginner's guide to Ancient Egyptian language. Seeing none, I asked the clerk if she knew of a book that a child my age might use to learn 18th dynasty classical Egyptian language. She asked if I meant hieroglyphics and I replied that I thought I should learn the language before trying to decipher the writing.

She raised her eyebrows and glanced over at my beaming father.

"Really?" she asked. "Why the 18th dynasty in particular."

I told her about my name and how I felt a special connection to my namesake and the world in which she lived. She asked my father if we had a few minutes to wait while she went to talk to someone upstairs. He agreed while we looked at replicas of amulets and other artifacts.

After a few minutes she returned asking us to follow her to the second floor. We passed a sign that said "Closed to the Public" hanging from a velvet cord and climbed a wide, curved, marble staircase. She led us down a long hall lined with dark wooden doors. Finally, we reached one that said: Ancient Language Department: Dr. Livingood, Chair.

Dr. Livingood sat behind a desk cluttered with piles of papers. Behind her, mountains of books overflowed floor to ceiling bookcases. Looking up from her papers, she removed her reading glasses, smiled, and said, "Well now! Who do we have here? This young lady," she gestured to the clerk who stood smiling in the doorway, "tells me that a little girl wants to learn the language from the classical period of ancient Egypt. Is that you?"

"Yes ma'am." I said confidently.

"I understand you have something in common with Tutankhamun's grandmother?"

"Yes ma'am."

"And what is that?" she asked with growing pleasure.

"Well," I told her, "What I have learned about Queen Tiyi was that she was a scholar, a musician, and a scribe. While very few people could read and write, Queen Tiyi not only could read, but she wrote poetry and music. I want to do what she did. I want to be able to read the papyri myself."

Dr. Livingood began to laugh, "I thought you were going to tell me that you shared a name! I can see that you are a serious scholar. I think I can help you become a scribe as well."

Dr. Livingood spent the next couple of hours showing me how to cross reference an Egyptian language workbook and the textbook that her graduate students used. She shared some of the basics and told me that Egyptian hieroglyphics was extremely difficult because it contained both phonetic and pictographic symbols. She told me to not get discouraged, but to call her if I got stuck. She assigned Chapter One, in which I would take short passages written in hieroglyphics, translate, then transliterate to find their English meaning. Dr, Livingood gifted me with an enormous text that my father had to carry due to its size and weight, a smaller Egyptian Language book, and the accompanying workbook.

My father and I both thanked her profusely. Then, giddy with anticipation, we headed home with our bounty. I couldn't wait to begin. I read about grammar and syntax and dove into the workbook. This replaced all my normal third-grade schoolwork much to the chagrin of my teacher. I pretty much disengaged with elementary school and became a budding researcher.

When my third-grade teacher tried to humiliate me for lack of homework and for daydreaming I simply retreated further into my own mind. Soon, I stopped speaking and participating at all and remained selectively mute for the next five years in school.

Though my participation in the normal world of an eight-year-old waned, I had another world apart that filled me with wonder. As I translated and transliterated, I gained a deeper and deeper connection to something that felt so comfortable and familiar—something that I began to experience more like a memory with each new lesson.

We visited Dr. Livingood many times. She praised me for my progress and told us that she had graduate students who didn't have the drive that I had. For me it was less a drive than a hunger. I felt as though something pulled me with each new lesson, each new page. I found that when I sat my enormous books on the table and began shifting back and forth from text to workbook, no spirits or entities bothered me. I felt safe and protected, as if something watched over me so I could learn significant things.

Sometimes, as I worked, I experienced strange thoughts that felt like memories. I saw myself in my studies—as if I could smell and touch a world thousands of years in the past. I sensed the heat of the Egyptian sun and the cool stone hallways through which I imagined myself walking.

Dr. Livingood told me that there were no vowels in the hieroglyphic writings so we can't accurately know how the language sounded. Yet, when I translated, I could hear it in my head. I knew how it sounded.... It was as if I remembered. Perhaps it was the vivid imagination my mother told me I employed to explain away my frequent interdimensional spirit encounters. Once again, experiences muddied my understanding of the corporeal and the ephemeral.

It didn't matter to me. It offered yet another escape from both the house, and my father's alcoholic violence. When we studied hieroglyphs together, he didn't fill his tumbler a second time. His knee didn't bounce up and down with anxiety. He didn't yell or suddenly shift into an unrecognizable creature. He let me tell him what I had learned, and we would talk until my bedtime. This provided a much improved "normal" for which I so longed. It also meant that when I went to bed, I might dream about a life in ancient Egypt instead of nightmares about my boneless father pursuing me alongside terrifying serpents.

# Chapter 15
# Susurration

(sü-sɛ-'rā -shɛn—*noun*: a soft murmur; whisper)

As our family grew, the strain of living in a place with frightening things, both living and not, continued to affect us. More and more, Daddy stayed late at work or went for drinks after work, arriving home later and later in the evenings, leaving family responsibilities to my mother. Grandma grew more and more crippled with terrible pain from what she referred to as rheumatism. She often dragged her bent body around her house behind a straight-backed chair. Her gnarled fingers had difficulty managing the beads on her ever-present rosary. As Grandma became unable to leave the house, or to tend to even her most basic needs, my pregnant mother stepped in to help. Mommy did all of Grandma's shopping and helped her cook meals. When Grandma's hands could no longer turn the can-opener crank, Mommy even opened the cans of chicken à la king that Grandma loved so much. Mommy not only cleaned our house, but also cleaned Grandma's. Uncle Jack worked nights, so we were rarely allowed in Grandma's house during the day in order for him to sleep undisturbed. This left us completely on our own when Mommy was next door at Grandma's.

By this time, I was eight years old, so I could take care of myself and the younger ones. I loved playing their games and teaching them little songs. My mother told me that I was a natural teacher, and that she never worried about the kids when she put me in charge. When my younger brothers and sisters asked me about scary things they experienced in our house, I would tell them what my mother told me; that their eyes were playing tricks on them. I told them this so they wouldn't be afraid, but then I made sure to keep careful watch on them to keep dark things away when they were my responsibility. I learned to stop voices and specters temporarily by willing them gone, and by pushing an imaginary bubble around myself so they couldn't touch me. I had no words for what I did, I'm not even sure If I did it consciously. All I knew was that it worked most of the time. When it didn't, I could distract and make more noise than anything unseen. Sometimes I could push my bubble out to repel frightening things, keeping my little brothers and sisters and myself safe when Mommy was not home.

One early autumn day, an ambulance came to carry Grandma away. She had fallen and shattered her leg. I recall her wails as they lifted the stretcher into the ambulance.

"I'm never coming back!" she screamed, "I'm going to die in the hospital!"

Though shocked by the scene, we tried to smile and wave to encourage her as they shut the doors and sped up the street with lights flashing.

That night I watched my father weep in my mother's arms after the doctors told them that Grandma was "shot through with cancer". It broke my heart to see *his* heart so broken at the prospect of losing his mother. Mommy comforted him with hugs and gentle words. Though she never really had gained favor with Grandma, she would miss the old woman too.

The next day Grammie Ethel picked us up from school in her big Cadillac. We never, even in rain or blizzards got a ride home from school, but always walked carrying an armful of books. Kate immediately grew suspicious.

As Grandma Angela's first granddaughter, Kathleen Mavourneen was held in the highest esteem. She could do no wrong. Grandma and Kate would sit together at her dining room table eating strawberry rhubarb jam on bread while playing cards for hours on end. I coveted the jam, but had no desire to play cards, finding the game extremely uninteresting. Kate knew that Grandma Angela loved her best. She also knew that something was going on with Grandma and resented Grammie Ethel for not filling her in before we got home.

When we arrived, we saw many cars lining the street in front of Grandma Angela's house. Grammie Ethel didn't let us go home to our own house but herded us into Grandma Angela's house. The place was filled with aunts, uncles, and cousins. Even Aunt Theresa and Uncle Eddie had come all the way from Madison, but I didn't see my parents. I began to realize the seriousness of the situation.

Pizza pies and bags of potato chips appeared on the dining room table. The ice box held many cans of cold Hamm's beer, and liquor bottles stood shoulder-to-shoulder on the kitchen counter. It looked like a party, but no one laughed or joked, and nobody went down to the basement bar to play pool like they usually did. Instead, they all stood around talking solemnly with beer cans or small glasses of whiskey in one hand, and some with a cigarette in the other. Kate grew more furious as Grammie Ethel took on the duties of hostess, cleaning up, and offering to refresh peoples' drinks. Kate hated how she usurped her favorite grandmother's home and sat silently glaring at her, arms crossed, next to the fireplace and Grandma's empty chair.

I stood in the doorway between the dining room and the kitchen as Uncle Gerald Pulled strands of hair loose from my ponytail, smiling and calling me "Terrible T, The Tough Tot." Suddenly an unopened can of chicken à la king fell out of a closed cupboard and landed with a thud on the kitchen floor.

Uncle Jack said, "Somebody mark the time, She's dead."

Everyone nodded their heads and noted that the clock said 5:47. When my mother called from the hospital twenty minutes later with the news that Grandma had passed away Uncle Joe told her that we already knew. My mother told him that Grandma died at ten minutes to six.

"No," he corrected, "It was 5:47. She knocked a can off the shelf to let us know."

Everyone just nodded again.

Grammie Ethel tried to console Kate as she gave her the terrible news. Kate pulled away and rushed into the bathroom, slamming the door hard. Some started to cry, saying, "At least she is out of pain now." They said Grandma Angela wouldn't have to spend time in purgatory but would go straight to heaven because she had suffered so much in life. I agreed, though when they started talking about her being a true saint, I became skeptical, recalling how she used to yell at us, and how she treated my mother so badly for the "sin" of marrying her son.

After a while Gramps arrived. He and Grammie Ethel took us next door to put us to bed. My parents didn't get home until after we had all gone to sleep. The next day nobody woke us up for school. They thought we needed a day off after such a difficult night grieving our poor dead grandma.

Sometimes—forgetting that she had gone—Daddy would look out the window next to his bed to wave goodnight to his mother where she used to sit watching *The Late Show with Fahey Flynn*. On more than one occasion he told us that he thought he saw her wave back before realizing that it was impossible. I did not think, in fact I knew that it was entirely possible *and actually likely*, given that she announced her own death with a can of chicken à la king.

Great Grandma Lyons died only a few short months after her daughter, Angela. Her other children chose not to tell her the bad news that her daughter had died because it might break her already weak heart. On her own deathbed, Annie Lyons wondered aloud why Angela had come to get her along with other long-dead relatives.

In the spring my baby sister, Mary Angela, named for my grandmother, was born. My mother had to miss my first communion because she stayed in the hospital recovering from the birth of her eighth child. In her absence, all my siblings got to stay with Uncle Jerry, my father's brother, and Aunt Pat, but I alone had to go stay with Uncle Gerald and Aunt Jeanette because they lived close to the church, and could more easily get me to CCD and communion practices. I missed my siblings and resented the fact that my first communion had been usurped. To remedy this, on my first communion day we all piled into the station wagon to go to the hospital. I wore my beautiful white dress, veil, fancy socks, and white patent leather shoes that Grammie Ethel bought for me. We all got out of the car in the parking lot to wave frantically as Mommy waved to us from a fourth-floor window.

Then the unimaginable happened.

Daddy told all the other kids to get back into the car and he took me into the hospital. Children were strictly forbidden in hospitals because we apparently carried deadly germs on our dirty little bodies. He spoke to a nurse in a white uniform with a pointed white nurse cap who smiled sweetly at me, telling me how lovely I looked. Two other nurses joined her, and we stepped onto the elevator. I stood in the far corner and the three nurses stood side by side in front of me to hide me from anyone who happened onto the elevator. The bell rang as the doors opened and they quickly whisked me into a conference room where my mother sat on a small couch holding my new baby sister, Mary Angela.

I couldn't believe my eyes! My mother told me how beautiful I looked in my first communion dress. She asked me to spin around so she could get a good look at me, then told me to sit down next to her. She kissed me on my forehead, then handed me the baby. Mommy put her arm around the two of us. I stared as Mommy and Daddy both smiled broadly. It astounded me how tiny the baby was, or how good she smelled, or how amazingly beautiful her tiny face looked. I instantly fell in love with my baby sister.

Mommy told me that this baby belonged to me, and that we had a very special bond because she came at such an important time in my life. I took this to heart and leaned down to whisper in Mary Angela's tiny ear. "I love you so much," I whispered, "I will love and protect you from everything for as long as we live. I will stick by you to show you how to survive in the world and in our family. I will love you forever.

I felt proud and special when Daddy and I returned to the car.

I didn't even mind it too much when he dropped me off at Uncle Gerald's before driving everybody else to Aunt Pat's.

When my mother came home from the hospital with baby Mimi, she handed her to me first. I knew the baby recognized me and I welcomed her home, even though home could at times be terrifying.

With my father gaining respect as Chief of the Organized Crime Task Force under Attorney General Bobby Kennedy, the birth of their eighth child, and Grandma no longer needing looking after, my parents contemplated moving.

After ten years of living in the haunted house we rented from my great grandmother, my parents began to search in earnest for a perfect home of our own. I remember the excitement I felt walking for the very first time into the spacious house they chose. With no wall or archway between the living and dining rooms, the openness of the main living area really struck me first. It seemed enormous compared to the small rooms in our old house. I also immediately noticed how so much more light filled the space, and how it had an air of peacefulness. Though I could not determine anything I could really put my finger on, or articulate, I simply knew that it just felt somehow warmer, clearer, lighter, and infinitely more quiet.

We all pitched in, along with aunts, uncles, and cousins, to move the trappings of ten people into the new home. As a housewarming gift, my mother's father helped with the expense of new curtains, carpet and furniture for the living room, but we filled our bedrooms and other spaces with the weathered items from the old house.

A fresh start in a new neighborhood brought with it many exciting opportunities. Instead of all my siblings crowding into two bedrooms, Mom assigned us to the four bedrooms upstairs. A long, narrow hallway connected the rooms with a tub room at the end, and a powder room next to it. Nothing about the new house caused fear or trepidation. Even the carpeted stairs seemed easier to navigate since they had two separate landings with turns, which meant you could never fall or get pushed down more than six stairs. I loved that! Plus, we found no need to watch out for a slinky lady or any other creepy *thing* on the stairs.

I never again heard my father holler from his place on the couch, *"HOLD THE RAILING AND WALK!"*

With multiple boxes yet unpacked, and the clutter of moving and sorting strewn throughout the house, we all finally fell into bed that first night—excited and fully exhausted. To my surprise and delight I had no trouble at all falling asleep in the new place. I slept undisturbed the entire night and awoke on my own at almost 10:00 a.m.! The aroma of coffee came from the kitchen below, but the rest of the house remained still and quiet. I scampered quietly downstairs to find only my mother awake. Not even the baby had begun to stir.

"Well," she said pouring hot coffee into her cup, "Looks like you and I are the first ones awake. How did you sleep?" Mom asked this question every morning of my life, but on this morning it held new and special meaning for the two of us.

"Fantastic!" I said. "I slept like a log." I looked around the bright kitchen with boxes of dishes and nonperishables stacked along the wall, under the windows, and on the counters. "This place is so quiet." I said with amazement. How come it's so quiet?"

Mom just nodded in agreement as she sipped her coffee. "Much quieter than the old neighborhood I suspect."

"It's so light in here ... and *quiet.*" I repeated, astonished.

Just then more children joined us in the kitchen. Everyone remarked on the peace and quiet, and on how well they slept. It was nearly 11:00 when my father awoke and joined us.

"I can't believe I slept that long, or that peacefully!" he remarked as my mother handed him a steaming cup of fresh coffee. His face appeared softer somehow, relaxed and not at all tense. He began to laugh, looking around at his growing brood.

"How do you like the new house?"

The room erupted with a clamber of exclamations from everyone all at once—all focused on the quiet and peace in that place. After a breakfast of cereal and milk, the work of unpacking continued. For the rest of the day, and every day after that I never ever heard my name called from another room by something other than a living person. I did not sense ethereal movement out of the corner of my eye, nor did I see or feel anybody in closets, or hallways, or on the stairs. Even the basement with its concrete walls and floor felt surprisingly light and airy.

My father colluded with his uncles to get a second-hand pool table and set it up in the basement. They spent many weekends shooting pool and laughing over beer or whiskey.

Mom's new washer and dryer were connected in the basement, as well. It never felt dark, or dangerous, or threatening. We often chose to play there on rainy days or when it became too hot to play outdoors. As unbelievable as it seemed for my brothers, sisters, and I, we felt completely safe and comfortable in the new house ... every last part of it.

As we settled in, we spoke more and more of how peaceful and still our new house remained at all hours of the day or night. Instead of feeling terrified to spend time alone I sought solitude there. This naturally led to discussions among my parents and older siblings comparing the new house with the old. Our stories emerged around the supper table, in the living room, while doing dishes, just before bedtime, or any time or place we gathered. A flood gate of awakening had opened.

My parents expressed amazement at the realization that all of us who lived in the old house experienced exactly the same spooky things to varying degrees. We *all* saw The Slinky Lady. We *all* heard night whispers inches from our ears. We *all* felt icy fingers touching exposed skin as we slept. We *all* saw endless movement in our peripheral vision. We *all* felt the weight of darkness and grief bleeding from the very bones and tangled roots of that house.

My mother confessed that she would tell us to ignore our "vivid imaginations" because she did not want to scare us. She worried that acknowledging our encounters with the dead—or whatever else lurked in the shadows in the old house—would frighten us. She had no way to really protect her children and didn't want to influence and terrify us. Hoping to shield us with denial, she prayed, dismissed, and just plain wished it would go away and leave us alone. But it never did.

My parents saw and understood that now. Our experiences became our stories, now that they were safely in the past. We were not, however, fully rid of that house yet. Uncle Gerald and Aunt Jeanette lived there now with their four children. We visited, though not often.

I vividly remember the first time we went back for a visit to the old neighborhood. My grandmother had died, but Uncle Jack still lived in the little house next door that he had shared with her. It felt remarkably odd to go to homes empty of the people who filled them in my young childhood; to see different lives playing out in such familiar spaces. Then I stepped over the threshold into Uncle Gerald's, my old house. Immediately, I felt a flutter in my gut as the hair on my arms raised. Though midday, with sunlight flooding through open windows, it suddenly grew darker as something profound shifted. I had been laughing with my cousins only moments before but stepping back into that house brought on insurmountable grief. I wanted to burst into tears. It had nothing remotely to do with nostalgia, though that's what my mother deduced, noticing the dark mood overtaking me.

"It's normal to feel sad," my mother said cheerfully, "It's fine to miss your old house. We had lots of love in this place." She looked around smiling.

"Love?" I thought, "Is that what you call it?"

I stood in the middle of a room filled with chattering relatives, yet utterly alone and isolated. I sensed something approach me. Frozen, unable to speak, helpless to break the mesmerizing trance that flooded my body and brain, I felt a rush of icy breath on the back of my neck, and imagined it grimacing. I knew that it recognized me. I sensed the foul thing circle me and move very close to my ear.

"*Tiyi*," it hissed. "*Tiyi*."

I closed my eyes attempting to prepare for whatever came next, when all at once my cousin Joey grabbed me.

"Antoinette Marie!" He always addressed me by my full given name. I opened my eyes relieved beyond words. The horrid thing vanished, and the room shifted again as I grabbed Joey's arm. With his help I joined the living and the party once more.

I visited with cousins and other extended family that afternoon, knowing full well that whatever had called my name lurked just out of sight, and yet quite nearby. I noticed the basement door as I passed through the dining room into the kitchen. The safety hook swung freely outside of its protective eye. I feared that the door might swing open at any moment. I knew Uncle Gerald and Aunt Jeanette had small children and wondered if they had any idea the danger it posed for them... or for every living soul for that matter. I walked by quickly trying to avoid looking directly at that door.

A couple of hours passed, and I found myself needing to go to the bathroom. Panic rose in my chest. The bathroom would isolate me from all the other people, leaving me a sitting target for that thing that knew my name. I was too old—it would have been weird to ask someone to go with me—so I steeled my resolve and headed to the bathroom off the kitchen. Someone else occupied it, and another stood waiting.

Aunt Jeanette, passing by with a bowl of chips lightly said, "Why don't you use the bathroom upstairs? You know where to find it."

Fortunately, she said it in passing without actually looking at me because I am absolutely certain that my face spoke loudly of my horror at the thought of going upstairs alone.

"I'm good." I said, continuing to wait nervously.

I began to tell myself that if someone else came along and waited outside the bathroom door behind me it might make it just a bit safer. Perhaps they would be able to tell if something bad happened, or maybe the dark thing wouldn't bother me with someone else close by. I might even try to maintain a conversation from the other side of the door. Unfortunately, as the bathroom opened up, nobody else came behind me. I knew I had to close the door, though I really did not want to. I had no desire to find myself alone, even for a few short minutes.

The moment I shut the door, I felt the room close in. It grew frigid and hollow. After discussions confirming our suspicions that we shared our old house with spirits, I no longer had the defense of telling myself that it was my imagination. Shivering, I fumbled to try to relieve myself as quickly as humanly possible. It wasted no time. Again, I heard, *"Tiyi"* whispered close to my ear. Mercifully, the energy dispersed with a loud knock on the bathroom door.

"Hurry up in there! I've gotta go!"

I quickly finished my business and wasted no time washing my hands but flushed and flew to the door thrusting it open with lightning speed.

"Jeez! My cousin said, "What's wrong with *you*? Are you okay?"

"Fine." I said rushing past him to find Mom and ask when we might leave.

She sat on the couch with my aunt, sipping a cocktail and munching chips. "We were just discussing letting Tommy spend the night with Jimmy. They have so much fun together."

I looked over at my little brother, knowing that he had never really experienced the spirits in that house. At five or six years old he had escaped full awareness of the darkness there. My mother, however, could not claim innocence. I looked at her incredulously, wondering how she could rationalize leaving her small child to fend for himself in that dangerous place. He would not know that he needed to avoid solitude, or to tuck his hands inside the pillow or covers. He would have no idea that he must never turn his back to the open room. My only hope lay on his young cousins who now lived there. They must have figured out how to stay relatively safe among the spirits. They had lived there for months now.

As the sun dipped behind the trees, we prepared to leave. I felt the dark entity's eyes boring into my back as I stepped onto the front porch for goodbye hugs and kisses. Its grip dissipated as I descended the porch steps. We all piled into the station wagon, leaving little Tommy behind, happily playing with his favorite cousin. We also, I thought, left him with the spirits of the dead, along with something else that knew our names. That thing may have never known human life, but craved the taste, seeking it in anger, fear, and darkness. I said a prayer that my little brother's guardian angel would be on duty that night as we drove away.

The next day Aunt Jeanette brought Tommy home in the late morning, earlier than expected. "He really wanted to come home." She explained.

Tommy looked exhausted as he snuggled up next to Mom. After Aunt Jeanette left she asked squeezing him tighter. "Did you have fun with Jimmy?"

"Yeah," He said unconvincingly, "I don't want to sleep over at Jimmy's house anymore though."

"Why not?" My mother asked.

"Well," he continued, "Jimmy slept on the bottom bunk, so I got to sleep on the top. Just as I'd start falling asleep, I heard him call me. When I looked over the side of the bunk to ask what he wanted, he pretended to be asleep. Then he'd call me again. So, I just ignored him and fell asleep. Then he kept tickling my back."

My eyes widened, and I shot an "I told you so" look at my mother.

"Well ..." said my mother.

"That's not all though." He looked upset. "When I finally fell sound-asleep, somebody grabbed my hand. I woke up and couldn't get back to sleep after that. Jimmy shouldn't play tricks on me like that should he Mom?"

"No," Mom said, looking at his older siblings with a clear warning to keep still. "It's not nice to play tricks like that. You don't have to sleep at Jimmy's anymore if you don't want to."

"Maybe he can sleep over here?" He perked up, "He won't play tricks on me if he sleeps over here."

"No, he won't." My mother assured him.

"*Of course* he won't." I thought casting a sideways glance at my older sister as we both nodded.

# Chapter 16
# Nightmare

(nīt- ,mer–*noun*: a terrifying dream in which the dreamer experiences
feelings of helplessness, extreme anxiety, sorrow, etc.)

SINCE GREAT UNCLE GERALD AND HIS YOUNG FAMILY lived in the family
home after us, we only moved our own things. We left behind a century
of remnants from the generations of my father's family who had occupied the home before us stored safely away in the attic.

After only a few years, Uncle Gerald passed away from the ravages
of lung cancer. His young wife, Jeanette, went into deep mourning and,
unsurprising to me, did not want to remain in the house alone with her
four small children. She prepared the house to sell outside the family
for the first time in more than a century.

Teenagers by this time, my siblings and I helped with the many
boxes of papers, pictures, and artifacts stored in the attic of the old
house. Aunt Jeanette and her four grieving young children were not
able to sort through the leavings. Uncle Gerald had come to my father's
aid when his father left during his childhood. Now it was my father's
turn to come to Gerald's family's aid—so the task fell to my family. Far
from a burden, the task of going through the dusty boxes filled with
ancient photographs of my father and his family was a treasure hunt
for my family. One afternoon, several of us gathered around a box of
tintypes and yellowed photographs, passing them from hand to hand as
we looked into the past.

"Holy cats! Look at this guy!" my sister Colleen laughed, "Look
Dave. You really take after this guy."

She passed the faded photograph of an elderly gentleman sporting sideburns, a bulbous nose and round cheeks to my brother.

"Very funny." Dave said, though his long bushy hair and juvenile attempt at a hippie sideburns and beard did make the comment hilarious.

He passed the photo to me. Laughing, I turned it over but saw no name penciled in—as with most of the pictures.

"I wonder who this is." I mused handing the photograph to Annie.

As she took it, and looked closely, all the color drained from her face. Her eyes grew huge and fear began to grow in them.

"What?" I asked, "What's wrong?"

"That's him." she replied, "That's the man in the corner.

We all quickly passed the mystery photo from hand to hand then went straight to my mother in the kitchen for some answers. Showing her the photo we implored, "Who *is* this?"

"I'm not sure," my mother said, glancing quickly away from her cooking pot and at the photo. "Maybe your father's grandfather. Ask him when he gets home. I'm busy right now."

We carefully sat the picture on the coffee table in front of my father's designated spot on the couch awaiting his arrival. Heeding my mother's warning to not jump all over him as he entered the door, we patiently waited for him to change clothes and settle down with his first cocktail before interrogating him about the mystery man in the photograph. Though mysterious entities no longer attacked my father, liquor became his new demon. We knew we had a brief window in which to get the answers we sought.

Without letting on about Annie's realization, we finally asked my father to solve the mystery.

"Who is this?" we all asked shoving the photograph into his hands.

My father smiled. "Well, will you look at that. That's my grandfather. We called him Pa."

We all fell silent, glancing from one to the other, as Dad began one of his many stories about great grandfather and how he threw greedy crooked politicians off his porch when they asked for bribes to award his business one of the many lucrative contracts following the Chicago Fire.

"What?" He asked, becoming aware of our shifting glances and silence, "What's going on?"

"Tell him!" we all clamored at once prodding sister Annie. "Tell him what you told us."

Mom had joined us in the front room by this time and sat next to Dad on the couch. She took the picture from his hand smiling. "What?" She asked.

"Remember the night I saw the leprechaun in the old house?" Annie began. My parents nodded smiling.

"I don't think it really was a leprechaun after all," she looked intensely at my mother, "Because that," indicating the photo in my mother's hands, "... is the man in the corner."

The photo fell into my mother's lap from her stunned hands as she and my father turned to look at one another in astonishment.

"Well," My father began, "that explains a lot. My grandfather died in that room when I was a boy. Grandma Lyons said that after he died, and for as long as she lived there, he would sit next to her and hold her hand as she fell asleep."

"Grandma told me that he remained in the house even when we lived there. I used to hear him on the stairs until I told him to not scare me." my mother added.

This incident opened up a floodgate of experiences and stories. We openly shared the terrifying things that my parents had attributed to "seeing things", "dreaming", or "our vivid imaginations" throughout our childhoods. My parents—in an attempt to not frighten us—made up excuses for every spooky incident we experienced. At last we knew now that we might begin to find the truth behind our haunted childhoods.

Every day after school, more ancient, dusty boxes, crates, and trunks appeared in our front room. They piled up under the windows by the radiator. Arriving home, we would change out of our school clothes, and then dive into that treasure trove of ancestors' photographs, birth, baptism, and death certificates, deeds, receipts, and endless scraps of paper that, when pieced together would tell the story of a century of Dad's family. We sorted them into piles to distribute to various other branches of our family for their own archives. Generally, the backs of most of the photographs displayed the names of the people in the photo along with a date to place it at a specific time in family history. Those that had no name or date would go in a pile for my father to identify.

"Ah ... that's Bootsie," He would say, "That's her first Communion dress. So, I suppose she must have been about seven or eight years old. That would make it 1938." Touching the tip of her pencil to her tongue, my mother would then inscribe the notes in pencil on the back of the faded, fragile photographs. I remember the awe I felt at Dad's power of recollection, while at the same time wondering why on earth Mom had to wet the pencil tip before she wrote.

One day we discovered a large, ancient steamer trunk. Opening it we found no photographs, but only stacks of papers that included a deed for the lot, and the original blueprints for the house. We also found ancient newspapers, political documents, and many more historical items. Many of the documents bore an unfamiliar name: Davidson. We knew all the names of our ancestors and relations—Ryan, Murphy, Walsh, and Lyons—but could recall no stories of family members named Davidson. Mom could not offer any answers either. Once again, we had to wait until Dad returned from work to provide them.

This did not, however, stop us from digging deeper into the mysterious trunk. At the very bottom we found a small packet of letters tied together by a rotting blue ribbon. My aspirations of becoming an archaeologist came out as I carefully extracted the letters and unfolded the fragile paper. Straining to read the faded ink, I realized that what I held in my hands were love letters from a time gone by. Each one was addressed to "Friend Davidson" and spoke with tenderness and affection. For some reason, I assumed that the letters came from a woman's hand, though perhaps I only read that in, as I imagined this love affair from the past. Each letter bore a simple signature that gave little clue as to the author: "Fondly, C." Who could "C" have been? Who was "Friend Davidson?" And how did these mysterious letters fit into my family's story?

Dad worked late that night, so bedtime loomed by the time we showed him the deed displaying the name Davidson. As expected, he knew about the Davidsons. He told us that they were two brothers who built the house in the 1870's. He didn't know a lot about them, except that they were local politicians who lived there together for several years before disappearing suddenly. Family stories included suspicions that the Davidson brothers were crooked, and perhaps even stole money from the city—or took bribes. All Dad knew was that they were *not good people*. When the house came on the market, my great-great Grandma Bridget Ryan bought the property through the Davidsons' attorney or representative. Nobody ever heard of them again.

"Well, what do you think of these?" I carefully handed the love letters to Dad.

He placed them on the coffee table and picked up the top one. He ran his hand gently over the surface of the letter feeling the long-dried ink and read the words aloud. Next he did something unexpected. His eyes filled with tears as he again ran his hand gently from top to bottom, then back again over the page. Resting it at last, he looked off into someplace far away in his memory. I prepared myself for another family story.

"Jackie?" he turned to my mother, "Do you remember that dream I had that one night?"

"What dream?" Mom asked, confused.

"The one where I felt like I went back in time. The one I asked you to remember because I knew it was very important?" He looked pleadingly to my mother.

"Oh yes, she said the one about Carrie or Carla or ..."

"Cara." Dad said.

"Cara." they both repeated, nodding in unison. Then he told us his dream.

> I had just fallen asleep when I found myself standing in the front room alone. I heard a strange voice calling over, and over again, "Cara ... Cara ... Cara ..."

Slowly the room began to shift before my eyes. I knew it was the same room, but it looked completely different. It had gas lamps and fixtures. It had strange wallpaper, and furniture from long ago. I felt like myself, but someone else at the same time. I viewed the scene as if looking through the bottom of a glass because anything out of my direct line of sight appeared distorted and blurred. I began to walk toward the stairs. My vision focused on each step as I climbed ever so slowly to the top. I turned and walked into the big bedroom. There I turned toward the bathroom but found a bedchamber in its place.

A woman with long, thick, curly black hair lay sleeping under a white sheet and quilt. I watched helplessly as I raised my hand. I remember a feeling of both terror and anguish as I realized I held a large knife in my left hand. I watched helplessly as my hand came down again and again, thrusting the knife into the sleeping woman. I watched as her blood spread over the entire bed, turning the white sheets red as the life drained out of her.

I stood looking at her lifeless body. Though I never turned to look at the face, I became aware of someone or something else in the room with me. I dropped the knife, then another man and I hoisted the lifeless form from the bed. Grabbing her under her arms, we began to drag her down the upstairs hall. Her bare feet left a trail of blood on the floor. Without speaking—and with my heart breaking—we dragged her to the top of the stairs, then slowly, one step at a time, down the stairs feeling a thump on each of those eighteen stairs. We turned down the downstairs hall and continued to bear the burden of her limp body slowly to the basement door. I watched my hand open the basement door using the very same door handle that I hated to turn, as I bore the weight of not only what I had done, but of her corpse as well.

Next, we struggled and strained as we carried her down into the basement. Looking to my left, I could see a roughly prepared grave. Bricks had been removed from the wall and lay in a neat pile on the floor. I saw a hole dug in the dark black dirt behind it. We shoved her body into the small space and, with our hands, packed dirt around her lifeless body. Then again, I heard the voice calling ... calling ... "Cara ... Cara ... Cara ..."

All at once I found myself standing again in the front room listening to her name over and over again, "Cara ... Cara ... Cara ..." as the room slowly returned to the way it looked when we lived there. Then I woke up.

"Do you remember Jackie?"

Troubled and pleading, he looked again at Mom. "I woke you up. I was so upset. I told you to please always remember that dream. I didn't know why; I just knew we had to remember it."

Forlorn, He looked down at the letter in his hand.

"Fondly, C." He said. "Cara."

My brothers, sisters, and I all glanced quickly, knowingly at one another.

"The Slinky Lady." We said almost simultaneously.

"The Slinky Lady." We all nodded to one another.

"What do you mean The Slinky Lady?" our puzzled father asked, glancing at our equally-confused mother.

We filled many hours that night taking turns telling stories of the strange and disturbing things we had all seen, or some of us saw, in that house filled with spirits and secrets. I felt relief for my own sanity as, one by one, we spoke of things that had remained unspoken, even unspeakable for so many years.

For the first time, I understood the grief that I had felt as a small child when I gazed into the eyes of the dreadful man in the closet. As Dad described the feelings of grief and self-loathing that he had experienced, I fully understood the pain Dad described in that dream. I had felt it too. I knew at that time that the man I saw, wringing his hands in utter anguish in the closet, had killed Cara. It perfectly explained his desperate and hopeless remorse, his lurking in deep shadows, wringing his hands for all time.

I also knew that Cara herself, traveled her final journey, with a regularity we could always count on night after night, into eternity, replaying the terrible violence and injustice she suffered, then to lie unknown for a century only steps away from the living, her murderers having escaped any consequence.

I also knew that her murderer joined her forever, locked in a hell of his own, having to relive his crime and forever wallow in grief and remorse. He damned himself to suffer in the same place as Cara, and was yet oblivious of her. Their intertwined spirits were contained in their own hell and tormented the living who dwelt there.

As we talked, one of my sisters recalled how Dad used to yell at us because the bricks were always falling from one spot in the basement wall. Dad, suddenly visibly disturbed, put his head in his hands as he told us that the place the bricks kept falling from was the exact same place where Cara had been buried in his dream. He felt stunned that he hadn't made that connection before.

At last it all made sense. Cara herself, or the spirit of Cara, wanting her body to be found, brought us repeatedly to her grave, and yet we never put it all together.

"Sweet Mother of God." Dad said shaking his head, "That poor woman, God rest her lost soul. Let's say a prayer for her that she might finally rest in peace."

We all bowed our heads and prayed the Hail Mary that poor Cara, The Slinky Lady, might find peace and go to Heaven.

The house had already held dark secrets and several ghosts when Bridget Ryan bought it as a wedding gift for her daughter Annie and her new husband Thomas before the turn of the twentieth century. Four generations of Dad's family added to the layers of spirits that haunt the house to this very day. So much pain. So much fear. So much remorse. So much sorrow. So much trouble. So many stories.

# Chapter 17
# Return

(ri- **turn**–*verb*: to go or come back, as to a former place, position, or state)

As the years passed, I grew up and moved to Michigan with a family of my own. The old house slipped into legend, becoming nothing more than stories to intrigue friends and raise shivers around campfires, or late-night gatherings. Invariably, someone would ask me if I had made it all up.

"That's what my mother used to tell me," I would reply, "And what I tried to tell myself as I watched full-bodied apparitions come toward me or walk down the hallway. That's what we all told ourselves, and each other until it stopped abruptly when we moved out. So, no, I didn't make it all up."

One weekend, my friend Mary Sue and I traveled to Chicago to meet up with an old friend of hers who had come from Germany to interview Holocaust survivors living in the Chicago area. Her interviews were part of a research project in which she participated at a university in Berlin.

We met at an apartment on the south side loaned to her by a colleague who traveled abroad at that time. That night over a bottle of wine I told stories Dad had told me about the history of Chicago, and then began to tell my own stories of my haunted childhood home.

"Is it still there?" They asked.

"Yes," I replied, "And it isn't too far from where we need to go tomorrow."

We agreed that, after the interviews, we would drive to my old house to have a look, and to see if it might still creep us out as much as the late-night stories had.

Most of the next day consisted of driving from one modest bungalow to another. Mary Sue and I waited in the car chatting as Bieber conducted her interviews. When she returned from her conversations with survivors, her face revealed the distress she experienced listening to old men and women tell of the unspeakable horrors they endured as children or young adults in Germany during the Holocaust. She did not want to talk about what she had learned, neither did we want to put her through repeating the horrors. We also knew how difficult it might be for us to hear, so we drove to the next address making small talk.

When the last interview concluded, we decided to make our way to my old neighborhood. Much had changed, but so very much still remained the same, even after more than thirty years. We turned down the one-way street past Jimmy's garden apartment. I pointed out where different friends lived, and where other childhood memories took place. I slowed the car and we crept past my old house.

"There." I said. Indicating the tall, unobtrusive home of my childhood.

The current residents had upgraded the old Victorian house immensely. It had new siding, new windows, and an entirely new look. A steep, narrow set of stairs and small covered stoop replaced the broad steps and full-length porch where long ago Dad had sat comforted by Mommy and Uncle Jack after something unseen nearly drove him to bash our heads in with a heavy lamp.

My grandmother's house next door, however, appeared completely unchanged, exactly as I remembered, a small red brick house set back from the sidewalk. It had the same door through which we ran to safety when Daddy grew unpredictably dangerous. The ornamental wrought iron railings also remained.

"We used to play "Jail" behind those small railings." I told them, chuckling.

I almost couldn't imagine how I fit my whole little self behind those curved bars. How I was once tiny enough to peer through them waiting for rescue during games of "Cops and Robbers".

Checking my rearview mirror to make sure we didn't block any cars, I cruised slowly to the end of the block. We turned right at the corner, then turned again into the alley behind the houses. Rolling past my grandmother's old backyard, I noticed that the cherry tree my grandmother cherished had disappeared. The hill on which we gained so much speed running, or sledding was actually merely a slight incline. I smiled and shook my head, remembering how it seemed so formidable as a little girl. I had always thought of Grandma's yard as enormous in the days of my childhood. Now it looked like any other small urban backyard.

We continued down the alley, stopping to gaze at the back of the house and my own former backyard. In place of the old back porch, and a ramshackle garage in a driveway of black cinders, we found a large swimming pool surrounded by a beautiful new deck. Though nothing appeared the same on the surface, I felt something familiar as I looked into the small upstairs window. I could feel in my bones that spirits still dwelled in the dark shadows in that place.

We came around the block again and turned back up the street. Both Mary Sue and Bieber convinced me to park so we could take a longer look as I told them more detailed stories of hauntings. I parked in front of my old, long-deceased neighbor's place and turned off the car. They listened and looked as I pointed out the exact locations of the stories I had told. Growing a bit apprehensive I wondered what people might think about three women parked, and just sitting in a car looking and pointing at their house.

"You should go up and ring the doorbell." Mary Sue suggested.

"No way!" I replied, "What am I supposed to say? 'Hi, I used to live here. Can I come in?'"

They both laughed, "No," said Mary Sue, "Just tell them who you are and that you grew up here."

"I don't know." I said nervously, "I'm not sure if I even want to go back in there ever again."

She went on, "You don't have to go in, but it might be fun to see if they have experienced any ghostly activity."

"Oh," I replied sarcastically, "So not only can I come in, but do you see ghosts? Right ... That makes a lot more sense."

"Just ring the bell." They both laughed, cajoled, and coaxed, until I gave in.

"Okay," I said, "But I really don't think this is a good idea, and you guys better come with me!"

I turned the key to shut off the engine, took a deep breath, and stepped on to the street and sidewalk where my spirit had escaped and played unencumbered by fear every night of my childhood. The streetlight marked the very spot where I first ventured out beyond the clutches of the terror in the house to which I now reluctantly returned. I did not feel fully convinced that this was at all a good idea.

I carefully climbed the steep stairs with Mary Sue and Bieber close behind. Standing at the door I waited a few seconds mustering courage, then rang the bell.

A charming man in his early to mid-thirties answered the door. "Yes? Can I help you?" he asked.

Through an extremely dry mouth I nervously said, "Hi. My name is Tiyi Schippers I ..."

Before I could get another word out, his expression changed from inquiry to delight. He raised his eyebrows and a huge smile filled his face as he interrupted, "Schippers! Schippers? Are you a Schippers who used to live in this house?"

I nodded yes.

"Please do come in," he said excitedly, "We have so many questions!"

I looked back to my friends who urged me forward, as he graciously bid us come in.

"I'm so excited to meet you.' He said, "And who are these lovely ladies with you?"

I introduced myself and my comrades as he ushered us inside.

"Let me show you around. We've really upgraded the place. You probably won't even recognize it."

He spoke the truth. Entering, I first noticed the openness and light in the place. The dividing walls had disappeared giving way to a spacious living area. Next, he showed us back to the remodeled modern kitchen. It looked and felt nothing at all like the place where I had stood long ago on a chair alone in the dark as some other worldly thing ran its icy fingers up my body taunting me and tasting the very depths of my soul. Everything appeared new, elegant, and lovely. Though I knew they must have upgraded the ancient wiring, I wondered if they, too, experienced lights flickering or going out randomly leaving their TV on.

"Just wait until you see what we did upstairs!" He said excitedly. "You won't even recognize it."

I felt butterflies in my stomach, and my heart began to race. I did not sense The Slinky Lady, nor the man in the closet, nor any other spirit I had known so well, but the thought of going back upstairs after so many years gave me pause.

As we reached the bottom of the staircase, I saw that it too had been replaced, but when I put my hand on the railing a flood of energy pulsed through my body.

"This is the same railing." I said.

"Wow!" He replied, "You sure have a great memory.'

I didn't tell him that it had less to do with *my* memory, and more to do with the house itself remembering. Though faded and obscured by the light that flooded the space through new large windows the spirits of my childhood remained. I held the railing tightly, and carefully walked up the stairs.

The remodel had eliminated all the small spaces including the long hallway where The Slinky Lady walked day and night. The new master suite had absorbed the small room and the closet from where the hopelessly mournful man watched me night after night. The bathroom where we ran, timing our visits by counting until The Slinky Lady returned, had grown twice its size with a large Jacuzzi tub and two massive skylights. I saw no place to which the man in the corner, my great grandfather, could retreat if discovered. The wholeness of the space appeared light and clean, still I couldn't help but sense something hidden just outside of view.

After many compliments and expressions of appreciation at the remarkable transition in the upstairs we headed back down the stairs to the main floor.

"Well this part is all done," he said with a sweep of his arms while descending the stairs without even touching the railing, "but we still have a little more to go. Let me show you what we plan to do in the basement."

I saw my friends flash me a sideways, knowing glance wondering how I might react. I took a deep breath and followed our host to the basement door.

At first, I noticed the door handle. Though every other detail in the house had undergone an update, the very same door handle made the exact same "click" in the exact same latch as it turned to open the newly painted original basement door. As he swung it open, I couldn't help but notice that the basement side of the door had never received a fresh coat of paint. I could almost imagine my own small handprints on the door where I frantically pushed it open to escape whomever pushed the bricks out from the foundation decades before.

"Be careful on these steps," he said as my feet fell on the same rickety stairs with a loose railing that my mother had navigated with baskets of wet laundry. "We want to redo the foundation and dig the basement a little deeper so we can finish this space and make it a rec room."

Stepping on the rough concrete floor I commented on how it hadn't changed a bit since we lived there. A new high efficiency furnace had replaced the enormous oil-converted-from-coal furnace of my child-hood. New ductwork and pipes crawled across the low ceiling, but every-thing else remained the same. As we walked deeper into the basement our host cheerfully described his plans for the remodeled basement. I felt unmistakable heaviness in the dank and dusty space. I walked toward the place where the outside door to the basement had once stood. In its place I saw a solid steel, permanently sealed security door.

I thought, *Had that door existed in my childhood we would never have dared each other to stand alone behind it for as long as we could bear.*

I tried to avoid glancing at the wall where long ago I had heard, then watched in horror as something or someone slowly pushed bricks out of the foundation and onto the basement floor. I shuddered remem-bering that terrifying scraping sound.

As we turned to go back upstairs, I realized that indeed bricks had fallen out of the wall exactly as they had for probably more than a hundred years. I tried to not appear startled.

"You know," the current resident said, "When we first bought this house all the neighbors told us it was haunted. They said there might be some kind of buried treasure hidden here."

"Well, I responded indicating the crumbling brick foundation wall, "If there is something buried, I'm guessing that you are going to find it right there."

My friends, remembering one of my more disturbing stories looked at that brick wall with the same horrified expression with which one might look at a moldering grave, which in fact was most likely accurate.

After we returned to the main floor we sat in the kitchen. Our host offered us a drink, asking if we could stay a bit so he could ask me some more questions. We agreed.

He told us that they had some pretty crazy things happen when they first moved in. He told of lights going on and off, of hearing foot-steps, and walking into cold spots. He said that he thought whomever haunted the place liked all the work he and his partner had done, because afterwards things settled down considerably.

I agreed that the house seemed much quieter than it had when I lived there. I did not, however, tell him all the frightening things I had experienced. I did tell him about my ancestors who had lived in that house, and what little I knew about the Davidsons. He became animated as I told him about the trunk, we had found in the attic that contained ancient papers, letters, and even the original blueprints from the house.

After a lengthy informative chat, we bade our leave with the promise of keeping in touch. I gave him my phone number and email information asking him to contact me if anything amazing turned up in the basement wall. I told him to look closely for jewelry. In order to not frighten him I did not ask him to look for bones or teeth. We hugged, and then I turned my back on that house and its multiple layers of spirits one final time.

Though I had promised to keep in touch, I never did. I never heard if they ever found anything in the basement wall and had no contact with the house at all until years later when I found the property listed on a real estate website. The video showed the beautifully remodeled Victorian home. Then in an effort to highlight the infrastructure, it showed the basement. Not surprisingly nothing had changed. The basement wall showed a small space where new bricks and tuck pointing had replaced the old discolored ones. Still the grave shaped area appeared to be crumbling.

Over one hundred years after her brutal murder, Cara continues to reach out from behind the basement wall hoping someone will find her, or perhaps hoping that someone will finally learn her story.

# Chapter 18

# Anamnesis

(a-ˌnam-ˈnē-sᴇs—*noun:* the recollection or remembrance of the past; reminiscence.)

As I began working on this book a deluge of vivid memories—some delightful, and others quite traumatizing—flooded into my consciousness. The whole thing started as an attempt to simply write down interesting and true ghost stories from far in my past. I immersed myself in the task of providing an accurate depiction of the spooky events that took place. I simply wanted to preserve my stories as I remembered them. In doing so I set in motion a revived connection with both the events that came to define the woman I am, and the spirits with whom I shared my unusual childhood. These spirits and events helped set me on my life's journey experiencing an ever-thinning veil between known and yet-to-be-discovered realities.

The spirits as well as my early memories came to me in both my dreams and waking hours. I found myself thinking about them all the time. Sometimes something would trigger a memory at odd and inopportune moments. Often my reaction to these memories was visceral. I could feel the effects of trauma not just in my mind, but in my body as well. My heart would beat faster, and I would feel butterflies in my stomach much the way I did so long ago when these things originally occurred. I began to recognize the spirits of my childhood standing in the shadows in my room when I would awaken in the middle of the night. Their urgency felt relentless and powerful. Over time it became my obsession to tell more than just *my* story, but also *theirs.*

One weekend my husband and I traveled to Chicago to visit my elderly parents. Both were in ill health, and I knew that I would not have them for very much longer. I intended to run the stories I had written by them to check for accuracy, and to discover if they knew of any I had missed. I also wanted to get as much of the back story as possible. Armed with a newly installed recording app on my phone, we settled into the task I had planned. When I read them my written memories of life in our haunted house, both Dad and Mom confirmed the accuracy of my stories. Then Dad began to elaborate. I clicked on the recorder as he recalled how the house seemed to just drag him down when he returned from work. He did not remember the incident with the lamp, or crawling on his belly up the staircase, though he remembered my mother telling him about that. He said he could never stay in that house alone. He remembered how during Mom's long hospital stays after childbirth—with all the other children farmed out—he would stay until closing time at his uncles' pub and sometimes even fall asleep in the car. Mom piped up saying that he probably passed out in the car, but he insisted that even if that did happen sometimes, other times he just could not muster the courage to go into that house alone.

Becoming agitated and visibly uncomfortable, Dad abruptly changed the subject. He began telling rich tales of our ancestors in Ireland and pre- and post-fire Chicago. He asked me to retrieve the massive family bible from its stand in the living room. My great-great-grandparents had carried it with them when they came to America from Ireland in the middle 1800's. Dad pointed out the handwriting depicting birth, death, baptism, and marriage information written in the margins of the yellowed pages. He told story after story about our ancestors whose faded faces I remember seeing in time-worn photographs and tintypes as an adolescent so many years ago.

Hidden deep in the pages we found ancient love letters from my great grandfather, Thomas, to his wife, Annie. This reminded me of the small carefully tied bundle of love letters to "Friend Davidson" signed by "C." Though I adored hearing all my family stories, I remembered that I had a different mystery I wanted to solve.

When Dad finished speaking and paused to gaze with wonder at the newly-discovered artifacts, I changed the subject one more time. I asked about the Davidsons from whom our ancestors bought the home in which the lovers Thomas and Annie spent their lives. Unfortunately, my father had little or no information to share. He only remembered that his grandmother and uncles told him that they were *not* good people. I asked him what he thought they meant by that and he said that he heard they worked for the city right after the great fire. He knew that many politicians at that time had, as he put it, "sticky fingers." The Davidsons served as Democratic precinct captains as well, and during those early days many party officials took bribes for influence or favors. He assumed, based on his knowledge of Chicago history, that the Davidsons may have gotten caught up in corruption and skipped town.

I couldn't help but think that, based on my *own* knowledge of Chicago history, this was not an unusual offense, and those who did these things not only didn't need to get out of town, but were rewarded richly by a system that fostered, even encouraged that level of corruption. I wasn't buying it. I suspected some other dark episode had occurred that led to the disappearance and disparagement of the people who occupied our family home before us. Though I had no empirical proof, based on my early experiences with the ghosts in that house, along with things they had begun showing me more recently, I had a pretty good idea of what may truly have become of them. I only needed a few details to begin searching the internet to find out if any trace of the Davidsons remained. I asked Dad about the old trunk we had rescued from the attic of the Chicago house. The information I needed rested in the bottom of that trunk.

"I'm pretty sure you can find it with all the other basement stuff stored in the garage," Dad replied.

My folks had downsized to a new more accessible home after all their children had moved out. Dad told me that they had stored the trunk in their basement until a torrential storm flooded theirs and all their neighbor's basements the previous year. Everything got soaked and moldy, so they had the basement emptied, gutted, and refinished. Shortly after that, my father's and mother's health took a downturn, so nothing had yet been returned to the basement.

My heart sank when I stepped into the garage to look for the trunk that held essential clues to the Davidsons and their fate. All the contents of the flooded basement stood stacked yards deep against the walls, and on metal shelves in the middle of the floor. The former contents of the flooded basement filled the two-and-a-half car garage to bursting. The pile included stacks upon stacks of precious books, tools, boxes of random artifacts, and remnants. Several trunks rested beyond reach in the middle of, and under large heavy objects and boxes. I had no idea which trunk might hold the key to unlock the mystery behind the haunting of my childhood home, but I felt a glimmer of excitement and hope realizing just how close I stood to an answer. Unfortunately, I realized that it would take many helpers stronger than myself, and far more hours than I had that afternoon to unearth the trunks. I realized that the mystery would have to wait for another visit. My sister, who aided in my folks' care, promised to ask some of the strong young folks in the family to help unearth the trunks in time for my next visit.

My frustration grew even more when I discovered that I had never clicked the actual Record button on my new app! Fortunately, I took some notes as my father spoke, though relying on a recording, I had left out many details. After driving five hours back to my home, I sat with my notes trying to fill in all the details I could remember.

The next day I contacted my cousin who lived closer to my folks, and who had taken it upon himself to record the family history and family tree. I told him some of the stories my father told, and how we had found letters and notes in the family bible. My cousin said excitedly that he had never heard some of those stories and didn't know a family bible even existed! I also told him that it appeared both my parents' health was deteriorating and suggested that he pay them a visit to video-tape as many stories as Dad could tell. He agreed enthusiastically and made a date to visit with my brother the following week to interview Dad.

More than a month passed before I visited again. This time the excavated trunks lay in easy reach on the floor of the garage. I opened one after another until I recognized the yellowed contents beneath the lid of the trunk I sought. Pulling up an old kitchen chair, I began painstakingly removing layer after layer that included newspapers of every major event of the twentieth century. The top layer held papers from Nixon's resignation. After a couple of hours, I reached the bombing of Pearl Harbor. I found headlines from the great depression, all the way back to the early twentieth century.

The deeper into the trunk I got, the stronger the smell of mold and mildew grew. It became clear that flood water had breached the ancient steamer trunk. Soon the papers themselves began to feel damp. I spread them out on cardboard boxes hoping to salvage as much of the treasure as possible.

At last I reached the final few inches at the bottom and found documents bearing the name "Davidson." To my horror, as I gently and carefully attempted to lift one document it disintegrated in my hand. The entirety of the Davidson history stored for more than a century waiting for someone to find it had turned to nothing more than ash and dust. The only things marginally intact were some receipts for insurance payouts from the Oddfellows, a heavy cardboard list of registered voters in the 27th Ward, 4th Precinct from November 1893 with several penciled in notes and names crossed out, a receipt from Dr. M. T. Moore for Mr. Davidson dated February 11, 1896, and a single postcard addressed to Mrs. C. Davidson of Mayfair, dated March 20, 1896. Nothing gave me a first name from which I could begin my internet search. The only confirmation, or partial confirmation of our experiences, rested in that one postcard.

I sat dolefully regarding the lost papers realizing that somewhere among those moldering shards rested a precious bundle of secret love letters from "C," Cara. It broke my heart to lose what I hoped might have become powerful artifacts to confirm or refute the story that the spirits tried to reveal over more than a century to all who dwelled in that house.

Though no other living soul accompanied me in the garage that warm afternoon, I began to feel as if I was not alone. I felt a chill on my neck and sensed someone very near, leaning into me as if to whisper something in my ear. After a lifetime of experiencing many remarkable encounters between realities—beyond the veil—I no longer felt fear or trepidation at the realization that one of the beings who tormented me as a child had something I needed to learn.

I took a deep breath, cleared my mind, smiled and reached into the decaying remnants of paper at the bottom of the trunk. I caressed a small handful of the long-ruined documents and began to remember.

When spirits connect with me it often manifests as a memory that is not my own. I don't see events play out over time as in a dream, but suddenly have a full memory of events shared by the spirit communicating with me. Think about a memory you have. You don't start at the beginning and go step by step through events, right? You remember the whole thing all at once. That's how it is when spirits communicate with me. Sometimes I hear words or see a shadow or wraith in order to get my attention, but when a spirit needs a story told he or she does not tell it, but somehow, I remember it.

The first part of this book consists of my own personal stories, and the family stories told to me on many occasions by my family members to whom they happened. Though I tell the stories using dialog I obviously could not have heard, I took great pains to keep it in the spirit of the history my family shared. These stories came from the living so I can vouch for their authenticity.

Part Two, however came to me in quite a different way. What follows on the next pages tells the stories of those whose lives ended long before I came along. It may be true that, as my mother often told me when I described hauntings, I have a vivid imagination. But when I wrote the following pages, they poured unplanned onto the page as stream-of-consciousness writing. Before beginning the first part of this book, I designed an overall outline, then outlined each chapter before writing it. I made sure to organize it so it made sense. When I completed it, I believed I had finished the book. But the spirits did not agree.

Part two had no such outline. Once I allowed the spirits of my childhood to reveal their stories to me, I began writing obsessively, sometimes barely aware of the words, as I typed for hours on end, stopping only to take short breaks to stretch my stiffened body. At first, they revealed their names to me, but after several long stretches of writing I looked back to realize that the story had shifted from third person to first. When I finished each chapter, I had to go back to edit it back into third person, sometimes reading words and events I did not recall writing.

During this process I wrote about places and things of which I had no prior knowledge. More times than not, I asked my husband to google a name of a restaurant, or a place, or even foreign words I had written to find they proved to be accurate.

Since these are not my own memories, and no documentation exists to prove the stories in the following pages, nor the way in which I learned them, I will have to designate them fiction. Having said that, I have tried to tell their stories as accurately and faithfully as the spirits shared them with me. I have willingly lent my pages to the ghosts of my childhood to allow them to reveal their long-hidden secrets—with heartfelt hope that they may find peace.

# Part 2

# The Spirits Speak

## Vivification

(vi‑ve‑fe‑ˈkā‑shen—to give life to; animate; quicken)

# Chapter 19
## Survivor

(sɛr-ˈvī-vɛr—*noun*, a person who continues to function or prosper in spite of opposition, hardship, or setbacks.)

JOSEPH GREW UP THE LAST OF FOUR BROTHERS born to an Irish laborer and a meek mother in a Southside Chicago tenement house in the 1850's. Since early childhood, he felt that someone had somehow dropped him into a foreign land. His older brothers grew up rough and quick to violence of all sorts. Joseph, on the other hand, having no taste for ruffians, became the target of their teasing and aggressive play. Joseph's mother tried to protect her last-born, but his father encouraged the older boys' cruelty, even to the extent of punishing his mother with a cuff across the face when she admonished the older boys.

"Stop coddling the boy!" His father would scream with a sudden blow to his mother, "You're going to turn him into a panty-waist! He needs to find his way in the world of real men, not tied to his mother's apron strings."

Sometimes a parental clash afforded Joseph enough time to escape his brothers' violence, the usual result was even rougher treatment by his brothers, however. Over time his mother simpered in silence when her husband and sons grew rowdy.

At an early age Joseph and his brothers had to work to help support the family. His father was a stockyard wrangler and meat packer, a filthy and blood-soaked occupation. When Joseph was only six, his father sent him with his brother Michael to shovel out cattle stalls. When Joseph fell behind, his pay lagged. They thought he might better handle a mop so at age seven he began mopping the slaughterhouse floor. The blood, death, flies, and stench turned his stomach. The boy turned pale and vomited frequently. When the foreman sent Joseph home early, his father beat him, shouting, "If you can't work, you shan't eat!" As the rest of his family feasted on bread and hearty soup his father made Joseph sit at the table and watch.

Risking a beating after blowing out the lamp, his mother slipped Joseph a hard crust of bread she had hidden in her apron pocket. She knelt down beside him where he trembled, wrapped only in a thin blanket on the floor.

"Hush now, my baby, my sweet boy, someday you will find your way in this horrid world..."

"Woman!"

She jumped quickly to her feet. "Coming husband, just finishing up here."

Before she disappeared into the darkness she bent down and kissed Joseph on his head.

"My sweet gentle boy." she whispered.

Joseph's brother Brian had escaped work in the stockyards by secretly saving enough money to buy his first bundle of papers from the *Chicago Tribune*. He had managed to beat the other boys away from a particularly lucrative corner near the Courthouse. Brian brought more money to the family than any of his other brothers because he had, as his father noted, "The gift of Blarney"—he could talk and sell anything to anyone, even his father. Brian convinced their father to let Joseph come along with him to hawk papers.

Joseph loved watching the rich and powerful people passing by in the city center. Their fine clothing and high falootin ways impressed Joseph. He loved the flourish with which his brother hawked the dailies, shouting out headlines, and making them up when they lacked excitement. Brian noticed right away how the rich folks, fine ladies especially were drawn to Joseph's big baby blues and shock of curly golden hair. Sometimes they would press a penny in his little palm after tossing one into the can to pay for the paper. At first Brian demanded Joseph hand any extra penny over—"Nobody should get something for nothing!"—but soon Joseph became adept at hiding his tips from his brother.

They stood on that corner in rain or shine, blistering heat, or in icy winds. They arrived before the sun came up and stayed until they had sold every last paper. Each morning Brian would have to buy a bundle of papers from the "Trib." They needed to sell every single one to make a profit. Brian's gift of Blarney, along with his adorable little brother, resulted in tips which the brothers conspired to hide from their father (who would drink up any extra pennies anyway).

One chilly evening Brian had an idea. He handed Joseph a single newspaper hiding the remaining papers along with himself around the corner. He instructed Joseph to shiver, which was not difficult because the wind piercing his thin jacket already had Joseph chilled. Brian told him to beg passersby to buy his last paper so he could go home to his poor widowed mother and a hot bowl of cabbage soup.

"Oh, you poor little darling," Cooed his first customer, "Such a pretty little boy. Here ..." She handed him a nickel, "Take this home to your poor mother and tell her to put a bit of sausage into that soup."

Brian and Joseph clapped each other on the back gleefully, then repeated their hook until they had dispensed with every last paper in record time earning nearly fifty cents extra! A true fortune!

That night, when Brian explained how they had concocted a scheme to dupe their marks, their father laughed heartily, and directed his comments to Joseph.

"Finally," he laughed cruelly, "Something you're actually good at. Looking pretty and pitiful!"

Joseph smiled concealing his hatred and resentment for his family as the rest of his brothers laughed. They smacked him a little too hard on the back, while his mother looked down at her hands in silence. Brian just smiled and nodded as he stuffed his mouth with soup-soaked bread, allowing it to drip down his chin.

That night as he pulled his blanket tightly around his frozen little body Joseph imagined himself as one of the dapper men to whom he sold papers. He longed to have important work, and to never again have to endure the company of his filthy, disgusting, and cruel family. He only needed to save enough money and to find a way to sever his connection.

After several months Brian decided that he and Joseph could make more money if they each had their own corner. Bigger newsboys had already claimed the best corners, so Brian had to enlist his older brothers to help clear a corner so he could set up shop. One night they beat a poor unsuspecting newsboy so viciously that not only did he relinquish the corner but quit the trade completely. This now required Joseph to carry his own heavy bundles, but it also allowed him to keep his own tips.

Late one Friday night as Joseph tried to sell his last "last" paper, a handsome gentleman smelling of cologne approached him offering two bits for the paper. Joseph wondered if the paper contained something special, but soon realized the man's actual purpose. He tousled Joseph's hair, then gently ran his warm hand down his neck.

Joseph nervously glanced around to see if anybody else noticed the stranger's odd attention. Nobody looked in their direction. A few people hurried up the street, intent only on their destinations.

"You are such a pretty little boy, now aren't you?" The man leaned down with his face very close to Joseph's.

"Would you like to earn even more than that?" He indicated the quarter Joseph held tightly between his fingers.

Joseph nodded.

"How about this?"

The stranger pulled a silver dollar from his vest pocket.

"I don't have any more papers mister." Joseph said nervously.

"I know, you just sold me your last one." he said smiling suggestively. "If you follow me and help me with a little something, I will pay you this dollar."

The man turned and walked briskly up the street. Joseph looked around to see if Brian was coming to walk home with him. The man turned down a dark alley and Joseph followed a short distance behind.

"Hurry up!" the man whispered loudly, waving Joseph closer.

The man stood with his back against a building as Joseph caught up.

"What do you want me to do mister?" Joseph asked, then he noticed that the man had opened his pants and pulled his enlarged pecker out into the night air.

Joseph backed away terrified, "N-no way mister! I'm not doing that!" he said as he took another step back.

The man laughed and reached out, grabbing Joseph by the arm. Joseph struggled against his strong grip as tears stung his eyes.

"Please mister!" He begged, "I'm not like that!"

"Don't worry sweetheart," the man said holding Joseph's arm in one hand as his other hand furiously pulled his own pecker, "You don't have to touch, just watch."

Joseph continued to struggle, unable to look away as the stranger pulled and panted until a white stream squirted out, landing on the filthy stones at their feet. When the man let go, Joseph ran down the alley toward the street. But the man called after him. "Wait! What about your silver dollar?"

Joseph stopped, turned to look back at the man, then cautiously returned to snatch the coin from his disgusting hand. Then Joseph ran away as fast as he could while the man laughed as he tucked himself back into his pants.

Joseph put the silver dollar in an old tin can that held his other secret tips. He hid the can underneath the tenement stairs where nobody but the rats ever went. That night when his father came home, Joseph, without a word, gave his father his usual handful of pennies, then sat down at the table with his ravenous and foul-smelling brothers. He wondered how much money his can contained now with the silver dollar added to it. Joseph knew he dare not pull it out to count, lest his father or one of his brothers confiscate it and give him a beating for being a cheat.

That night when at last he heard his brothers and his father snoring loudly, he silently reached into his drawers and grabbed hold of his own pecker. He started to move is hand up and down thinking about the stranger in the alley. To his surprise it grew warm and hard, and felt amazingly wonderful. He continued to pull until he heard Michael snort and turn over toward him. He lay perfectly still and silent, feeling his pecker pulse in his hand, then squeezed hard until it convulsed on its own. He felt the warm stickiness in his hand and pulled it to his face to get the smell of it. It felt wonderful. He rubbed the goo onto the back of his drawers and turned over. Smiling, he drifted off to sleep.

Over the course of the next several months, Joseph earned twenty silver dollars from the man, who no longer had to hold onto Joseph's arm as he watched him pull his own pecker. Joseph began to grow excited anticipating their meetings, waiting and watching for the man to come along as his last papers sold. Sometimes Joseph would just stand there like a fool long after he hawked his last paper hoping the man would appear. These encounters started making Joseph feel good between his legs. Sometimes he felt his own pecker twitch as he watched the man.

One night the man noticed Joseph enjoying his activity and asked if he would like to try. Joseph shook his head stepping away slightly.

"Here," The man said smiling gently, let me help you."

He reached down and gently grabbed Joseph's pecker in his large hand and rubbed it up and down right through his drawers and trousers, all the while with his own pecker poked out long and hard from his opened pants. Joseph caught his breath. The man's eyes sparkled as he looked closely into Joseph's face.

Joseph's breath quickened, his face flushed, and he began to tremble. The man moved his hand faster and faster over his clothes, then slipped his other hand into Joseph's trousers touching his skin directly. The man's cool hand met the heat of Joseph's young penis, and it instantly exploded. The man kept his hand inside Joseph's pants as he again began pulling his own.

After he, too, exploded the man said to Joseph, "Maybe you should pay *me* a dollar tonight?"

Then he laughed and handed Joseph two silver dollars and blew him a kiss. Joseph ran home faster than ever—feeling both dirty and thrilled. That night in his blanket with his family sleeping nearby, he reached down to touch himself thinking that indeed his mother, or at least somebody, had turned him into a panty waist. And, God help him, he liked it.

Throughout his adolescence Joseph continued meeting the man whose name he never learned. In their encounters the man showed him many wild and thrilling ways to pleasure his and another man's body. He learned about new delightful dark places to touch, fondle, and taste. Soon they took their encounters off the street and into rooms where they could remove all their clothes and touch each other with abandon. Not only did the man continue to pay Joseph well for his services, but he also brought him gifts of cologne, fine clothes, and even a silver pocket watch.

Joseph could no longer hide these things from the prying eyes of his family in their tiny tenement flat. On top of that, he could no longer stomach their very existence. One day he unearthed his can of coins from under the stairs, found a rooming house far enough from his family tenement to avoid discovery, and secured a room. To her great delight, Joseph paid the landlady for two months' rent in advance. Then, he headed to Marshall Fields to buy a new suit of gentleman's clothes.

Returning to his room, he paid the nickel for a hot bath, slathered himself with the cologne the man had given him, and dressed in his new clothes. He bundled up his old clothes and dropped them into the rag bin in the alley as he strutted out into the bright September sun, a new-made gentleman.

With coins filling his pockets, he strode past the corner where only a week before he had hawked *The Chicago Tribune* to rich folks. A younger boy held out the paper shouting the headline. Joseph flipped a penny into his can and, smiling broadly, snatched the paper from his hand.

Joseph considered the hulking and ornate Courthouse, then walked around the corner to view the Chamber of Commerce building.

"That's where I'm going to get a job." he declared to no one in particular, "But first I think I will have a decent meal."

He turned and headed straight for Anderson's Restaurant when a handsome young man caught up to him on the sidewalk. The stranger tipped his hat and smiled the most delightful smile Joseph had ever seen.

"Good morning." He said passing Joseph as his silver tipped cane clicked on the walkway.

Joseph quickened his pace, "Good morning." He said tipping his own hat. "Sure is warm for September." He hoped to keep up a conversation with this handsome stranger. "I'm new in town. Hoping for a position at the Chamber of Commerce."

The stranger stopped, turning to Joseph in the friendliest way, said, "Welcome to Chicago. My name is Charles. I work at the courthouse for Mayor Mason. I'm on my way to lunch. Would you care to join me?"

Delighted, Joseph agreed. The two young men had a deliciously, long lunch at Anderson's topping it off with two glasses of port. They laughed and talked easily. Joseph recognized the way Charles looked at him with shining eyes and a suggestive smile. Joseph made a point of "accidentally" brushing Charles' hand as he reached for things on the table. He absently let his foot run into Charles' under the table. With every touch he felt that same warm feeling in his body that he had first learned in the alley as a small boy.

Each seemed to really enjoy the other's company, and so they made an agreement to meet again for lunch on Friday. Joseph gazed deeply into Charles' eyes as he shook his hand firmly and yet gently, reaching up to touch his shoulder with his other hand. It made him feel excited and warm. He couldn't wait for Friday.

# Chapter 20
# Dandy

dan- dē–*noun:* a man who is excessively concerned about his clothes and appearance.)

NINETEEN-YEAR-OLD CHARLES DAVIDSON STRUTTED down Clark Street sporting the new bowler he had just picked up from J.M. Loomis Hatter to replace his summer *boater.* Though it cost a pretty penny, it fit perfectly—even with the rakish tilt he gave it as he tipped it to folks passing by. Having just been appointed as an assistant to a secretary for Mayor Roswell B. Mason, Charles had the world by the tail. He loved politics and all the perks that came with it. Important people knew his name. He had a quick mind and strikingly handsome good looks. He stood taller than most of the other men in his office and made sure to dress impeccably in the latest 1871 fashion. Charles liked to think of himself as the epitome of a gentleman.

The morning sun rose overhead on an early October Friday. Charles had some work to do at the courthouse before meeting his new friend Joseph for lunch at Anderson's Restaurant. The whole city was a veritable tinderbox due to the lingering heat of summer and the drought that had gripped the city for most of the late summer and fall, but this did not cross the mind of young Charles. He was mostly excited to see Joseph. Joseph had, like Charles, impeccable taste in attire as well as stunning good looks. He knew that heads would turn whenever they found themselves in each other's company.

Something about Joseph made Charles feel excited and nervous. Their conversation had proved interesting and easy, and he loved spending his time with Joseph who hoped to get a position as a clerk at the Chamber of Commerce on LaSalle Street.

Charles watched the clock as it approached noon, the hour when he would get to meet Joseph. At last the hour struck and Charles jumped up excitedly from his desk.

"Look at you all a tizzy," an office mate noted, "Looks like you must be meeting a pretty lady for lunch."

"Not at all," Charles replied annoyed by his office mate's breach of privacy, "I'm meeting my friend Joseph if you must know."

His colleague, properly admonished, turned back to the paperwork on his desk as Charles grabbed his bowler and silver tipped cane and made his way to Anderson's.

Joseph waved happily to him from the corner table where he waited. He stood up and shook Charles' hand warmly while gripping his arm with his strong left hand. This sent a charge through Charles' skin and into the depths of his belly. The same tingle returned as Joseph accidentally brushed Charles' hand while reaching for the butter plate.

After lunch the two young men shook hands again and made a plan to meet the next week for drinks at the pub after work. This plan, however seemed doomed from the start.

Late Sunday night, Charles began to hear the courthouse bell ringing furiously. An emergency! He rose from his cot and stepped out into the warm night breeze in bare feet and his nightshirt. Horror gripped his mind as, looking southward, he saw a wall of fire at least sixty feet high spanning, it seemed, the entire horizon. It looked as if the devil himself had come to Chicago and brought with him all the fires of hell.

Charles stood with his jaw agape mesmerized by the spectacle before him until he noticed the panicked throng on the street below fleeing the flames. Someone shouted up to him, "Run for your life! The fire is moving faster than a horse can run!"

Charles, terrified, returned to his flat and ran in frantic circles trying to figure what to grab, and what to leave behind. The smoke now filled his room, stinging his eyes. An orange glow pierced the dark in his room. He stripped off his nightshirt and got dressed in his best suit, quickly tucking his stockings into his garter, he then pulled on his lace-up ankle boots. He grabbed his coat and ran down the stairs toward the street. Remembering his new bowler, he turned and sprinted back up to his room two stairs at a time. In his room he headed toward the drawer that held his records and papers but noticed his silver topped cane resting next to it. Grabbing only the bowler and cane, he ran back down the stairs and joined the melee in the street. It was pandemonium as thousands of terrified men, women, children, and animals flooded the streets heading toward the river.

The fire continued to rage as the clang of the courthouse bell rose above the shouts, cries and wailing children until ... It eventually stopped completely. Charles guessed that the fire must have reached the central downtown. He found himself alone among a growing throng of terrified citizens waiting to make their way across the Randolph Street Bridge to safety on the other side of the expansive Main Stem of the Chicago River. He thanked the powers that be that his poor dear mother and father resided safely in Heaven and didn't have to witness or endure this terrifying event.

Though the crowd was clearly panicked, only a few ruffians tried to push their way through the crowd toward the front of the line to cross the bridge to escape the raging conflagration. The brutes were met with the fists of fathers and husbands trying to get their own families to safety. After nearly an hour, Charles found himself in the tsunami of humans, wagons, and horses swept across the Randolph Street Bridge. While most people kept moving northeast away from the river Charles stopped to gawk at the terrible disaster that befell the city he loved. He watched the fire approaching closer and closer to his perch along a railing overlooking the fire beyond the river, until he heard a great kerfuffle from up-river. He heard loud screams and shouts and saw people on his side of the river starting to run. He scanned the scene to determine its cause when he heard people shouting,

"Run! Run for your lives! The fire has jumped the river!"

*Impossible,* he thought, *the river is nearly a full city block wide.*

Joseph's heart sank as he saw parched rooftops and dry trees burst into flame less than a block away from where he stood on the north side of the river. Terrified, he began to run in the direction the crowd moved, glancing behind him from time to time to watch the inferno approaching. All civility vanished as people fled in a panic for their very lives. Strong men pushed and shoved children, mothers carrying babies, and even the elderly out of their way if they didn't run fast enough. "Every man for himself" it seemed as the fires of hell swept down onto the terrified rabble.

Charles swung around with raised fists as someone grabbed him from behind. He must have looked like a wild man ready to destroy whomever thwarted his escape.

"Charles! Charles! Thank God it's you!"

Joseph threw his arms around Charles and held him tightly. Then, without shame, kissed him on his cheeks as all the terror and confusion of the night melted away into pure love. Charles wanted to kiss him passionately right there on the street, but he noticed several burly men scowling and watching them suspiciously.

Without hesitation Charles threw his arms around Joseph, declaring loudly for the bystanders to hear, "Oh my brother! My brother Thank the good lord you got away from the fire unscathed!"

Thinking they were brothers, the disapproving glances passed, along with the threat of a beating for being sodomites. Charles and Joseph clung to each other as they joined the now-slowing march toward grasslands beyond the fuel stoking the great conflagration.

People gathered around wagons and in small groups sitting on the beach grass stunned and exhausted as the fire continued to burn. It took two days for the blaze to cease. The city hissed like an enormous serpent when rain began to fall on Tuesday evening, finally quenching the terrible fire. The U.S. Army arrived with canvas tents and set up mess stations and first aid tents. Charles and Joseph took shelter in each other's arms at night under wool blankets distributed by the army. During the day Charles led Joseph through the refugees searching for someone from City Hall with whom to connect.

After several days Charles found some colleagues from the mayor's office. They suggested he go to the Congregational Church where the mayor had set up operations since the courthouse had been completely destroyed. Mayor Mason had placed the Chicago Relief and Aid Society in charge of the relief efforts. Charles introduced his *brother* Joseph to the mayor's secretary for whom he worked. Immediately, they both were brought on to help coordinate the relief efforts. Tens of thousands of dollars began flooding in from across the country.

Charles and Joseph found a rare vacancy in a rooming house in the unscathed part of the city and rented a single room with one small bed together. The Irish landlady didn't bat an eye at two young brothers seeking shelter together after the great fire. The first night they found their bodies touching they could barely breathe. They just lay facing each other inhaling the same air and sharing the same warmth.

Charles felt embarrassed and tried to pull away as his manhood became aroused. Then Joseph reached down and touched him. Charles had never in his life felt pleasure like that. His breath caught in his throat and he felt a quiet moan emerge from the depths of his being as Joseph stroked and caressed his genitals. When Joseph leaned in and put his mouth over Charles', slipping his tongue deeply inside, Charles could no longer contain himself and burst forth in Joseph's hand and onto the bed sheets.

"Oh no." Charles whispered, "The sheets. The landlady."

Joseph shushed him placing a finger that smelled of ecstasy gently to his lips.

"Don't worry. I'll take care of it."

Then he took Charles' hand and placed it on his own manhood. Frightened but overcome with passion, Charles touched Joseph the way Joseph had touched him until Joseph, too, exploded in the bed. Satiated, they drifted off to sleep in each other's arms. They woke late in the morning by loud knocking on their bedroom door. Mrs. O'Toole called to them.

"Are you going to sleep the day through? I'm going to clean up the breakfast dishes. If you want to eat, come down now."

Giggling like schoolgirls they kissed again, then dressed hurriedly for breakfast.

Charles and Joseph worked side by side helping to keep track of the donations and distribute them to the right places, which sometimes meant the pockets of decision-makers. Charles saw no sin in keeping small amounts for himself and Joseph since he too had lost everything in the fire.

Rebuilding of the city began immediately after the fire. With each new political administration came greater opportunity, and the brothers grew more politically powerful. They moved out of the boarding house and out of reach of Mrs. O'Toole's meddling eyes. Though she often commented on how neat and fastidious the Davidson brothers kept their room, making their bed up tightly each morning, even stripping their own bed on Monday mornings dropping their soiled linen directly into the washtub, discretion was paramount. Charles had never felt happier in his whole life. Even though he had lost everything he had earned and saved in the fire along with papers, clothes, books, and even a tintype of his long dead parents, he felt that he had gained something beyond words in Joseph. They had each other, and a whole new identity as brothers that could conceal their forbidden affair for as long as they lived.

When Charles tried to ask Joseph about his past and his people, Joseph changed the subject, telling Charles that it brought him too much sadness.

"Let it suffice to say," Joseph once told him, "That whatever terrible things befell me in my life before have led me to you, and that is all that I care to consider."

Charles loved Joseph deeply and purely despite the depraved nature of their affair. He wanted nothing more than to make his lover happy, and to live out their days in peace.

# Chapter 21
# Entente

(än-'tänt–*noun:* an alliance of parties)

CHARLES AND JOSEPH TOOK A ONE-BEDROOM FLAT on the second floor of one of the new brick two-flats rising from the ashes on the near north side of the city. Buildings and infrastructure sprang up like radishes as Chicago forged ahead, rebuilt, and emerged as a city that rivaled even New York. Working out of the mayor's office afforded special privileges and opportunities for Charles and Joseph. They knew how to get contracts awarded which brought them many clandestine cash-filled envelopes from grateful plumbers, brick layers, and builders.

As the city thrived, so did the Davidson brothers. In the late 1880's they met an architect at a political function held by the newly powerful Democratic Party. The architect spoke of an opportunity to build beautiful spacious homes northwest of the city center in an area called Portage Park. He said that streetcars would soon reach out that far and offered Charles and Joseph an opportunity to purchase property at a steal where they could build a glorious home.

Charles and Joseph loved the idea of having a house of their own. Even though they had more privacy in their flat than in the boarding house, they still had to be very careful to not make suspicious noises or behave too affectionately toward one another lest their downstairs neighbors find out that they were lovers, not brothers after all.

The next Saturday they hired a hack to drive them out of the city along the Northwest Plank road into Jefferson Township. From there they headed east over a rutted unfinished track into the idyllic prairie land northwest of the growing city. Land was plentiful and inexpensive. Joseph and Charles spent the afternoon walking among the tall grasses loosely scattered with mature elm trees. They chose a quarter acre less than a stone's throw from the plank road. The excited real estate broker said the streetcar would soon extend along the plank road bringing with it all of the opportunity and commerce that the expanding city of Chicago could offer.

Charles and Joseph stood side by side as the broker yammered on, turning to survey the expanse of space. Neither of them had ever experienced this kind of vast openness. The sky overhead shone with the deepest blue, spotted with random puffy white clouds. Birds called from the branches of the elms. The only human sounds came from a distance away where ditch diggers opened the ground for water and sewer pipes.

Charles and Joseph felt like pioneers settling a new land. The house they would build here would be the very first in Portage Park. They could do as they pleased outside of the prying, judgmental eyes of either neighbors or strangers. They decided to make it a jewel and a showpiece.

Shaking hands with the broker, they agreed to meet the next week at the First Chicago Bank to sign papers for a building loan, and to secure a deed. They also agreed to contact an architect to begin to design the home of their dreams.

When asked for identification at the bank Charles and Joseph explained that they had lost all their records and identification in the great conflagration. This was common in the years after the fire, so no one questioned their familial connection. Their employment in Mayor Harrison's office, substantial clout with the Democratic Party, along with an envelope of cash, ensured that they procured the deed they needed without difficulty at the courthouse.

Their architect designed a two-story, three-bedroom home with a full attic, basement, and a fashionable front porch. The porch would span he length of the house, so they could sit on hot summer evenings, feel the breeze off the prairie, and watch birds. The world would come to their doorstep as Portage Park developed. A front parlor with large windows would open onto the porch, a formal dining room with a leaded bay window would lead from the parlor, and a separate study would serve a quiet space. At the back of the ground floor, a state-of-the-art kitchen would include a built-in icebox that opened up to an enclosed back porch where the ice man could make deliveries without entering the house and tracking in mud. They splurged to include the most luxurious water closet graced with a porcelain bathing tub with water heated in copper tubes that coiled past the furnace and around the chimney. A separate coal bin with outside access would keep the coal from soiling the interior of the house. The large furnace would heat the entire main floor in a matter of minutes—even on the coldest winter day. Construction began early that spring.

Throughout the season they would sometimes pack a picnic basket, then hire a hack for a drive out to the building site. It thrilled them to watch the construction progress under the skilled hands of strong, bronze-skinned, sweating men who spoke Italian. Charles and Joseph made sure to behave toward one another like brothers, and to the foreman and workers in the manliest ways to avoid scrutiny.

When at long last construction ended and they could move in, they hired a team of men and horses to transfer their things to their beautiful new house from their flat near the city center. Together they perused the Sears Roebuck catalog for the finest home décor, including the latest fashion of fancy gas lamps and damask draperies. They ordered built-in glass and oak cupboards in the kitchen, shelves and more cupboards in the pantry, and a beautifully crafted built-in credenza with ornate brass fittings in the dining room. They fully furnished all three bedrooms with wardrobes, featherbeds, side tables, draperies, and rugs, but secretly decided to share the large L-shaped master bedroom in the front of the house. The connected but separate bedchamber was unnecessary, but an added bonus, nonetheless.

Life was good for the Davidson brothers. More homes began

springing up around them, along with markets, pubs and restaurants. Throughout their thirties, the pair were alone together in their beautiful home at night, while they raked in a fortune at City Hall during the day. Despite the distance between their home and those of their neighbors, and no matter how friendly Charles and Joseph behaved toward others, suspicions began to grow. Neighbors, and even colleagues began to wonder about the two handsome and successful gentlemen who remained single as they approached the age of forty. People also noticed that neither brother ever spent any time in the company of ladies. Charles caught the grocer snickering and whispering to other patrons as he left the market with his grocery basket over his arm. Neighbors started whispering or ignoring them as they walked up the newly made street in the evenings. Some pulled their children abruptly away, closed their doors, or obviously turned their backs as Charles and Joseph passed by. Even though Charles had been elected as the 26th Ward Precinct Captain, during his rounds meeting with voters, he noticed a new wariness among his constituents.

No matter how carefully they behaved in public, living alone together was beginning to draw unwelcome attention. They needed a way to conceal their forbidden love for one another. The answer came one day in an ad in *The Tribune*.

**Beautiful Girls**

**looking for a new life in America**

**European Picture Brides**

**Contact....**

"You want to get *married!*" Charles asked aghast.

"In name only." Joseph explained. "We could set her up in the bedroom at the top of the stairs, or even in the study. You could move your things into the connected bedroom, and we could still be together. We can take the dividing wall out of the closet shared between the rooms. When she's asleep, you can slip through the closet to sleep in our bed where you really belong."

"But won't you have to bed *her* too?" Charles felt a strong wave of jealousy.

"No." Joseph caressed Charles' face. "Maybe once to consummate the marriage, but if she's young enough we can convince her that sexless marriages are perfectly normal. She won't know the difference at all." Then he added, "You know that it's you I love, and you I will only long for forever."

Charles hung his head, pouting, "Why can't I be the one to marry the picture bride?" he asked, "Why does it have to be you who gets married?"

"It doesn't have to be me. Would you rather it be you? I'd really rather you marry her anyway, so I have less to pretend. You are so much better at keeping up appearances. I have no doubt about your faithfulness, my love. I'm not worried at all about some foreign woman under our roof."

Smiling contentedly, and contemplating their perfect ruse, they sat in their overstuffed chairs holding hands as Charles drew deeply on his pipe.

They agreed that the next day they would find a photographer so that Charles could sit for a formal portrait to send to the picture bride broker. Seeking a wife was the perfect cover for their illicit and unnatural love affair.

Weeks later, they received a letter from the broker along with a photograph of a lovely, olive skinned, Greek girl with dark eyes and a full mop of dark hair braided high on her head. Barely out of childhood at seventeen, Chara seemed the perfect match for Charles ... and Joseph.

Together the brothers composed a charming letter to Chara and her family, agreeing to pay the broker's fee and a reasonable dowry. They offered to reserve a cabin on a steamship from Greece to New York, also a train ticket for a Pullman car from New York to Chicago. Then Joseph kissed the sepia photograph of a very handsome, and distinguished looking Charles Davidson, and dropped it in the corner mailbox.

A little more than a month later they received the first letter from Chara addressed to "Mr. Charles Davidson" in which she spoke fondly to her intended. Thereafter, weekly letters from Greece expressed a growing fondness for Charles. The brothers could not determine if Chara had dictated the letters, or had written them herself, but each greeting said, "Friend Davidson," and each was signed, "Fondly, C."

Chara had a kind and gentle way of expressing herself. She wrote of the joy they would share when they could, at last, be in each other's company. Charles and Joseph composed their responses together over glasses of port, increasing the flirtation and ramping up the romance with each new letter. The lovers courted Chara through the post and did it expertly.

The Greek girl wrote more letters in response, matching the flirtation. This went on for a full year. Joseph surprised himself at the level of excitement with which he met each new letter. He would read them multiple times, feeling a growing fondness for this mysterious Greek woman. Every day he would gaze longingly at the portrait they had received from Mr. Costas. Joseph imagined the sound of her sweet voice speaking the words that appeared on the pale blue stationary. He relished the evenings he and Charles spent composing return letters.

*This*, thought Joseph, *is a truly romantic love affair via post.*

He counted the days until Chara herself would come into their lives. Though Charles seemed mostly anxious or uninterested, Joseph cherished and saved every letter that she signed, "Fondly, C". He had begun to move his things from the master bedroom into what would become his own room when the picture bride arrived. Joseph kept those letters tied together with a blue ribbon hidden deep in the top drawer of his bureau.

Six months later, in the middle of October as the autumn chill began to grip the city, Charles and Joseph met Chara for the first time at Union Station. They recognized her from her picture even though she looked much younger than eighteen, exhausted, and a wee bit frightened. They found her scanning the crowded platform. She searched for Charles, glancing frantically back and forth from the crowd to his picture in one hand while holding two carpet bags in the other. The Davidson brothers approached her, smiled, and bowed when they finally connected with Chara. They tried to communicate with her and found that she had learned a few English words and expressions.

"Miss Chara?"

Though he pronounced her name wrong, saying the soft "C" as a hard "K," Chara found it charming. She did not embarrass him by correcting his pronunciation. She kept repeating, "Yes. Thank you. Hello. Hello. My name is Chara (pronouncing it the way he had). You are Charles? I am so very happy to be meet you. Thank you, Charles."

Chara's subtle and mysterious beauty combined with a gentle air that Joseph thought would serve her well in the world of the brothers Davidson. As Charles took her arm, she smiled shyly. Joseph found a porter and arranged for her trunk to be delivered to the cab station. When he returned to Charles and Chara, they were clumsily attempting hand gestures to indicate their desires. As Joseph bent to pick up her travel satchels, his eyes met Chara's. Joseph saw something in them that gave him pause. She looked at him much the same way that Charles did. Unexpected emotions arose in Joseph and he returned her glance unflinchingly until the bustle of passengers rushing for trains—and Charles himself interrupted them—breaking their visceral connection.

The unlikely, and unwary trio hailed a hack to their home, and the new life that loomed before them.

# Chapter 22
# Hunger

(hɛŋ-gɛr—*noun:* a compelling need or desire for food, to have a strong desire.)

HUNGRY. IF ONE WORD COULD DEFINE CHARA'S CHILDHOOD, that word would be *hungry.* Chara began her life on the shores of Lake Kopais outside of the Greek village of Haliartus. Her papa met an untimely end during a struggle with a Scotsman at the offices of The British Lake Copais Company just days before her birth. Her Mitéra, still mostly a girl herself, wore black every day for the rest of her life.

Chara and her Mitéra joined her grandparents in a sparsely furnished three-room stone cottage for the first years of her life. The goats occupied the ground floor, the food stores on the second, and the family room above. Her Yaya cooked eels, ducks, and fish that Papou caught at the lake. She added goat milk, cheese, and the scraggly vegetables that grew in their small garden, a poor rocky area. When Chara was four, the lake was drained, creating arable land to grow currants for Christmas puddings in England. This meant food for Chara and her family grew more and more scarce. Soon the lakeshore retreated further from the village and the ducks ceased to come. Chara's family had little food, and no means to buy food.

Four-year-old Chara did not understand why she could not eat all the vegetables they pulled from the garden. She felt her belly crying for food one day, and so she climbed up into the food storage looking for something to make it stop. She would never forget the beating she received when her Mitéra caught her there eating raw potatoes.

"How will we grow more next year if you eat all the seed potatoes!" Mitéra screamed, whipping Chara with a switch until her Yaya grabbed her hand.

That night Yaya scolded Mitéra for beating the child simply because she was hungry. Both women wept softly as they lay near little Chara who had curled up on her own small sleeping pallet. That night, Chara whimpered herself to sleep from her stinging skin as well as the terrible pain in her belly.

Yaya made thin broths of onions and beets to feed the family. Sometimes Chara would pull small clods of dry grass from the hillside, then run off to hide as she ate it, dirt and all. She did not care that she choked on the sharp leaves, or that the dirt tasted of manure. It kept her belly from crying at least for a little while.

Before Chara reached her twelfth year, Papou died. His body simply wasted away. She remembered seeing his ribs and hips jutting out, and his legs looking as thin as sticks when she watched Yaya wash his corpse with wine. Mitéra picked wildflowers from the highlands, fashioned a wreath, and placed it on Papou's head.

Chara tried to hold back her tears as the men carried his open coffin along the rocky road to the burial ground. Yaya, however wailed, beat her chest, and tore her hair as they lowered his rough coffin into the dry earth, then she packed away her colorful shawl and joined her daughter wearing only black.

Chara missed the amazing tricks Papou did with his hands, tapping and turning them over and back in elaborate patterns. She missed the sound of his voice singing old folksongs or laughing so hard that before long everyone in the cottage joined him—whether or not they knew what was so funny. She missed his humming that grew more and more mournful as he mended the nets that would never catch another fish or eel. She longed to feel his rough fingers get caught in her tangle of dark, curly hair as he playfully rubbed her head. Most of all, she missed the humor that seemed to disappear when he died. Yaya stopped singing during her mending or cooking. Mitéra ceased to smile or sing old love songs. The tiny stone cottage had become as much a tomb as the place where they had left Papou's body.

Yaya followed Papou to Heaven before summer came again. Mitéra shed not a single tear as she washed Yaya's body with a small amount of wine mixed with water. They had used most of their wine on Papou.

Chara thought it fitting because, unbeknownst to Yaya, Chara had seen her many times pour thin soup into the bowls for her family, then secretly add more water to her own bowl, sacrificing her nourishment for that of her husband, daughter, and granddaughter. Now, even in death, Yaya's portion was watered down.

Mitéra began to do washing and mending for the English and French men who dug the trenches to drain Lake Kopais. They paid her in bread and sometimes a few coins. Occasionally, when she delivered the clean washing she would be away for a long time. On those days there would be more to eat. Chara never saw Mitéra eat the extra food she brought back to the cottage on those long days. Instead she sipped tea and watched Chara devour the delicious meats, fish, olives or figs.

After a few years of subsisting on the dwindling garden and the food and coins in trade for washing, some of the old women in the village began to shun Chara and her Mitéra. Village girls threw stones at Chara and called her terrible names as she walked along the path that once bordered the lake.

As Chara developed into a woman, the French and English men began to notice her, making comments as she went for water. Mitéra would become furious and pull Chara close, shouting at the foreign men in their language. She would accompany her scolding with lewd gestures toward the men. When they returned to the cottage, Mitéra would slap and beat Chara, and scream, "Don't walk like a whore! Never smile at the workers!"

Chara did not know what Mitéra saw. She did not intend to flirt with the men. She did not invite their catcalls. She grew to hate Mitéra and wished beyond anything that Yaya had not died, or that her ghost would come in the night and scold Mitéra for mistreating her daughter.

Chara cried herself to sleep more nights than not as Mitéra's beatings became more frequent and more severe.

Mitéra spent longer and longer days at the British Lake Copais Company serving many more of the workers. She looked worn down and grew tired and irritable. Soon she developed painful sores on her face and body until, after a while, the laundry work stopped. Mitéra took to her bed shivering with fever and moaning in pain. The larder quickly emptied, but when Chara offered to take up the laundry Mitéra slapped her.

"It's only laundry!" Chara protested. "Why do you hate me so? We need to eat something!"

Mitéra began to weep, "Ah but would it have been only laundry. My girl, My beautiful Chara. Men want only one thing from women. I will not let them ruin you like they have me."

Then weeping, Mitéra slipped into unconsciousness. Chara did not understand her mother, she attributed the confusion to fever and illness. Mitéra never regained consciousness. She died during a terrifying fit five days later. Chara found herself all alone.

She remembered the washing in wine, and flower wreath ritual, but possessed neither wine nor flowers. She had no relatives, and no money, and no way of getting either. The other villagers shunned her Mitéra as well as Chara for reasons only they knew. Chara sat on a small wooden stool outside the doorway to the tiny stone cottage with her dead Mitéra lying up the steps inside as cold as the stone walls. Chara didn't even weep a single tear but sat wondering what to do next. Two days later an older man from The British Lake Copais Company came to call.

"Where ... is ... your ... mother?" He asked, slowly accentuating every word hoping Chara might understand his language if he spoke very slowly.

Chara just looked at him blankly.

"YOUR ... MOTHER." He thought maybe shouting would help her understand. Then he spoke a word she knew, "*Mitéra!*" He shouted

"YOUR MOTHER!"

Now Chara understood. She motioned for him to go inside. When he entered the dark room, he let out a loud gasp, and came rushing back out into the sunlight.

"Oh my God! How long has she been there like this?"

Though Chara did not fully understand his words, she did understand his shock.

"Days?" she said in tentative English, "Two" she held up two fingers!"

"Two days!" the Englishman, appeared horrified, "What happened?"

"Died." Chara said in yet another English word she knew. "Hello, you're welcome."

She attempted a smile.

"You people are crazy!" he exclaimed. "She's got to be buried! She needs a funeral."

Several of the English and French men gave money to the villagers for the burial. They provided wine, money and food to Chara, even though she did not intend to take up their laundry.

She walked under her Mitéra's black veil in silence as the village men carried Mitéra's coffin up the hill to lie with the rest of her family. The old priest refused to bless the burial so one of the Englishmen wearing a stiff white collar spoke a few foreign words and made the motion of a cross over the coffin as they lowered her into the hard, cruel earth. Chara did not shed even a single tear.

A few days later, as she walked through the village, one of the girls who had thrown stones at her on many occasions noticed Chara and motioned for her to come over to where she and several other village girls gathered. Reluctantly, Chara made her way to the group. They giggled excitedly as a large man wearing a bright red fez smiled and talked loudly while showing them several photographs.

"You should do this Chara," said the stone throwing girl, "You are perfect for this!" Then she turned to the strange man, "Here! This is the girl I told you about: Chara."

The man bowed deeply. He spoke her language, but with a strange accent, "Would you like a rich husband? Would you like to travel away from this poor tiny village?"

Chara nodded. Either prospect sounded welcome. "Where?" she asked, "Who would want to marry a poor peasant girl like me?"

"Ahhh," the man said, "Allow me to introduce myself. My name is Mr. Costas. I am a broker, a matchmaker if you will, for beautiful young girls like yourself and handsome, rich American men. I set up an arrangement whereby you and your prospective groom write letters and send pictures to one another. I have many Greek men who have gone to America to make a better life who would like to marry a beautiful Greek girl like you."

Chara had no interest in Greek men. She saw the way the men in the village treated her Mitéra before she died. "Greek men?" she spat dramatically in the dirt.

"Not only Greek men." said Mr. Costas, "Here look at this fine gentleman. He lives in Chicago and has a powerful job in the government."

Mr. Costas shoved a picture of Charles Davidson toward Chara. She grew intrigued. The man in the photograph appeared quite fine and handsome. His striking features and intense eyes seemed to speak to Chara.

"And this man?" she asked, "How much for this man?"

Mr. Costas laughed, "It costs you nothing. The gentleman pays for everything including your passage on the steamship. You will live in luxury and have plenty to eat for the rest of your life.

"Plenty to eat" was all Chara heard. She agreed to participate and become a picture bride. Mr. Costas told Chara and the other girls to clean up, wash their hair and face, and dress in their finest clothes for a portrait the next day.

The next morning, Chara leaned over the basin and washed her hair with cold water, olive oil, and lavender. She brushed it until it shone, sweeping it off her forehead. Then she braided and pinned it back high on her head. She searched through her Yaya's trunk to find a brightly-colored skirt and white blouse with multicolored ribbons that had belonged to Yaya long ago. Dressed in her best finery, she strode to the village square. There she saw several other peasant girls, all dressed in their finest costumes, gathered around a large camera box on a three-legged stand. The girls giggled and whispered—except one who wept and begged her father to not send her away. The girl craned her neck toward a village boy standing nearby. Her father slapped her and told her to be quiet. She lowered her head and wept quietly as Mr. Costas produced documents for all to sign.

After a long time, he told the girls, one after another to stand still and smile at the box while he snapped their photograph. That night as she lay on her sleeping pallet, she practiced saying "Hello," "You're welcome," and "Charles."

Chara had no choice but to take up her mother's duties doing the washing for the men at The British Lake Copais Company. They treated her kindly, and paid her well to collect, wash, and return their soiled clothes every week. Chara immersed herself into the work. She found that scrubbing the filthy shirts, pants, and underthings against the washboard staved off her fears about marrying a stranger in a strange country. She had nothing to leave behind really, but the prospect frightened her, nonetheless.

One of the Englishmen, Albert, spoke Greek quite well. He spoke to Chara very kindly of her Mitéra. Chara did not understand what he meant when he told her that she should not hold any ill will toward her Mitéra because she did what she had to in order to keep herself and her daughter alive. Chara did not judge her Mitéra for doing the washing for the men that dug the trenches that caused their village to starve. She knew nothing else of which to be ashamed.

The more contact she had with the foreigners, the more English words she learned. When letters came from Charles of Chicago, America, Chara took them to Albert. She listened with delight as he translated the charming love letters her Charles had written. Chara told him what she wanted to say in response. Albert handled the pen exquisitely and wrote in a beautiful hand "Fondly," then Chara wrote "C." The writing appeared lovely and flowing, unlike the angular Greek writing Papou had taught her as a little girl. Chara began to believe that the life before her would be as magical and appealing as the script on the pages that traveled between Haliartus and Chicago, America.

Chara lived alone for months in her tomblike stone hut. Nightly, she dreamt of Charles and a life free from the cruel disdain of her neighbors, her empty belly, and her cracked and bleeding knuckles worn raw from the mountains of washing. Finally, Mr. Costas returned with passage for the steamer to New York, along with train tickets from New York to Chicago. Chara hoped she would thrive in her new life. She believed that her husband would love her as tenderly as he described in his letters. She knew she would make a good wife for the handsome and charming Charles. Most of all, she was ready to leave Haliartus and hunger forever.

# Chapter 23

# Passage

(**pas-**ij–*noun*: an act or instance of passing from one place or circumstance, to another)

ALBERT GAVE CHARA A USED STEEL STEAMER TRUNK in which to pack her few possessions to take to America. Chara thanked him, but seeing its size wondered just how she would ever fill it. She stood alone with the opened flower paper-lined trunk in the middle of the floor looking around the bare rooms. She thought she could take Mitéra's worn black dress, since she had buried her in her good one. She could take the colorful skirt and ribboned blouse she had found in Yaya's cupboard along with the crocheted wool coverlets that as a small girl, she had watched grow from Yaya's own hands.

When Chara looked into Mitéra's box, she found remnants of a life before widowhood and before Chara. She found a lovely embroidered shawl, a short jacket, flowing blouses, and skirts. Mitéra must have secretly saved these things since she was a girl. Chara shook out the dust and took them outside to beat in the warm Greek sunshine. These would be her travel clothes to start her new life.

On the day Mr. Costas came with the cart to carry the picture brides to the harbor, Chara squeezed herself into her Mitéra' dress and girdle, stockings, and leather shoes. Mr. Costas loaded her trunk and the two carpet satchels she had filled with bread, wine, olives, currents, figs, and a picture of Charles Davidson into the cart. Chara, alone in the empty rooms, studied the stone cottage one last time. She sat down in Papou's place at the table and spoke to her ancestors.

"I take you with me to my new life in my heart and in the stories I will tell my children. I ask your blessing for a good life, and your protection from the evil eye and anything that could bring me harm."

Then, feeling a growing lump in her throat and tears welling in her eyes, Chara walked out of the only life she had ever known, leaving the rough wooden door open to the world.

Chara looked to see if Albert had come to send her off. Not finding him she watched sadly as the other picture brides kissed their families goodbye amid tears from old women and men alike. All of the brides except one smiled excitedly and waved as the cart made its way over the rocky road toward the harbor several hours away. Chara felt pity for the distraught girl she recalled from the portrait session. The girl sobbed, pleaded, and reached toward a sobbing boy who ran after the cart until he could run no more. Not knowing what to say as the girl fell into quiet despair with tears wetting her face, Chara simply tried to comfort her with an understanding smile and nod. She wondered how sweet it would feel to leave something you would miss. Chara, on the other hand, had nothing at all to regret leaving Haliartus or all of Greece for that matter.

The Haliartus Picture Brides hung close together on the dock as groups of other girls from other villages gathered preparing to embark on their journey across the sea. Chara breathed in the sea air and relished the feeling of the warm late September sun on her skin. She took out the picture of Charles to memorize every feature so she could identify him when at last she reached her destination. She knew the journey would take weeks, but could not begin to fathom the adventure that lay ahead.

Once aboard, a steward showed the group from her village to the place they would spend the first part of their journey in steerage. Many people packed into the dark, foul smelling area lined with narrow steel bunks with bare mattresses. The man assigned a bunk to each of the immigrants except Chara. She began to panic fearing a change of heart on the part of Charles, or a problem with her ticket.

"Excuse me sir," she said to the man, "I have no bunk assigned to me. Is there a problem with my passage?" She showed him her ticket and documents.

"Not at all Miss." he said cheerily, "Forgive me, but you are in the wrong place."

He asked her to follow him back up the steel stairs and through a narrow room that had long tables and benches in the center with a few chairs along the walls. Chara clung tightly to her satchels as she followed, terrified that he would lead her back down the gangplank and off the ship. Instead he led her to a vented door halfway down the room that opened to a small semi-private cabin on the deck above the steerage passengers. This cabin contained a tiny round window and two bunks made up with linens, a wool blanket and a small sewn bag of feathers she would later learn was a pillow. Along one wall she saw a set of drawers and a little table that had an opening cut in the top to hold a large bowl and pitcher securely in place. At the foot of her bunk she found the trunk that Albert had given to her. Chara's heart leapt at her good fortune. She had never in her life experienced such luxury. She sat on the bunk bouncing slightly causing the steel springs that held the mattress to squeak merrily.

Before long another young woman joined her. She wore fine silk clothing and an elaborate bonnet. Chara smiled and nodded to her not sure if they spoke the same language. The other woman turned up her nose with an extremely unconvincing half smile.

"Well," she said at last, "I suppose we will just have to put up with these horrible accommodations all the way to New York."

Chara was flabbergasted. *Horrible accommodations?* she thought, *This girl has no idea about horrible accommodations.* Chara remembered the conditions her fellow picture brides would have to endure a deck below

"This is just fine." Chara said. "We can make do."

Later that evening the cabin steward announced "Dinner".

Chara did not know what to do so she waited for her cabin mate to make the first move. She stood up and opened her large trunk that had a set of drawers on one side and a place to hang nearly a dozen dresses on the other. She called out to the steward to bring clean water and washed her face and hands. She took out an ivory comb and smoothed her hair, then opened another drawer to reveal powders and perfumes in bottles and applied both.

She turned to Chara who sat in silent awe watching her every move. "Aren't you going to get cleaned up for dinner? You look a mess."

Chara felt ashamed. She had no powders or perfume. She had only a wooden brush with horsehair bristles that pulled at her tangle of long curly hair. She did not want to remove her braid lest it become more wild and unruly. She decided to splash her face in the bowl of water and patted her skin dry in the same way as did her cabin mate. Then Chara followed her through the door where she saw about twenty people, mostly men, sitting at the long tables. She recognized some of the French and English words they spoke as they drank from large mugs and talked over one another.

"Here, sit here." Chara's cabin mate patted the bench next to her. "Looks like we ladies are going to have to stick together."

All the men rose to their feet as the two women sat. The men greeted them politely, then made small talk with each other as the men ignored the girls. The men talked of prospects, business, and other things of which Chara had no knowledge.

The cabin steward put bowls of potatoes, bread, butter, and a salty meat stew on the tables as the captain joined the group. The men waited until the women had served themselves before scooping heaping helpings onto their plates.

"Some wine Misses?" a very young-looking cabin boy asked as he tipped a large jug over their empty mugs.

"Thank you." they replied and began their first meal aboard the steamship.

Chara's cabin mate introduced herself as Birdie and began telling of her summer holiday in Athens with her wealthy Yaya and Papou. Her father had a thriving business in New York where she was born.

After the meal the men excused themselves to go out onto the deck for a smoke and some brandy. The handful of ladies sat in the chairs in the common room and exchanged stories.

When they heard about Chara traveling all the way to Chicago to meet her future husband they seemed surprised.

"I thought all picture brides traveled in steerage," one said with suspicion directed toward Chara.

"Oh," she explained, "My Charles Davidson is a very rich and powerful man with a position in the Chicago America government."

"Oh, Chicago." one woman said with a smirk, "I can only imagine what kind of power he has in the windy city." She turned to another lady, "Crooks and ruffians is what I've heard about the politicians in Chicago."

Chara did not know what she meant but could see that the woman seemed to disapprove of her. She had already had enough of that from her neighbors back in her village. She excused herself and returned to her cabin secretly spitting on the doorjamb to keep away the evil eye, or the evil thoughts of the judgmental ladies.

The steward had already lit the lamp when she entered her cabin. She lay down on top of the blanket on her bunk fully clothed with the feather sack next to her head. Birdie chuckled when she came in and saw Chara in such a state, but her laughter held no malice.

"You've never traveled before, have you?" Birdie asked kindly.

Chara sat up and shook her head.

"It's okay," she went on, "I've crossed several times. I'll help you. First you need to get out of those smelly clothes and get into your nightshift."

Chara did not know about nightshifts, and certainly didn't have one in her trunk. She tried to stop her as Birdie unlatched and opened Chara's trunk.

Looking at the contents inside Birdie appeared surprised and a bit shocked.

"Oh dear." she said. "This just will not do at all. Here," she went to her own trunk, "I think we are almost the same size. I have far more than I will ever need during the passage. Besides, my mother will take me shopping at Stewart's for a whole new fall wardrobe when I get home."

Birdie handed Chara a beautiful long-sleeved white nightgown. It had white roses embroidered on the yoke with tiny pearl-like buttons that went from the lace neck to the bottom of the full bodice. The sleeves gathered at the shoulder then again at the wrist fastened by another tiny button surrounded by more embroidered white roses. Chara had never felt fabric so soft and light. Her Yaya had embroidered vivid and bold colored flowers on the jacket Chara wore as a child, but she could never have imagined the elegant beauty of white roses on fine white cotton.

"I cannot." Chara began as Birdie broke in.

"Stuff and nonsense!" She said. "We can't have you walking the streets of New York in your village attire. You'll be far too easy a mark for every con man and flimflam artist in the city. Besides," she went on, "It will be fun! Like dressing up a pretty doll."

Birdie sat down on Chara's bunk and gave her a friendly squeeze around the shoulders. Chara felt apprehensive. In her life, she had experienced little kindness without conditions.

Chara thought, *perhaps this is an omen of how it will be in America. Mr. Costas set me up to correspond with Charles. Charles certainly sounds and looks charming and kind. Albert helped me with the letters and gave me the trunk. Now Birdie wants to give me beautiful clothing. Maybe only Greeks hold ill intentions for me.*

During the three-week passage north along the European coast, then across the open Atlantic Chara and Birdie became good friends. Birdie helped Chara learn more English words and phrases. She showed Chara how to dress her hair the way the finest ladies did in America. She shared her silks, dresses, and hats. When the air grew cold at sea, Chara felt grateful for Yaya's brightly colored shawl, though Birdie said it did not match the blue satin dress she had given her. Instead of facing Birdie's disapproval, Chara, who was smaller than Birdie, secretly wore her own dress underneath the fine clothes that Birdie had given her. This helped protect her against the cold sea air.

Chara shared her currants, olives, and figs with Birdie even though more than enough food was served three times a day in the common room. She gave the stale flatbread to the steward who said it might make an excellent bread pudding. Her belly never cried from hunger. If it weren't for the cold, Chara might have thought she had died and gone to the Elysian Fields. Then the storm came.

Chara awoke to a loud roaring sound. She heard the shouts of men over the sound of the wind, rain, and crashing waves. The cabin was pitch black.

"Birdie!" she called out.

"I'm right here!" She shouted back. "I will try to light the lamp."

Chara stayed huddled on her bunk with her blankets pulled up to her chin as the ship lurched back and forth. She felt her stomach turn as it rose and fell with the sea swells. Birdie cried out as something crashed. Then Chara saw the flash of the flint, followed by a small flame. She watched it swing back and forward as Birdie tried to lift the glass and light a lamp fastened to the steel wall.

"Quickly!" Birdie ordered, "Get dressed as warmly as you can. Double up your stockings and wear an extra waistcoat."

The two young women frantically pulled on clothes as the ship tossed them from one bed to the other. Once dressed they made their way to the common room where chairs lay out of place on the deck. A few seated passengers clung to tables that were secured to the floor as the ship rose and fell with the swells. Someone handed Birdie and Chara a strange device telling them to strap it onto their chests. They helped each other with the cumbersome straps and clips, then sat on a bench and held on for dear life.

Through the roar of the storm and the sounds of sailors shouting on deck, Chara began to hear another terrible sound. She heard a multitude of people screaming and wailing from below. Chara stood and shouted, "The people below!!! What about the people below? What is happening to them!?" The other passengers just looked at Chara with terrified eyes.

A sailor grabbed Chara by her upper arms. "Don't worry Miss. We've battened the hatches to below. They won't be bothering the likes of you. Now sit down and hold on until this storm blows itself out."

He roughly put her back in her seat, then returned to the deck before Chara could explain that she had no fear *of* them, just fear *for* them. She looked at Birdie who had always seemed so knowledgeable and worldly. Now she appeared like nothing more than a frightened child who longed for her mother. The men, too, seemed frightened. Chara alone felt more anger than fear for her countrywomen locked heartlessly below in the terrible storm. She knew that, without the protection that Charles gave her, she too would be bearing whatever fate those below suffered. She felt grateful and guilty all at once. For the first time she began to question whether or not she deserved to become the fancy wife of Charles Davidson. She wondered if she would ever fully belong in the life ahead of her. She wondered what Mitéra, Yaya, and Papou would think of her abandoning her neighbors this way. Then she remembered the way they treated Mitéra and her back in the village. She wondered if the stone throwing, name calling girls below didn't regret their cruelty as they faced their fates.

Before dawn the storm subsided. Without the raging wind, Chara could clearly hear moans and cries from below in steerage. She couldn't bear that sound another second.

"What about the people below?" she shouted at a sailor, "You've got to check on them. Please!"

"Yes Miss," he replied. First, we need to get you folks safely back in your cabins, and some of the flotsam and jetsam put back in place. Then we will be sure to make certain that all souls are safe."

Chara couldn't believe that he needed to first tend to objects before checking on the moaning human beings in steerage. Helpless, she returned with Birdie to their cabin. They spoke not a word as Birdie removed her life jacket and outer clothing and sat on her bunk. Chara did the same, still listening to the sounds of misery below.

At last Birdie spoke, "Well at least we have only a couple more days to go. I've had passages where it stormed nearly the entire two weeks at sea! Anyone can survive a storm for a single night."

Chara hoped that was true. She hoped that every man, woman, and child with lesser means had indeed survived that terrifying night unscathed. She hoped that she would never again have to experience the terror that the storm had wrought.

When at last they reached the Port of New York, Chara and Birdie prepared to disembark. Birdie emptied Chara's trunk, leaving all her worldly possessions in a small pile on her bunk, telling her that she would have no use for those old things in Chicago. She filled it with her own dresses, nightgowns, shoes, stockings, jackets, and even a fancy hat. Before closing it, however, Chara put one wool afghan from Yaya on the top. She rolled up her mother's shawl and stuffed it into one of her satchels along with a tin of powder, lip paint, and a small bottle of perfume from Birdie. Then Chara followed Birdie on to the deck to watch the ship dock.

Chara felt amazed at the enormity of New York. She had never seen such buildings and so many people in one place. She noticed a strange stench she had never smelled before as well. As she walked down the gangplank arm in arm with Birdie, she saw a nicely dressed middle aged couple waving and calling to them from the dock below.

"Wave! Cried Birdie, "That's my family. They will make sure you and your trunk get to your train."

At first Chara did not see the other picture brides whose journey had no doubt been much more difficult than hers. She did see groups of anxious and hopeful men from young to old grasping photographs scanning the disembarking passengers for their own future brides.

On the dock Birdie introduced Chara to her parents. They all spoke Greek with the same inflection as Mr. Costas, which gave Chara much relief. Birdie's father disappeared to secure a carriage. As they waited for his return and their trunks to be carried down, Chara noticed the steerage passengers begin to disembark. She could barely recognize the cheerful and eager young girls as they dragged their weary, filthy, and stinking bodies from the ship to the land. Unlike Chara and the other cabin passengers, new immigrants were told to form lines where their papers could be checked, and their names and status entered into the official record.

The immigration officials on the dock had apparently assumed that Chara and Birdie were sisters coming home, and thereby never checked Chara's papers, nor listed her as a new immigrant. Chara smiled at her good fortune, and thanked her ancestors for delivering her safely, and without obstruction to the new world.

Birdie's parents treated Chara as their own daughter. She spent the night at their elegant townhouse where Chara had the first hot bath of her life. She had never experienced such sensuous pleasure as the perfumed warm water on her body. She slept in an enormous, unbelievably soft bed with her head resting on a pair of fluffy down pillows.

In the morning a servant brought Chara coffee with sweet milk and sugar, and pastries that melted in her mouth. She was beginning to think that America would bring her a long and happy life. Before getting dressed for the last leg of her journey to Chicago she picked up the now-ragged photograph of Charles Davidson and practiced what she would say to him.

"Yes." "Thank you." "Hello." "My name is Chara, you are Charles?" "I am so very happy to be meet you." "Thank you, Charles."

Kissing Birdie goodbye and promising to write, Chara boarded the train for three more days of travel. Again, Charles had provided her with a first-class ticket that included her own private sitting and sleeping room.

A man with skin as dark as midnight carried her bags in white-gloved hands. He showed her to a tiny room with two velvet benches facing each other. She sat watching the countryside through the large windows. In the evening he showed her to another car where she dined at a small, white cloth-covered table with candles in silver holders. More silver forks, spoons, and knives than one person could ever use were arranged neatly on top of a gleaming white towel beside a china plate trimmed in gold. Two different glasses rested above the plate next to a beautiful china cup sitting on a saucer—both also trimmed in gold. In the middle of the small table, a crystal vase held a single red rose bud.

The waiter, another very dark man wearing a short white coat and white gloves, brought her a small plate with a strange, sweet orange fleshed fruit on top of a mild tasting liquidly curd. After he cleared that away he poured a tall stemmed glass of bubbly wine that tickled her nose and made her a little dizzy. Next, he brought a plate with a gigantic slab of juicy meat and a whole baked potato, cut open and topped with a large dollop of sweet butter and sour cream. Chara had never seen so much meat on a single plate. She thought that if Papou had eaten this even once in his life his body would not have wasted away, this much meat would have fed all four of them so that none of their bellies would have had to cry in the night.

She cut small pieces from the edge and chewed, closing her eyes as the juices filled her mouth. It tasted nothing like the occasional mutton Yaya cooked in stews, nor the salty meat on the steamship. When the dark man returned, she offered some of the meat to him, pushing the plate in his direction, smiling, and indicating the other utensils on the table.

At first he thought she had enough and wanted him to clear it away, but when he realized her offer, he began to chuckle. He leaned down and spoke softly so nobody else could hear. She didn't understand everything he said, but she did understand that while he thanked her for her kindness, he was forbidden to taste her food. Still, she had eaten but a small part of the meat. When he took her plate away, she hoped he would use it for his own dinner later. She sat watching the other passengers' reflections in the window glass as they ate great amounts of food from their china plates. Soon the dark man returned with a glass of sweet, brownish wine and a small piece of dark brown cake covered in a darker brown sauce and sprinkled with white powder.

A small flower made of sweet cream rested on a mint leaf next to the cake. Chara cautiously dipped her finger into the dark brown sauce and white powder and put it to her lips. The sweet richness exploded in her mouth. She let it rest on her tongue which gave her a most pleasurable sensation.

Opening her eyes, Chara noticed other passengers shoveling forkfuls of the delicious cake into their mouths without taking even a moment to savor its exquisite pleasure. She wondered at the notion that perhaps in America this level of pleasure had become commonplace.

Returning to her tiny room, she found that someone had pulled a fully made bed down from the ceiling. A washstand held a basin filled with warm water, and a soft towel hung on a rack beside it. She pulled down the fringed shade to cover the window and undressed placing her garments carefully on the bench below the bed. She slipped into the white embroidered nightgown that Birdie had given her and prepared to climb up into the bed. On the pillow she found a small piece of sweet, minty chocolate wrapped in silver paper. She climbed under the crisp sheets, rested her head on the soft pillow the way Birdie had shown her, and put the chocolate in her mouth. Smiling, she let the gentle motion of the moving train lull her to sleep.

For the next two days Chara repeated the routine of American train travel. She would find her bed and compartment arranged and rearranged each time she returned from the dining car. She learned the names of the waiter, porter, and conductor, and they all greeted her by her name, "Miss Chara." On the last night of her journey as she lay awake listening to the train whistle and the rhythmic clicking of wheels on the tracks, Chara thought that she could live the rest of her life in contented bliss riding the trains in America. A part of her wished she did not have to get off the train in Chicago, and yet another part couldn't wait to meet Charles in person, and to begin their life as Mr. and Mrs. Charles Davidson.

# Chapter 24
# Ménage

(mā-ˈnäzh–*noun*: a domestic establishment; household.)

CHARA SMILED DURING THE LONG CARRIAGE RIDE with the brothers Davidson as they chattered on about themselves, their house, and the life that awaited them. She liked them right away, though she only understood a fraction of what they said. Charles sat next to her and Joseph sat on the seat facing them. She noticed how Charles engaged his brother with love and admiration, and how Joseph returned the same sentiment. Finding this delightful and charming, she liked them even more for it.

After a bumpy ride of more than an hour, they reached their destination. Joseph jumped down from the carriage first. He gently took Chara's hand, helping her to the street, smiling sweetly, and looking into her eyes. She knew it was Charles she would marry, and yet felt a flutter of excitement when Joseph touched her.

She stood for several minutes admiring the grand house in front of her until Charles said, "Welcome home." and excitely took her hand to climb the steps. The expansiveness, beauty, and decor of the Victorian home took her breath away. She did not know what to do, or what to say, and so stood in silent disbelief.

After the coachman brought in her bags and trunk Charles dragged them up a tall staircase with a beautifully carved railing that curved at the top of the stairs and wound around a long hallway. Joseph disappeared toward the back of the house and Chara stood motionless in the middle of the parlor awaiting further direction.

Before long Charles came back down the stairs and Joseph returned from the back of the house. They smiled broadly and asked her if she liked it. She smiled and nodded affirmation. Joseph's bright blue eyes sparkled as he gazed into her lovely dark eyes. Her beauty far surpassed the photograph he had treasured for over a year.

"Sit down." Charles said as he sat in one of a pair lovely over-stuffed chairs with floral upholstery.

As she went to sit in the chair next to him, Charles became agitated.

"No," he said indicating the dark green velvet sofa across the room. "Not here, there."

Slightly flustered for already having made a mistake, Chara smoothed her skirts and sat on the edge of the cushion on the ornate sofa. Joseph returned to the parlor with a small silver tray holding three beautiful crystal glasses filled with a light brown liquid. He held the tray down, resting it on one hand with his other hand gallantly behind his back. Chara's heart leapt as his beautiful blue eyes met hers.

"A glass of port for the lady." he said with great dramatic flair.

Then he turned to Charles and, with the same flourish, served him his drink. Next he took his own glass from the tray. Placing the tray on the small table between the two chairs, he seated himself, and lifted his glass toward Chara. "A toast to our beautiful picture bride!"

She did not understand what he said, but knew they honored her. They both lifted their glasses to their lips and she did the same. The sweet liquid warmed her throat and body as it descended from her mouth to her stomach. Chara had tasted wine on many occasions, but nothing like this. She licked her lips and took another sip—closing her eyes to savor the nutty flavor and warmth of it.

When she opened her eyes again, she saw Charles and Joseph gazing at her, appearing pleased.

"You like the port?" Joseph asked.

"Port." she repeated holding up the glass, and nodding. "Yes port. I like port."

The brothers laughed with delight.

"She is one of us!" Joseph said to Charles. "A perfect match!"

Chara, still confused, finished her drink trying to understand what was going on between the Davidson brothers. They certainly had an unusually strong bond. Though it seemed a bit odd to her, she enjoyed the way Joseph had referred to her as theirs. She thought that she had found a family at last, a wealthy and powerful one at that. A sense of contentment and security consumed her for the first time since Papou died.

Suddenly, Joseph sprung to his feet startling Chara who stiffened on the sofa.

"What are we thinking?" He clapped his hand to his head, "You have been traveling for weeks! Let me run a warm bath for you and make something for you to eat." Charles, still sipping his port, smiled at Chara as Joseph disappeared up the stairs. After several minutes he returned indicating for Chara to follow him. He led her to a narrow, warm and steamy dressing room. A luxurious, white dressing robe hung from a hook next to two larger similar robes.

"This is for you." Joseph indicated the smaller robe. "The bath is in here."

He led her through another door where she saw a deep claw-foot bathtub, warm water filling it directly from the wall. Great mounds of white suds reached nearly to the brim.

"Put your clothes in this basket and I will get them to the laundry," Joseph said, pointing to a tall reed basket near the door. Then he left.

Chara removed her clothes and slipped into the soft robe to enter the bathing room when she heard a soft knock on the door. She shyly opened it a few inches to find Joseph on the other side smiling the most beautiful smile she had ever seen.

"Here," he said slipping a fresh glass of port through the crack, "Have this with your bath. No hurry, soak as long as you like."

He had lit a lamp with a tall chimney and had also placed several candles on a high table near the tub. Joseph's words came too fast for

Chara to understand, but she knew he wanted her to be comfortable and enjoy the bath. She placed the delicate glass carefully on the table, slipped out of her soft robe, and stepped into the sensuous, soapy water. The scent of gardenias and rosemary filled her nostrils. She sank down until the warm water covered her shoulders and neck, closing her eyes, savoring the quiet. After a long time, she reached out and took the glass of port in her hand and sipped the syrupy wine in ecstasy.

After nearly an hour, she heard Joseph again at the door.

"Use the tap to rinse off after your bath." he said through the closed door.

Chara sat up quickly, afraid she had done something wrong, or that Joseph would enter the room and find her naked.

"Hello?" he said softly, "Are you okay in there?"

"Okay." she repeated.

"Can I hand you a towel?" he asked opening the door slightly.

She crouched down in the tub to hide her nakedness until she saw that his eyes were closed tightly.

"Here," he said holding a large fluffy cloth in her direction, "Dry yourself off and come to the dining room for dinner."

Chara grabbed the towel from Joseph's hand and pushed the door shut in his face. She heard his laugh as he left the dressing room. "Dinner" was a word she knew well. The port had gone to her head, but her belly came alive with the word. She couldn't wait to eat. Chara dried herself and pulled her robe around her body, tying the sash tightly at her waist.

Charles sat at the head of the table with Joseph sitting beside him. She saw another place setting on the other side of Charles, across from Joseph. Both men smiled and bade her sit. She clutched her bathrobe, clearly uncomfortable.

"It's okay," said Charles smiling with kindness in his eyes, "We are family, manage as you will."

He patted the cushioned seat of the tall-backed chair. Cautiously she sat, making sure to keep her robe securely closed.

"Oh my!" Joseph exclaimed, "Your feet!" he pointed to her bare feet under the table. "You will catch your death!"

Then he turned to Charles. "Dinner can wait until our lady can properly prepare for her first meal in our house."

"Of course, of course," Charles replied, "How thoughtless of us. Please Miss, let me show you to your things so you can get dressed."

Charles led Chara to a room at the top of the stairs where her trunk had been placed beside a lovely carved wardrobe that already contained several articles of clothing. Bowing, he told her to take her time, then to join them downstairs. Despite her limited English, his flamboyant gestures helped Chara understand. She chose a skirt and blouse that had belonged to Birdie. Staring at the bed, Chara wondered what expectations Charles would have.

When she returned to the dining room, the brothers had drunk most of a bottle of wine. They both laughed and chatted happily until she entered the room. Seeing her, both Charles and Joseph stood. Charles pulled out her chair and bade her sit before either of them sat themselves. Again, they raised a glass to her.

As the trio toasted Chara said, "Yes. Thank you. Hello. Charles. Joseph. I am so very happy to be meet you. Thank you, Charles. Thank you, Joseph."

They all laughed, then began eating the bounty of meat, vegetables, and cheese from large platters on the table.

That night when Chara returned to her room, Charles gave her a key to lock her door. She was grateful, and far less anxious— not knowing what would be expected of her. Chara dressed in Birdie's nightgown and climbed into the warm soft bed ... Her very own warm soft bed. As she closed her eyes she smiled and spoke to her ancestors.

"Look at me," she whispered, "Look at me in this place."

She smiled contentedly and closed her eyes.

Weeks passed. Charles and Joseph took Chara shopping, to restaurants, and concert halls. They seemed to truly enjoy dressing her up and taking her all about town. Months passed with no talk of marriage. Chara learned English with surprising ease. Perhaps spending time with Englishmen in Greece gave her an ear for it. Soon she was able to shop for groceries on her own. They taught her how to use the modern appliances in the kitchen and relished the fact that she enjoyed a tub bath every day.

Joseph and Charles showed her how to prepare American food. She enjoyed the great variety of ingredients, the endless supply of fresh beef and large vegetables, so easily available to her at the local markets. She began to take great pride presenting three-course meals to her family. One evening at dinner she boldly asked Charles if he still wanted her for his wife. He and Joseph shot each other a startled look, then Joseph began to chuckle. Charles glared at him sternly. Chara did not see the humor in her inquiry. She was supposed to marry Charles and instead they had been living like siblings for nearly half a year. She did not mind it. They had a wonderful time together, but she wondered if she should expect more.

"A wed-ding...." Charles stammered, "Yes, well indeed we should have a wedding."

He looked at Joseph, "So how should we go about this wedding?"

The next week all three rode the streetcar to the courthouse to obtain a marriage license. The clerk asked Chara to produce her immigration papers, or some form of identification. Confused, Chara explained that she did not possess any such documents.

Charles described the "picture bride" arrangement, and the contract signed with Mr. Costas. The clerk explained that Chara should have received immigration documents at the Port of New York.

Chara's eyes filled with tears as she recalled watching the steerage immigrants, including her fellow picture brides, standing in line at the docks waiting to get inspected and registered. She thought about how Birdie had dressed her in fine clothes and ushered her past the rabble directly to her parents. No record of Chara's immigration existed. No record of her at all existed anywhere including the place of her birth. She had no living relative who could vouch for her. She had no way to prove who she was, or even *that* she was. The clerk refused a license until they produced documentation.

"Well, I guess that's it." Charles said as they left the courthouse. "It's okay," he went on clearly relieved, "This does not change a thing. We can just continue on as our little happy family. Why don't we all find a nice place to take lunch."

Chara said nothing. She could see how relieved Charles appeared realizing that they could not wed. She felt not only invisible, but rejected and unlovable as well. Charles never focused his attentions toward her, but mostly toward Joseph, his brother. She thought that she had somehow displeased him. The letters he had sent during their courtship by post demonstrated a romantic and loving heart. Each new response had become more intimate, as did her own letters back. She could not understand how such a warm correspondent could prove such a cold companion.

At lunch Chara remained quiet, barely touching her food as Charles laughed and chatted merrily with his brother.

"Chara?" Joseph asked noticing her melancholy, "You've not touched your food. Usually you have such a hearty appetite."

Chara put her hands in her lap. And lowered her head as tears began to run down her cheeks.

"Now!" he went on, "What's this? We can't have tears from our beautiful little picture bride." He daubed the tears with his napkin.

"I am sorry," Chara caught her breath stifling a sob, "I have displeased you. I will go away if you wish so you can find a proper wife."

"No! No. No." Joseph leaned close.

She glanced up to see his kind face close to hers. Their eyes locked as he spoke very softly and lovingly.

"Oh, dear sweet Cara." She loved the way he said her name. "Cara, You have displeased no one! We love you. We do not want you to go away. If it's a wedding you want, then it's a wedding you shall have."

She noticed Charles watching their interaction in stunned silence.

"You forget!" He turned to Charles flashing his broad smile and shining blue eyes, "We are the Davidson brothers! We know how to get things done in this town."

He lifted Chara's chin. "After lunch we will go to buy a beautiful wedding gown for our little picture bride. You can trust me to find us a way to have your wedding."

She smiled warmly at Joseph, then turned to Charles, her fiancé, who had still not responded to Joseph or her. He just sat there stunned and speechless.

At the department store, Charles and Joseph sat in chairs chatting and laughing with one another as the attendant helped Chara try on wedding dresses. First the attendant laced her tightly into a whalebone corset, then she tried on dress after dress. Donning one gorgeous dress after another, she would emerge from the dressing room seeking their approval. At last they chose the perfect dress. It was ivory silk with a high collar and twenty-five silken buttons on the bodice. Ruffles of the most beautiful lace decorated the wrists of the long sleeves. The same lace covered the front of the skirt along with decorative pleated silk accents and embroidery. They purchased satin high-button shoes, silk stockings with a lace garter, and an ivory satin hat with a short lace veil that covered her eyes. The brothers applauded as she appeared in all her finery.

Charles and Joseph carried her packages and hailed a carriage to take them all the way back to their Portage Park home so they wouldn't have to worry about being jostled on a streetcar.

The next month, the Davidson brothers hired a cook and several servants to prepare a reception for the wedding of Charles and Chara. That morning Chara bathed in scented bubbles while the brothers went out to purchase libations. Later Chara sat at her dressing table in her corset, gazing into the mirror at the woman she had become. She parted her hair in the middle and pinned it back the way she had seen so many American women do. She powdered her face, and applied lipstick Birdie had given her. Then one of the servants helped her into her dress, shoes, and hat.

She heard happy voices in the parlor, but had no idea who would attend her wedding, only that they would be friends and political colleagues from the city, along with their wives. She grew nervous at the thought of being on display and hoped that the party would not last too long into the evening.

The hired maid tied a small bouquet to Chara's wrist with a silk ribbon, then bade Chara good luck, and headed downstairs. Chara choked back tears wishing Papou, Yaya, and Mitéra could see her like this. Wishing that Yaya and Mitéra could be there to help dress her for her wedding instead of a strange woman.

She spoke aloud to them, "My family, I am about to become a wife. I am afraid. Please stand beside me and keep me as I keep you in my heart."

Chara kissed two fingers, then turned them toward her image in the mirror, sending the kiss to her ancestors. Then she smoothed her skirts and bravely left her chamber and descended the eighteen stairs toward the waiting group.

Charles and Joseph stood side by side dressed in fine suits smiling lovingly at Chara. When her eyes caught Joseph's, her heart fluttered, and her cheeks flushed. She quickly turned her gaze to Charles who appeared happy but nervous.

He took her arm at the bottom of the stairs and led her through the foyer to the entrance to the parlor. Both the parlor and dining room were filled with smiling guests. The couple stopped under the archway. Servants had decorated the rooms with ribbons and large bouquets of white flowers. Everything was lovely.

Instead of a priest, a red-faced, portly gentleman wearing a long black robe approached them. Charles let go of Chara's arm. They stood side by side as the robed gentleman began to speak.

"Cara, (He said her name the way the Davidson brothers did.) do you take this man to be your lawfully wedded husband?"

Chara nodded and whispered shyly, "Yes I do."

Then he turned to Charles, "And do you, Charles take this woman to be your lawfully wedded wife?"

Charles said, "I do."

"Then, by the power vested in me by the county of Cook and the state of Illinois, I pronounce you man and wife."

Joseph stepped forward and clapped Charles on the back joyfully, "Good man!" he said, "Good man."

When Joseph reached out to shake the red-faced man's hand, she saw him pass a wad of bills, saying, "Thanks Judge. Let me get you a drink."

Then he turned to Charles, "May I kiss your bride?"

Charles nodded smiling sheepishly as Joseph leaned down and kissed Chara sweetly on the lips. Then he turned, smiling his most endearing smile, and disappeared into the crowd. Chara felt secretly guilty, wishing that it had been Joseph who had written to her. She realized that Charles had not yet kissed her, but Joseph had. She felt shame for her thoughts of Joseph, her new husband's brother, but knew that she had little control over her own heart. She hoped her marriage to Charles would quell the longing she felt for his brother, turning that passion toward her husband instead.

Chara said very little as guests kissed her cheeks, shook Charles' hand and wished them well. They ate from many plates filled with small portions of meat, fowl, bread, cheese, fish, pickles, and sweets. In her honor, Joseph surprised Chara with a plate of large olives and figs imported from Greece to remind her of home. Though his intentions were kind, the gesture only made her miss her family even more. But here she stood: In Chicago, America, a new-made bride among strangers ... about to begin another phase in her life's journey. Sipping sweet sparkling wine from a stemmed glass, she couldn't avoid astonishment at how far she had come from the tiny stone hut where she survived on clods of grass and seed potatoes.

Chara retired to her chamber before all the guests had left. She sat at her dressing table taking the pins out of her hair when she heard a gentle knock. Her heart jumped, thinking it Charles coming to bring his bride to his bed. She opened the door to find Joseph there holding a white box tied with a blue ribbon.

"Joseph!" she whispered, trying to hide her delight, "What brings you here?"

"A gift for our picture bride." he said softly, smiling as their eyes locked. "A gift for your wedding night." Then he kissed her again and quickly descended the stairs.

Chara sat back down and opened the package letting the blue silk ribbon fall to the floor. Inside the box she found a lovely white silk dressing gown.

She smiled and stripped out of her wedding dress, laying it carefully across the bed in which she would not sleep this night. She stood naked in the lamplight regarding her small form. She lacked the curvaceousness displayed in all the American magazines and newspapers. Her olive skin was not the milky ideal she had witnessed at social functions.

Chara sighed deeply and pulled the soft garment over her head. Its narrow straps fell off her shoulders, and the neckline that revealed the curve of her breasts. She tied the ribbons around her waist, then sat back down to wait for Charles.

She began to hear a heated conversation coming from the parlor. She had never heard Joseph and Charles argue. She listened closely to determine its cause. After several minutes she heard footsteps on the stairs, then the door to Joseph's chamber open, close, and lock. More time passed before she heard another set of footsteps on the stairs. These came up slowly, stopping briefly by her door. She held her breath, expecting Charles to knock and invite her to his bedchamber. Instead the footfalls continued down the hallway where she heard another door open, close, and lock. She waited a long time for Charles to return, but he didn't. As her body began to chill, Chara removed the nightgown, and folded it carefully back into its box. Still naked, she draped her wedding gown over a chair, and climbed into her own bed alone. Curling up under the quilts and coverlets, she closed her eyes and thought of Joseph. She pictured his beautiful eyes sparkling as he looked deeply into hers. She imagined him lying beside her. She imagined his warm hands on her breasts, her belly, and between her thighs. Her own hands found their way to the places she imagined his would venture. She stifled her moans to keep them from escaping her walls. Once she had released her own pleasure, she turned her face toward the wall her bedchamber shared with Joseph's.

"Good night Joseph." She whispered. "Good night "εραστής" *Erastis*, my love."

The next morning, Chara awoke to more arguing, this time coming from Charles' bedchamber.

"You cannot do that to her!" Joseph shouted at Charles. "What must she be thinking!"

"I'm sorry," whined Charles, "I tried, but couldn't." He began to cry, "I am so humiliated. How can I ever face her?"

Then the voices grew softer. Chara, feeling compassion for Charles, and ashamed at her own betrayal alone in her bed the night before, rose quickly and dressed. She tiptoed to the kitchen to prepare coffee and breakfast. Later, when Chara found herself alone in the kitchen with Charles, he began to apologize.

Chara put a finger on his lips to stop him. "Shhh," she smiled, "We had many, many wine last night. Also, a very long and full day. No, you have to say sorry."

Charles was relieved at the kindness Chara showed. He smiled, embraced her, and kissed her on the forehead. But as she turned her face upward to return his kiss, he turned quickly away. Chara felt the ache of rejection once again. Then Joseph entered the room and embraced her enthusiastically.

"Good morning Sister-In-Law," he said kissing her on the head. Then he turned to Charles, "Look what the new bride made for us! Thank you, dear Chara." He poured a cup of coffee and left the kitchen. Alone again, Charles and Chara stood across the room from one another with nothing more to say.

"Eat." Chara demanded. Then, pouring a cup for Charles, Chara turned back to the stove.

After cleaning up breakfast, Chara returned to her bedchamber where she carefully folded her wedding dress and wrapped it in tissue paper. She placed it in her trunk along with Yaya and Mitéra's things, then closed and latched it. Pushing the box with her wedding night gown under her bed, she set about the business of the day.

That night they lit the gas lamps and sat together in the parlor as they had so many nights before. Charles sat in his chair smoking his pipe and reading a section of the newspaper while Joseph sat in his chair reading another section. Chara sat on the sofa embroidering a new towel. Soon Joseph excused himself to retire to his bedchamber. Charles looked slightly panicked as he watched Joseph ascend the stairs. Chara did not lift her eyes from her needlework, though her heart began to beat faster.

Several minutes ticked by before Charles tapped out his pipe in the ashtray and rose from his chair. "Well, my dear, shall we retire?"

Chara's cheeks flushed hot and red. She placed her needle work in the basket next to the sofa and rose to her feet.

"After you." Charles gestured with a sweeping bow as Chara reached for the curved railing to ascend the stairs ahead of him. She felt his eyes on her back, and tried to focus instead on the cool, smooth-polished railing. Stopping at her bedchamber door Chara turned to bid him goodnight.

"I will give you time to ready yourself in whatever manner you would like. I will do the same. Come to my chamber when you are ready. I will wait for you." He smiled sheepishly and gave her a peck on her hairline. Nodding, she closed her chamber door, lit the lamp, and undressed quickly. Again, she stood naked before the dressing table mirror until she began to shiver, both from the chill, as well as anticipation. She bent to retrieve the box holding the satin gown that Joseph and given her, and quickly let it fall over her body. The chill raised her nipples so that they grew clearly visible beneath the soft fabric. For the second time, Chara adjusted the ribbons around her waist, and the sleeves from her bare shoulders, and slipped into felt house shoes. For the first time, she quietly made her way down the hall to Charles' chamber door.

She tapped lightly on his door, praying that Joseph would not hear her, or them. Charles opened the door. He wore silk pajamas under a dressing gown. He looked down at her shivering form. She saw him notice her nipples, blush, then look away. She wrapped her arms around her chest ashamed of her body and how it made him turn from her.

"Here," he said softly, "You must be freezing. Get into the bed."

He turned down one side of the bedclothes and held her hand as she climbed up into the high bed. She adjusted her long hair on the pillow in an attempt to make herself presentable as Charles returned to his closet to hang his dressing gown. She watched as he lingered for several minutes in front of the open closet door.

"Charles?" she said softly.

He turned, closing the closet, and came to the bedside. There he turned down the lamp and climbed in on the other side. Their bodies did not touch. He lay on his back next to her. Chara could hear the sound of his breathing as it came faster.

"Charles," she said again, then turned toward him and put her hand on his chest.

She felt him inhale sharply, then turn on his side toward her, grasping for the hem of her nightgown. She lifted her bottom so that the delicate fabric would not tear as he jerked it to her waist. She lay on her back, spreading her legs, as he frantically climbed on top of her and began to thrust himself against her body. She barely took a breath noticing that his manhood remained flaccid no matter how hard he pumped against her. Her thighs began to ache. She knew that she would find bruises in the morning. Still Charles continued. At last he fell off her with a whimper and returned to his back. She lay motionless next to him as his body and the bed began to move. To her great surprise and shame, Charles pleasured himself in the bed next to her.

A lump filled her throat and hot tears fell silently from the corners of her eyes.

"Did he think her so hideous that her body could not bring him any pleasure?" she thought, "Did he find her so repulsive that he had to satisfy himself with his own bride in his bed beside him?"

Chara's shame and humiliation grew into a burning hot coal at her very core. She squeezed her eyes shut as Charles convulsed with a moan and fell still. He turned his back to her in the bed, and muttered, "Good night dear."

Chara tried to control her body as it began to tremble. As Charles' breathing grew slow and even. She inched herself close to the edge of the bed with her back to him. She pulled her knees up close to her chest, squeezed her eyes shut, and cupped both hands tightly over her mouth. Chara tried not to cry.

"What have I done?" she thought through silent sobs, "What in the name of all things holy have I done?"

She awoke alone in Charles' bed with bright sun shining through the front windows. She listened, hoping with all her heart that Charles had left for work. Hearing no movement in the house, she quickly climbed out of his bed, pulled the covers over the place where she had laid, and smoothed it as if trying to erase any sign that she had been there. She picked up her slippers and tiptoed quickly to her own bedchamber. Once inside she closed the door and turned the key in the lock.

Chara climbed into her own bed and curled up as small as she could make herself. She stayed there for hours, praying and talking to her ancestors. She thanked God that Yaya and Mitéra had never suffered such humiliation, then sadly remembered how Mitéra had gone to the English and French men. She finally admitted to herself what Mitéra had done to survive after Papou and Yaya died. She began to sob thinking of how both Mitéra and now she herself had fallen into shame for the sake of survival. Chara's shame was the price she would have to pay for meat, fine clothes, and hot baths. Chara, just like her Mitéra sold her body and her dignity for food and warmth. She could not blame the village girls for throwing stones at her when she was younger. They must have seen what she herself couldn't until now. She thought about all the other picture brides who traveled below her in steerage, while she ate well and dressed in finery above them in her cabin. She wept more thinking of them married to men who cherished them and gave them babes to suckle at their breasts. She wept until she could weep no more, then fell into a fitful sleep.

She awoke to soft knocking on her chamber door. Terrified that Charles had come to take her again to his bed for more humiliation she sat up and said,

"I am not well."

Then she heard Joseph's voice, "Chara, I have brought you a cup of tea and some bread. You have slept the day away."

As Chara passed the mirror on her way to open the door she noticed her swollen red eyes, and puffy face. She called through the door, "Thank you Joseph, but I am not well. I must be alone here now I think."

Joseph asked if she needed a doctor. Chara caught a sob and replied, "No doctor. Just alone please."

Joseph told her that he would check on her later. He also told her that Charles would be away until late in the evening. Chara returned to her bed. After a couple of hours, as the evening light began to dim, Joseph knocked again.

"I know you are not well," he said gently, "I made you some broth, and drew you a bath. I think both might make you feel better. Please open the door."

Chara pulled on her dressing gown and opened the door slightly. She kept her eyes cast to the floor. Joseph tenderly lifted her chin toward his concerned face. Unable to look at him for her shame, she closed her eyes as he held her face in his kind hand.

"Oh, my poor sweet little picture bride!" he said lovingly, "What on earth did he do to you?"

Tears began to fall from Chara's closed eyes. Then she felt Joseph's kiss. He kissed one eye then the other as more tears fell. He kissed her forehead and cheeks as her chest began to heave with sobs. He pulled her into his arms and kissed her wet face over and over until his mouth found hers, and stopped, slowly pressing his warm lips softly to hers. Then he paused, pulling back slightly. Chara opened her eyes to see Joseph with his own tears falling from his perfect blue eyes. She saw only pure love in those eyes, and she threw her arms around his neck, falling limp in his arms.

Joseph picked her up and carried her down the stairs to the bath he had prepared all the time whispering with his lips close to her ear. "My poor sweet Chara ... My sweet little bird. It's okay now. It's okay."

Chara, exhausted, stood limply with her eyes nearly closed while Joseph gently removed her dressing gown. As he helped her into the bath, he saw the dark bruises on her legs.

That *bastard!*" Joseph exclaimed, "He *brutalized* you! Oh my God! That miserable *bastard ruined you!*" Joseph began to cry. "Don't worry sweetheart. He will not touch you again."

Chara closed her eyes to hide her shame. She did not want to see Joseph angry with his brother, but she also could not bear the thought of him knowing that his brother had not ruined her but had found her so repulsive that he could not touch her. Chara felt hideous, dirty and shameful. She slid down in the water to hide her miserable body from Joseph, fearing he too might reject her.

Instead, Joseph pulled a kitchen chair into the bathing room and placed it at her head. He took a pitcher, dipped it into the warm water and poured it over Chara's tangled hair. Then he poured scented soap into his hands and began massaging it into her hair. His fingers became entangled and Chara began to weep.

"Am I hurting you?" Joseph asked worriedly with his hands resting in her hair.

"No ... no not at all. It's just my Papou ... my Papou used to gather my tangled hair in his hands. He loved me so much." Chara began to cry softly.

"I love you Chara." Joseph leaned down close to her ear whispering, "I love you, sweet little bird."

Chara and Joseph ate broth with bread, then he helped her back to her room. Seeing her mangled bedclothes, he went to straighten them himself as Chara slipped into a nightgown.

"Here you go little bird, a perfect nest."

Then he helped her into bed and pulled the covers up around her shoulders. He kissed her one more time, then left her chamber, closing the door behind him.

Chara fell into a deep and dreamless sleep. The next morning, she heard angry hushed voices from the parlor. She feared what Joseph would say, and what Charles would do. Then she heard footsteps coming firmly up the stairs, followed by a sharp rap on her door.

She sat abruptly up in bed, "Yes?" she called through the door.

She heard someone clear his throat, "Um, it's me Charles ..."

Chara pulled the bedclothes tightly up to her chin, terrified.

"It's me, I'm sorry for what happened the other night. I think I must have drunk too much port. It will never happen again. Um ... hmmm. I am terribly sorry."

Then he paused for several moments. "I will leave you to yourself dear. I hope we can continue as before."

Chara was flabbergasted! *As before!* she thought, *Does he mean before the wedding or before the bridal night?*

After that, Charles spent most evenings away from home. He excused himself with talk of political demands, but often when he did return it became quite clear that he had spent hours at the tavern.

Joseph carried on as well. He and Chara took their evening meal together and sat in the parlor in the lamplight. Their conversation stayed light. Chara felt grateful that Joseph never spoke of that evening when he found and rescued her. But at night, alone in her bed, she remembered Joseph's kisses. She remembered the taste of his mouth, and the loving way he bathed her, and washed and combed her hair.

She would feel her body come alive as she imagined him lying in his bed only a few feet from hers separated by the chamber wall, and the small gold ring on her finger. She cursed fate for giving her Charles as a husband while she loved his brother Joseph.

Then very late one night, she heard a soft tapping at her door. She sat up, suddenly wide awake terrified that Charles had come, drunk, to demand she go to his bed.

"Yes?" she whispered tentatively.

"Chara, are you awake? I can't sleep."

Hearing Joseph, she quickly and quietly jumped out of bed and turned the key to open the door. He stood there in the dark outside her door leaning in.

"Can I come in?" he whispered, looking back over his shoulder toward Charles' bedchamber. "Can I come in for just a minute?"

Chara opened her door and let him in, closing, and locking it behind him. As soon as the key turned, he took her in his arms and kissed her long on the mouth. Chara pulled back.

"Joseph?" she whispered, "Joseph please. Think ..."

"I cannot think," Joseph whispered kissing her neck," I can only feel right now. I love you little bird. I have loved you since the first letter I wrote to you. I have loved you since the first time I looked into your eyes at Union Station. I have loved you every minute of every day that you have lived here, Chara. Sweet picture bride. My little bird."

He swept her up in his arms and carried her to the bed where he laid her down. Then he fell into her with such tenderness that she melted with him, moving in unison with every wave of pleasure until they both exploded in a spasm of ecstasy and tears.

They remained there trembling and holding on to each other with all their might until they heard the first bird of morning announce that the dawn grew near.

Joseph carefully pulled on his nightshirt, then returned to Chara lying in bed smiling.

He kissed her saying, "Thank you little bird. Be sure to lock the door when I leave."

Then he stealthily returned to his own chamber. She listened for the sound of the key in his lock, then rose and locked her own door.

Chara and Joseph took great care to hide their encounters from Charles. Even though he had little to do with Chara, and clearly had no interest in her affections, she remained his wife after all, with Joseph as his brother.

This arrangement continued for years with Joseph coming to Chara in the wee hours of the morning until one month she began to suspect that she had become with child. She told Joseph who went into a panic.

"Oh no! What will we tell Charles?" he paced back and forth in the parlor, "Charles will kill us both!"

As Chara sat on the sofa watching Joseph, she wished to God that it was he she had married.

"Okay," he said at last kneeling before her, "I know a doctor. I will take you to see him. He will help us."

"Help us how?" asked Chara frightened.

"He will tell us if you are expecting and help us if you are. That is all I am going to say. We will go tomorrow when Charles is at work."

That night Joseph did not come to Chara. She lay alone in her bed dreading tomorrow and a visit to the doctor.

The next morning after Charles left, Chara and Joseph took the streetcar to Lowell's Drug Store on Montrose where they saw Dr. Moore. He examined Chara in a back room of the drug store. Then, while she got dressed behind a screen Dr. Moore spoke to Joseph.

"Well, congratulations your wife is going to have a baby." He said offering Joseph a cigar.

"N-n-no, thank you," Joseph's panic showing.

"Is this a problem?" the doctor asked.

"You have no idea," Joseph stood and began to pace. "We cannot have this baby. I can't explain, but we just simply cannot have this baby."

Chara came out from behind the screen. The doctor motioned

for her to sit in a chair as Joseph continued to pace furiously.

"Ma'am," he spoke gently to Chara, "Is this true?"

Chara wanted nothing more than to have Joseph's child. She imagined telling Charles that they loved each other and asking him to free her so she and Joseph could marry and raise a family.

But Joseph dashed her hopes. He bent over the doctor and said, "This is my *brother's* wife! Not mine. He will kill her and me both. Can't you do something? I've heard you help the Polish women with too many mouths to feed. Please! I beg of you! Help us now or you will hear of us dead!"

Chara looked on in shock at Joseph's words. Fear began to fill her heart.

"Yes! Please!" she added seeing the fear in Joseph's eyes. "He will kill us both."

The doctor furrowed his brow disapprovingly. He looked at Chara in a way that made her feel ashamed. Then he addressed Joseph.

"Not that I approve of such immoral behavior, but how would your brother even know?" the doctor asked.

"He *will* know. He has not touched his wife in years."

The doctor's face softened as Chara's eyes filled with tears. She felt worthless, rejected, and evil. Even Mitéra would be ashamed of her. She buried her face in her hands.

"Alright then," The doctor wrote an address on a slip of paper. "Come to my residence tonight at eight o'clock. Bring twenty dollars."

Joseph took the slip of paper and shoved it in his pocket. Then he and Chara caught the streetcar home.

Mercifully Charles did not come home that night before they went to Dr. Moore's residence. Joseph waited in his parlor as he took Chara into a back room. The doctor gave her laudanum that made her feel woozy and nauseous. He had her remove her bloomers and lie down on a hard table, then told her to open her legs. He moved the lamp close to view her shame as she squeezed her eyes closed.

Joseph jumped to his feet when he heard Chara cry out. A kindly woman bade him sit down, telling him that it was all over now and that his wife would be just fine. Instead of sitting, Joseph paced until Chara appeared with the doctor. She looked pale, shaky, and weak. As she took a step toward Joseph, she faltered. Joseph reached out and caught her in his arms.

"Oh, my poor little bird." He said holding her arm.

The woman gave Chara a vial of laudanum. "Take this for pain." she said.

The doctor cautioned them to make sure Chara rested until the bleeding stopped, and to take care to not let this happen again.

Joseph paid the doctor who gave him a receipt indicating far less than the amount he had paid. Then Joseph hailed a hack to carry them home. When they arrived, Charles had sat in the parlor. He scrutinized them closely as they entered.

"Where have you been ..." He inquired, "... and what is wrong with you Chara?"

He rose from his chair, but Joseph stopped him before he reached Chara.

"Don't bother, brother. We went to the tavern and Chara had one too many. I'll make sure she gets to bed safely."

Charles sat back down watching Joseph help Chara up the stairs. When he had put her to bed, Joseph returned to the parlor.

"Since when do you two go to the tavern?" Asked Charles suspiciously.

Joseph poured a glass of port and plopped into his chair. Picking up a section of the newspaper he said nonchalantly, "It's such a warm night for February. We felt bored and just wanted to get out. I got a carriage because Chara can't hold her whiskey." He winked at Joseph. "She should pass out pretty soon. That will give us the rest of the night."

Charles smiled coyly as Joseph winked at him and took his hand.

"C'mon brother," he snickered, "Let me take you to bed."

Chara remained in bed the next day. Joseph flippantly explained to Charles that Chara had never experienced a hangover, and that he would bring her a cup of soup to help her shake it off. Then he kissed him in the kitchen.

"It's been a long time since you kissed me here." Charles said,

"Where?" asked Joseph playfully, kissing him again on the mouth. "Here?"

"No, silly. In the kitchen. I miss how things were before the picture bride."

"Ahh," said Joseph, taking Charles' hand. "But then how would we keep our secret?"

Then he kissed Charles one more time and carried hot soup to Chara in her bed. When he lit the lamp, he saw dark circles under her eyes. He stroked her hair and kissed her forehead.

"Poor little bird," he said. "Here, you need some nourishment."

Joseph held Chara's head and spooned warm beef broth into her mouth. Then he sponged her head with a towel and collected the blood-soaked rags and wrapped them in it. Telling her he would return in the night he put out the lamp and closed the door. He hid the rags in the towel as he quickly descended the stairs. Avoiding Charles, he walked through the hallway past the basement door, through the dining room, into the kitchen, and out the back door where he dropped the bloody rags into the burn bin. Turning he noticed his neighbor, Mrs. Pulaski, watching him from across the alley. He smiled and waved, then dropped a lit match into the barrel.

"Awfully warm for February!" he called to her as the flame grew.

She simply smiled, brushed her hand toward him, then turned to go back into her flat.

"She didn't understand a word I said," he spoke aloud, then added "Damn Pollocks." and ran up the back stairs.

It took several weeks before Chara began to feel like herself again. Charles noticed and inquired about her feeling under the weather. Joseph attended to her making sure she ate and rested, until over time, the ordeal fell behind them. They resumed going to restaurants and shows. Things seemed to have returned to the happy times before the wedding. Joseph and Charles laughed together again, and playfully teased one another. Chara loved seeing them like this. She began to relax into her role as the picture bride all over again, but Joseph stopped coming to her. Although she knew that her pregnancy had scared him, she longed for his touch. When she caught him gazing at her lustfully, Chara's heart jumped. When their eyes met, she nearly melted.

Charles stopped staying out late at night, so their evenings consisted of a shared a meal followed by the threesome sitting together in the parlor as before. Each night Chara tried to wait for Charles to retire so she could have a few minutes alone with Joseph, but the brothers always outlasted her.

One night after many weeks Chara awoke to hear Joseph moving around in his room. She began to grow excited waiting to hear the sound of his door unlocking, followed by his familiar, and long-awaited knock. She did hear a door close, but not his chamber door. It sounded more like his closet door. She thought that perhaps he had grabbed a dressing gown since the weather had grown unseasonably chilly for spring. She waited expecting to hear him at her door, but he did not come.

She thought that perhaps he felt ashamed after asking her to rid herself of the babe and didn't want to burden her with his lust. Yet his lust was exactly what she craved. As she thought of the pleasure, she felt with Joseph inside her, she began to tremble, feeling a throbbing between her legs. She thought she could reach down and relieve that throbbing with her own hand when she heard Joseph move again on the other side of the wall.

Surprising herself, Chara boldly crept out of her room. She stopped outside her door in the hallway, listening to make sure Charles didn't stir, then she made her way in the pitch black of the little alcove leading to Joseph's door. Reaching out until she felt the wood, then she knocked three times very quietly. Hearing nothing, and shivering violently, she knocked again. This time she heard Joseph stir and come to the door. When he opened it Chara pushed into the room.

"Chara," he whispered, "Chara wait."

But before he could finish Chara let her nightgown fall to the floor. Joseph caught his breath as he saw her glowing skin, so lovely in the pale moonlight. Overcome with love they fell onto his bed.

"Sh-h-h" Joseph whispered, "Charles."

But Chara did not think of Charles. She did not think at all as she let herself drown in Joseph's touch. She drank in his skin and his breath. She watched every grimace on his beautiful face in the light of the spring moon. She whispered his name. She whispered, "Erastís, my love".

As the first light of dawn began to streak the horizon, Chara slipped from Joseph's bed, and with the sweetest, longest kiss left him lying, fully satisfied, to creep back to her own bedchamber where she fell into a deep contented sleep.

## Chapter 25

# Denouement

(dā- ,nü-'mä–*noun:* the final resolution of the intricacies of a plot.)

CHARLES AWOKE IN THE PREDAWN HOURS OF THE NIGHT. He turned over and reached for the familiar comfort of Joseph beside him, but found the bed empty, save for himself. A waxing gibbous moon cast long shadows across the floor in the room just outside the bed chamber. Charles grew concerned. More and more frequently Joseph would leave the bed they shared, returning to his decoy room designed to hide their love affair from Chara. Joseph explained that he experienced disturbing dreams that caused fitful sleep. He told Charles that when the dreams woke him, he chose to finish the night in his separate bed in order to not disturb Charles whose work grew more demanding as his position in the party rose.

Charles worried about Joseph, remembering how his own dear mother experienced the same fitful sleep and frightening nightmares brought on by pain shortly before her death. He hoped that this fate would not also befall Joseph. He knew that he could never endure the loss of the one person who loved him as much, and perhaps even more than his dearly departed Ma.

Charles wiped a tear from his eye with the back of his hand wondering if he should check on Joseph. He didn't want to disturb him in case he had returned to sleep, until he heard sounds coming through the closet the two rooms shared. Charles thought that maybe he could comfort his lover and help him out of the dreams that haunted his nightly rest.

Charles shivered from the early spring chill as he placed his bare foot on the floor beside the bed. He did not waste time in search of his dressing gown or bed slippers, but instead walked silently across the thick Persian rug onto the bare floor in front of the closet door wearing only his nightshirt.

He continued to hear sounds of distress from the other room, bed springs squeaked as Joseph tossed in his sleep. Charles quietly opened the closet door and pushed aside the garments hanging in the way to hide the secret passage into his lover's room. Once all the way inside the closet he heard hard breathing.

"Oh, my poor Joseph," he thought, "He must suffer so."

He wanted to rush in to hold his poor Joseph. Knowing that his selfless lover thought only of him, Charles was pained by the idea of Joseph leaving him to his sleep while he himself suffered alone through the night. Charles reached for the door handle from inside the closet and began to slowly turn it. Then he heard something unfamiliar. He heard what sounded like a woman sighing, followed by a soft coo. Charles opened the closet door just wide enough to see the tall bed in the moonlight.

Charles stood in the shadow of the closet witnessing his lover and his wife in lustful embrace. He stepped slightly forward thinking he should become enraged and try to stop them but could not for the life of him muster that response. Instead he felt only hopeless, endless, abject misery of an unfathomable depth. He took a small step forward, but when the moonlight reached his eyes, his wish to conceal himself drove him back into the shadows. Just a few feet away, Joseph and Chara made love.

Charles stood watching in his nightshirt, wringing his hands in utter grief. He had lost Joseph. The friendly companionship and security that Chara had brought to their home dissolved before his eyes in grunts and quiet moans.

Like a beaten dog, Charles slipped back through the closet to the master bedroom. He sat on the red velvet gentleman's chair staring off toward the empty bedchamber where he and Joseph had lived together as lovers for years. He continued to wring his hands, trying to determine what he should do next as the sun began to rise on the early April day.

In the first light of morning, Chara kissed Joseph sweetly on his lips, then slipped out of his bed to sneak back to her own before Charles began to stir. Joseph smiled contentedly, and—rubbing his eyes—sat up in bed. To his horror he saw that the closet door stood open about two feet. Just enough to have the entire bed in view.

"Oh Jesus!" Joseph exclaimed. "Charles!" He rose quickly, grabbing his dressing gown and rushing down the hall to the master bedroom. Finding it locked, and fearing for what Charles might do, Joseph beat on the door shouting for Charles to open it.

Chara, startled by the row, huddled in her own bed frightened by the shouting and banging. Though by this time her English had become fluent, she still could not quite discern what the brothers' shouting indicated. They had each locked their bedroom doors. Charles would never have come for her in the night. He had made that very clear after their first and only night in his bed. She thought it unlikely that Charles may have discovered her nightly encounters with Joseph. She listened for a clue to the trouble, but as angry voices turned to mournful sobs, they grew more muted. Chara decided to remain behind her locked door until the crisis passed.

No matter how Joseph pleaded, Charles refused to unlock the bedroom door. Joseph returned to his room and made his way inside through the secret passage in the closet. He found Charles in the chair staring mournfully forward as he wrung his red hands furiously. Joseph rushed to the chair and knelt before Charles, reaching for his hands and pleading.

"Charles! Charles!"

Charles lifted his foot and angrily kicked Joseph with such force that he tumbled backward. Charles rose, red-faced, from the chair with a fury that Joseph had never seen.

"I *saw* you!" He growled, "I saw you with *HER!*"

"Jesus!" Joseph said getting up from the floor, "Please! It doesn't mean I love you less. It means we can *all* be a family."

"You BASTARD!"

Charles flew at him with arms and hands flailing for Joseph's face. He threw him back to the floor, pulling fistfuls of hair from Joseph's head. Joseph stood up and rushed at Charles, landing several blows to his face and belly. Charles crumpled to the floor, weeping. "Bastard! Bastard!" He repeated. "How could you betray me so cruelly?"

Joseph slumped into the red chair and put his head in his hands, trembling.

"I'm sorry Charles. I'm sorry. I love you both." He said, "God help me I love you both."

"I want her out of my house!" Charles, still furious screamed, "Out today!"

Joseph pleaded, "Where would she go? We are her only family on God's green earth. You can't send her to the streets!"

"She can whore with some other man, NOT MINE!"

"*Yours!!!*" Joseph was incredulous, "Is that what I am! YOUR man? Your toy? Your property?"

Joseph turned away then flew back around angrily, "I *belong* to no man! I refuse to have another possess me ever again in my life! I am my *own* man, and if you send her away you will never see me again for the rest of your life! You will die alone and in misery a lonely, bitter old Nancy!"

Joseph stormed from the room and returned to his own— slamming the door violently, muttering obscenities, and turning the key in the lock. Then he stomped to the closet where he slammed that door with equal force, then pushed the bureau, scraping across the hardwood floor to block the closet door and the connection to Charles.

Chara cowered in her locked room hoping against all hope that Charles did not have another key. She could now tell that the men fought over her affair with Joseph, but so much of their conversation confused her. She always knew that the brothers had an unusually close, and affectionate relationship, but she had nothing with which to compare it, having never known brothers either back in Greece, or in America. The closest thing to a sibling she had experienced occurred with Birdie during her passage to America several years prior. Though they corresponded following her departure, they stopped within a year as Chara immersed herself in her home and life as Mrs. Charles Davidson.

She knew that she had betrayed her husband with his brother but couldn't understand the shouts of belonging to each other. She knew that *she* belonged to Charles. But after their wedding night, she also knew that she repulsed him. She thought a life of hunger had made her too skinny for an American man's taste. He made an excuse to not make love with her that night or any other, though she knew that she herself caused his disgust.

Charles paced furiously back and forth in the master bedroom as Joseph dressed to go out. Without a word, Joseph stomped down the stairs two at a time and flew through the front door, slamming it behind him. He stood in the street trying to figure out what to do next as a Polish couple passed on the sidewalk smiling at him.

Joseph managed an awkward smile, before heading to the North-west Plank Road—now called Milwaukee Avenue—for a cup of coffee laced with a couple of shots of whiskey. He stayed away all day, and well into the evening to punish Charles.

Charles called out to Chara through her locked door, his voice filled with rage and disdain.

"Wife!"

Chara shuddered. He had never referred to her as "wife" unless introducing her to his political colleagues or constituents.

"Come out and make coffee and breakfast for your husband!"

She knew she deserved a beating but feared what Charles might do in anger. Saying nothing in return, she dressed nervously. She waited a long time to hear the sound of his angry footsteps on the stairs before she opened her door. If she had to endure a beating at least it would not take place at the top of the long staircase where she could tumble to her death.

As quietly as possible, she descended the stairs watching Charles fume with rage as he lit his pipe. She had never seen him smoke in the morning either. Her terror grew.

Chara avoided walking directly past him and slipped quickly down the hallway along the staircase, into the dining room, then nearly sprinted into the kitchen. Listening for any sounds of movement, Chara tied her apron around her waist, and lit the modern gas stove. She put the cast iron skillet on the burner to heat up, and the kettle on to boil. Then she poured coffee beans from the Maxwell House can into the stone mortar and began grinding the beans as quietly as possible with the wooden pestle.

When the kettle whistled, she poured the boiling water over the coffee in the steel press and set it aside to steep.

Chara set the asbestos toaster on the stove and removed a loaf of bread from the copper breadbox. She took a great long knife from the block, sharpened it on the stone, and then checked to make sure Charles remained in the parlor. She saw him, calmer, reading last night's paper and puffing on his pipe. Chara returned to her work. She cut slices from the loaf, wrapped it back in a cotton towel and returned it to the breadbox. Then she opened the icebox in the back wall and removed a slab of bacon. Using the same sharp knife, Chara cut several long slices from the fatty pork. It sizzled as she dropped it into the hot skillet. She selected two large eggs from the bowl on the table and broke them carefully into the grease to cook alongside the bacon.

Chara placed the slices of bread carefully on the toaster to brown. She used a fork to turn the bacon and a flat spoon to flip the eggs. As they cooked, Chara used the fork to flip the bread over to toast both sides. Then she took butter, salt and pepper, sugar and cream and quietly placed them on the long table in the dining room.

Chara returned quickly to the kitchen to transfer the food from the heat onto a china plate before any of it overcooked. She removed the bacon last because she knew Charles liked it hard and crispy. Then she pushed the coffee plunger down in the pot. She poured the hot coffee into a cup, placed it on a saucer, and gingerly carried both breakfast and coffee to the dining room table. Calling to Charles to come eat, she disappeared around the corner back into the kitchen to pour herself a cup of coffee to drink at the kitchen table. She feared sitting alone at the table with Charles, dreading what he might do or say without Joseph there to defend her.

Charles took his time finishing an article about the World's Columbian Exposition that had recently opened. He had hoped to attend with Joseph and Chara all dressed in their finery catching every eye as they promenaded up the Midway. Now, it seemed all that was dashed to smithereens due to the awful betrayal of Joseph and Chara, and under his own roof, only steps away from where he slept unsuspecting their treachery. He grew angry again as he sat down before the food Chara had prepared for him.

"Wife!" he called again angrily.

Chara poked her head around the corner of the kitchen door, frightened.

"Do you need something Charles?" she asked meekly.

"Will you not sit at the table with your husband?" he said threateningly.

Chara picked up her coffee cup and walked tentatively to the table. She chose a chair at the opposite end, far away from Charles and his ferocity. A beast that he had hidden away for as long as she had known him had broken free and sat ready to pounce and devour her at any moment. His face was red, nearly purple with rage. His foot bounced nervously under the table, jiggling the lace tablecloth. Chara said nothing, barely sipped her now-tepid coffee, watching his every nuance for any sign that she should run.

Charles ate his food without comment. Normally he would thank her and tell her how delicious it tasted, but this morning he chewed silently while glaring at her. Finally, he pushed his plate away and spoke.

"Tonight, you will come to MY bed, Wife." his voice sounded more like a growl than his normal voice.

Chara became anxious. She wished he would just say her name the way both he and Joseph mispronounced it. She had never corrected them, seeing it as a new name for a new life. Now she wished Charles would say it instead of addressing her as "Wife." She knew it indicated his contempt for her and his ownership of her. She felt a very real threat in the cold, angry way he spoke at her.

Charles pushed his chair back and removed himself abruptly from the table. He took his pipe and newspaper and climbed the stairs. She rose and stood in the hallway looking up the stairs and listening for his footsteps to move down the hall. She heard his bedroom door open, then slam and lock. Chara remained there, terrified, wondering if Joseph was gone for good, leaving her to whatever terrible punishment awaited her in the hands of Charles.

She returned to the kitchen and cleaned up the breakfast dishes. She put on her hat and jacket, took money from the jar for household supplies, then pulled on her gloves and retrieved her shopping basket from the corner of the back porch. Chara walked in the April sun the two blocks to the market. As the streetcar clanged past, she contemplated using the grocery money for an escape into the city. She quickly abandoned that thought, realizing that she had no place else to go. Instead she hoped that Joseph would have found his way home before she had finished the marketing. The grocer greeted her in a friendly way as Mrs. Davidson. She managed a smile wondering if she should tell him of her fear.

"What would I say?" she wondered, "I can't tell him my husband might beat me for sleeping with his brother."

She knew of course he would agree with Charles, and probably never greet her again, but shun her like the villagers did to her mother and her so long ago.

*Besides,* she thought, *I have it coming. I am, after all, the whore my mother suspected.*

Forcing back both tears and memories, Chara purchased a fresh whole chicken, carrots, potatoes, and some fresh herbs. She splurged on expensive celery that had just come into season. She hoped that maybe a delicious meal, along with a little time, might help calm Charles' anger.

Chara took her time returning home. She did not relish the thought of finding herself back in the tension-, anger-, and fear-filled house. She entered through the back porch in case Charles had returned to the parlor in her absence. She found that Joseph had not come home and wondered if he ever would. Chara pushed the thought out of her mind, tied her apron, and began preparing the evening meal.

She tore hunks of day-old bread and tossed them in a bowl with salt, pepper, and the herbs, and placed it in the sun to dry out. While the skillet heated up on the stove, she sharpened the steel knife for the second time that day before slicing onions and celery. She scooped a dollop of butter and another of bacon grease into the skillet and watched it melt. Then she scraped the onion and celery into the pan to soften. The kitchen began to fill with a delicious aroma as Chara stirred the vegetables into the pan.

While they cooked, Chara removed a glass bottle of milk from the icebox and poured a small amount into a tin cup. She put it next to the burner on the stove to warm. Next she opened a can of yeast and scooped some in a crockery bowl. When the milk had warmed enough, Chara stirred it into the bowl of yeast and placed it on the window seat in the warm sun to bubble.

She washed the chicken with cold water in the kitchen sink and pulled the few remnants of feathers that remained around the wings after the butcher's wife had plucked it, placed it in another bowl covered with a damp towel and squeezed it into the icebox along with the milk. Then Chara returned to the stove. She scraped the vegetables and every drop of the pan drippings into the bowl of bread and tossed it together. Steam rose in clouds as she poured a glass of water into the hot skillet. She stirred it, then poured the liquid into the bowl of dry bread, mixed it with her hands, and set that aside. When the yeast and milk bubbled, she added handfuls of flour and salt and kneaded it on the kitchen table until it felt soft and elastic. From her girlhood, she remembered how to pat and toss the dough to make flatbread. Her neighbor in Chicago showed her how to make American bread to please Charles and Joseph. She found that she too preferred the soft, white spongy American bread far more that Greek flatbread. She baked nearly every day.

Chara did not know what to do with herself while the bread rose. She did not want to venture into the parlor or any place in the house other than the kitchen for fear that she would arouse Charles and create even more tension. She sat at the kitchen table, then decided to sit outside in the early spring sunshine. The air still had a chill to it, so Chara took Yaya's shawl from its hook on the back porch, pulled it around her shoulders and went out back to sit on the steps.

Occasionally she returned to the kitchen to knead the bread dough, returning as quickly as possible to her place in the yard. Chara listened to the now-familiar sounds of the growing city. She heard dogs barking, people laughing and talking, and the clang of the streetcar bell. She saw the growing neighborhood where new homes seemed to sprout up every day. She remembered how difficult all this noise seemed as the neighborhood grew. She recalled how different it sounded from the village of her childhood. She did not miss the cruelty or the hunger, but did miss Papou's laughter, and Yaya's warm loving smile. She even missed Mitéra before life had broken her spirit and her body. Chara shook herself out of her melancholy and returned to the kitchen to finish the meal.

The kitchen smells had enticed Charles back to the parlor. He ignored Chara as he retrieved a short glass from the cupboard and poured brown liquor into it nearly to the top. He returned to his chair next to Joseph's empty one and sipped and stewed, looking out the front windows at the street. Chara suspected that he watched for Joseph hoping nearly as much as she for his return.

Joseph found himself wandering the streets downtown. He had ridden the streetcar for more than an hour to get as far away from Charles as possible. He recalled meeting Charles for lunch at the dawn of his independent life after escaping his drunk father and cruel brothers. He thought that maybe the ragged, and toothless old man hawking papers on the corner might be his brother Brian, if he wasn't already dead. He recalled how the man who had paid him for sex and taught him everything he knew about sexual pleasure had staked a claim on him even before he'd had a chance to grow out of childhood. He grew angry as he thought about how somebody had owned him at every stage of his life. Despite his misguided thinking he had never truly experienced freedom. Even Charles, whom he loved, felt ownership of Joseph. He turned into a tavern and began to drink.

～

Charles fumed in the parlor. He would punish both Joseph and Chara. He knew Joseph loved Chara, he could see it every day in the way they looked at one another. How had he been so stupid? He had assumed that Joseph loved Chara platonically the same way he did. He would hurt Joseph by hurting Chara. He intended to have his way with her that night roughly and noisily, hopefully with Joseph listening helplessly in the next room. He wanted Joseph to feel the humiliation that he had felt when he chanced upon them together the night before. He did not relish the thought of brutalizing Chara. Her birdlike body repulsed him. He found nothing about her or any other woman that could arouse him. He hoped that his anger and vengeance would serve that purpose when the moon rose.

Chara patted the bread into round rolls and placed them in the oven on a baking sheet. Then she stuffed the chicken with the bread mixture and sewed it inside. She put the chicken in a roasting pan and waited for the rolls to brown. Meanwhile she selected a sharp paring knife and began to peel the potatoes. A terrible fear in her heart brought a fluttery feeling as she recalled the beating she received as a little girl for eating the seed potatoes. Squeezing her eyes shut, she called on the ghost of Yaya to please not allow Charles to beat her too harshly that night. She looked at the clock, dreading the passing time.

Joseph, now drunk, staggered back into the street toward the streetcar. He would not leave tonight but wait until he could withdraw money from the bank, then he and Chara could slip away to Saint Louis together—escaping Charles' wrath.

Charles and Chara ate in silence as the sun set over the city. She could barely swallow, anticipating what Charles had in store for her. He drank more whiskey during the meal which caused his eyes to become cloudy and cold.

Chara stood to clear the dishes as the tall clock in the hall struck seven.

"Leave them!" Charles demanded, "Leave them there and come with me."

Chara, shaking with fear, followed him as he walked slowly up the eighteen stairs. He stopped at the top and told her to get into her dressing gown. Entering the small room Chara attempted to close the door, but Charles blocked it with his foot.

"Take off your clothes now." he said with slurred speech and terrifying eyes.

Embarrassed and filled with terror, Chara undressed as he watched, sneering, teetering in the doorway. She felt repulsive as she watched his cruel eyes assess her trembling body. Opening the wardrobe, Charla chose a nightgown. There, hanging side by side, she saw the silk gown Joseph had given her on her wedding night, and the embroidered gown Birdie gave her on the passage to America. Choking back a sob, she ran her fingers quickly over Joseph's soft gift, then quickly chose, and pulled the nightgown that Birdie had given her over her head. Then Chara pivoted, shivering before her furious husband.

"This way!" Charles grabbed Chara roughly by the wrist and drew her into his bedroom. He slammed the door shut, turned the key in the lock and put it in his vest pocket. He made her stand barefoot and shivering while he sat in the red chair contemplating his next move. Should he whip her with a belt until her soft skin bled from the welts? More than pain, he wanted to humiliate her in recompense for the belittle-ment he had felt watching her whoring with Joseph. With growing rage, he rushed toward her and pushed her back onto the white comforter, onto the bed he shared with Joseph. She flopped down like a rag doll without attempting to defend herself at all. This startled Charles, spiking his furor.

"You filthy whore!" he screamed as he tugged at his trousers, "I will show you who you really are!"

Chara already knew who she really was. She had known it from the first time her Mitéra had brought home extra food. Though she denied it then, she came to understand that her survival required payment to a whore, her own Mitéra. Chara turned her head and closed her eyes and Charles pushed up her nightgown and thrust her legs apart.

Seeing her womanhood there spread out on his bed, Charles retched. She recognized the disgust on his face as he stumbled to the washbasin where he vomited his dinner and the many glasses of whiskey he had consumed that day. Chara did not dare move a muscle, nor speak, but lay fully exposed, shivering in the chilly evening air.

Charles slumped back into the red velvet chair in full view of Chara with vomit on his chin, and his flaccid manhood dangling out of his opened trousers. He began to weep. He couldn't keep Joseph and couldn't beat Chara. He couldn't even humiliate her. Instead, he humiliated himself. His life was over. As terrible grief again washed over him Charles said softly, "I do not deserve to live."

Frozen in her own position of shame, Chara remained still. Consumed by fear, Chara could not make out the meaning of Charles' words. She feared that any movement might force her angry husband to hurt her more.

"Cover yourself up woman," he said shouted, "I am done with you."

Chara crawled toward the head of the bed and slipped under the sheets. Her body shivered. She tucked her cold feet underneath herself in an attempt to warm them. Chara did not dare to sleep as long as Charles remained in the chair. She lay silently, praying to hear the sound of Joseph returning home. She knew the key to the room was in Charles' vest pocket. Hearing him snore, she had no intention to risk waking him by fumbling for it. His head fell forward in a stupor. As the sunlight abandoned the treetops outside the window, Chara's breathing relaxed and her eyelids grew heavy.

Charles woke with a snort. Disoriented, his head snapped up as he tried to recall why he sat in the chair with his pants open. Then seeing Chara sleeping peacefully in his bed—her long black hair across the pillows he shared with Joseph—he remembered. Humiliation at her whoring with Joseph returned. Disgust at her female parts filled Charles with renewed rage. A seething hatred rose from the depths of hell, sped through his veins, and into his still-drunk mind.

Charles stood as quietly as he could on disobedient feet and slipped through the closet into Joseph's room. Joseph, still in his business suit, lay snoring on his bed. Charles crept out the door, into the hall, and downstairs. He lit a lamp in the kitchen to find the remnants of last night's dinner strewn on table and sink. He spotted the long carving knife near the breadbox. Picking it up, he fingered the cold steel blade. Scraping the edge on his thumb, Charles found it exceedingly sharp. Silently carrying that knife through the parlor, up the stairs, he stepped deliberately down the hall to his bedroom. He didn't dare run the risk of waking Joseph by slipping through the closet again. Turning the handle quietly, he found it locked. Then he remembered the key in his vest pocket. As carefully as he could, Charles unlocked the door and entered the room. He left the door ajar and walked to the foot of the bed. Chara, his usurper, lay sleeping.

Tears streamed down his face as he drew closer to her head. Chara lay so vulnerable, so peaceful, and, in Charles' mind, so unwholesome there. Whore. Home breaker.

*He wished more than anything that she had been content to be a sister. Then, none of this perversion would have happened. He wished to God that their arrangement could just go back to the joyful days when Chara*

*first arrived. They had enjoyed each other's company, as the brothers'*
*popularity in the city increased. But all that was lost, never to return.*

Charles raised the knife above his head, noticing it catch the
fading moonlight. Then, with all the force he had, he thrust it deeply
into the sleeping woman's chest. An odd sound escaped through the
hole he had made. She opened her eyes and looked at him, pleading in
horror as he raised the knife and thrust it into her body again. Her body
lurched, but she didn't try to defend herself. She just lay there, allowing
him to stab her over and over as the life melted from her open eyes, and
her blood drained from her body turning the white bedclothes bright
red.

Exhausted, Charles dropped the knife beside the bed, backed up,
and plopped down into the red chair. His hands, dripping with Chara's
blood, hung limply on each side of the chair. Charles stared at the
ghastly sight, feeling nothing but grief. Outside the window, the sun
touched the trees.

Before long, Joseph pushed the master bedroom door open.
Seeing Charles in the chair in shock and dripping with blood, Joseph
ran to him.

"Jesus! Charles! What in the name of God happened to you!"

Charles, eyes glazed as if in a trance, stared straight ahead toward
the bed. When Joseph turned to the tableau of death on the bed, he
shrieked in agony.

"Oh sweet Jesus! Charles! What did you do?"

Stumbling to the bed, Joseph wailed, "Chara! No! NO! NO!"
through tears and sobs. "Sweet Chara! How could you have done this
to her?"

He turned back toward Charles, "You will hang for this! You will
hang! Oh, sweet Jesus! We will both hang!"

Joseph fell to the floor at Charles' feet, saying, "I brought this on,
I did this. Charles. Not Chara. Oh God in Heaven, not Chara."

Joseph sobbed, resting his head in Charles' lap. Catatonic,
Charles sat without moving, his hands hanging limply over the arms of

the velvet chair.

⁓

Suddenly Joseph sat bolt upright. "We have to do something about this."

Charles did not respond. Demanding engagement, Joseph slapped his brother to bring him to his senses. Unshaken, Charles directed his uninhabited eyes to Joseph. Charles' body remained limp and defeated.

"We can take care of this," Joseph went on. "We have to hide the body and dispose of all these bloody bed linens. Charles. I need your help." Joseph hatched a scheme to remove bricks from the basement wall to dig out a void big enough to bury Chara. He carried a lamp into the basement and found a place behind the furnace wall. He took a pick and began stabbing at the mortar between the bricks. At last, a brick fell to the floor. Then another. Soon he had opened a space big enough to hide Chara's bloody corpse. Joseph used a coal shovel he found resting against the furnace to dig the black dirt out of the opening.

When he felt the hole would suffice, Joseph ran back up the stairs to find Charles still sitting in his chair facing the lifeless, gruesome corpse of Chara. Joseph ran past him and tried to lift Chara from the bed. Though she was small, he could not lift her alone.

"Charles," he said grunting, "Please. You've got to help me, or we will both hang!"

"I do not deserve to live." Charles said beginning to whimper like a child.

"Charles!" Joseph shouted, "I *need* your help. I do not want to hang! Please help me."

Charles slowly rose from the chair he had occupied for hours and stepped to the bed. He grabbed Chara under one arm, and Joseph grabbed the other. Together they walked backwards out to the room and down the upstairs hall dragging her lifeless body between them. Her tiny feet thumped as they dragged her down each stair, leaving a trail of blood behind them.

"Jesus!" Joseph muttered as they carried her down the down-stairs hall toward the basement door. It had swung closed after Joseph returned upstairs for the corpse. Struggling to keep hold of her blood-slick corpse, Joseph pushed the basement door open with his hip. They pulled her down the open wooden stairs, past the coal bin, and laid her down on the cold floor at the foot of her newly-dug grave in the wall.

Charles whined and wept as they shoved her into the cold, damp earth. Joseph scooped dirt from the basement floor and packed it in the spaces around her, packing it tightly with the coal shovel while Charles stood weeping.

"There." Joseph said. "Now we need to clean up the blood. Charles, get a bucket and soapy water to scrub the hallway and stairs while I fit these bricks back in the wall and take care of all this extra dirt." Charles just stood there, "Come on," Joseph took him by the hand and pulled him up the stairs toward the kitchen.

Dinner dishes and leftover food still cluttered the kitchen and dining room. Joseph ignored it, retrieving a bucket and rag from the back porch. Filling the bucket with soapy water, he led Charles to the top of the basement stairs.

"Start here and scrub every spot from here to the bedchamber. Get busy! We must have this finished by nightfall."

Charles knelt and began mopping up the sticky blood. The water in the bucket turned pink, then red, as Charles scrubbed all the while repeating to himself, "I do not deserve to live. I should crawl on my belly like a snake. I am no good. I do not deserve to live."

He changed the water before starting on the stairs. Climbing one step at a time, each of the eighteen steps.

"I am a snake," he growled, "no better than the foulest serpent." He dropped the bloody rag and bit down hard on the edge of a stair. "I do not deserve to live. Even God cannot help me. I do not deserve to live." He washed the bloody floor next to the bed as Joseph added the last touches of mortar to the wall.

Charles stood next to the scene of his terrible damning deed and noticed the knife still lying on the floor where it had fallen under the bed. He picked it up and sat on the bed reeking of blood and death. Charles closed his eyes and cut deeply into first one wrist and then the other.

He sat on the edge of the bed as his blood ran out and intermingled with the blood of his victim, Chara. The room began to swim, as he passed out and fell backward onto the bloody linens. There his lifeblood drained from his body as he died in the same place as Chara.

Joseph climbed the basement stairs and noticed that Charles had cleaned up the blood in the downstairs hallway. Not seeing him on the stairs he assumed that Charles had gone up to finish in the master bedroom. Joseph looked at his trembling hands covered in dirt, blood, and mortar.

"Jesus!" he muttered, "Jesus, Mary, and Joseph! You're shaking like a leaf."

He went into the kitchen, turned on the tap, and began scrubbing his hands and arms. Realizing that he was covered from head to foot he turned off the tap and went to the bottom of the stairs.

"Charles." He called, "I'm covered with mud from the basement. I don't want to track it over the floor. I'm going to jump in a quick bath, then I will help with the rest of this mess. I'll only be a couple of minutes."

Charles didn't answer. Joseph returned to the basement overcome with dread. He tried to not look at the place in the wall where they had hidden Chara's corpse. But could not look away. He stoked the furnace with a shovel of coal feeling Chara watching him from beyond the wall. Then he stripped, even removing his underwear. He rolled his filthy clothes into a bundle and shoved them into the blazing furnace, shut the furnace door, and sprinted up the basement stairs nearly losing his footing twice.

Joseph opened the warm water tap, climbed into the tub as it filled, and began scrubbing his skin so hard that it turned beet red. As he poured water directly from the tap over his head, he began to sob uncontrollably.

*Sweet God in Heaven! Poor, poor Chara. What have I done! What have I done?* He thought about Charles. *What have I done?* Then he spoke aloud, "Not me! Charles! Charles did it! Charles murdered Chara, not me."

He began to sob again, remembering that his actions had driven Charles to such a terrible act. He felt that no matter how hard he tried to be his own man he was fated to always be at the mercy of somebody else. He had no real hand in his own fate but existed only in the shadow of others. Then he thought of Charles and the mess that still needed tending.

"I will not hang for this!" he shouted as he pulled the plug. Watching the blood and dirt swirl around the drain Joseph stepped out of the tub and wrapped in his bathrobe. Seeing Chara's robe still hanging there, he began to weep again, then pulled himself together, and headed upstairs to help Charles. Joseph called to Charles as he climbed the stairs and began to grumble when Charles did not answer.

Joseph burst into the master bedroom, where he was met with yet another horrific scene. He fell to his knees screaming beside the lifeless body of his lover and friend sprawled in a pool of blood on their bed. Charles' vacant eyes stared at the ceiling, his arms stretched out to each side, and his legs dangled over the side of the bed.

Joseph began to retch.

He crawled to the red velvet gentleman's chair across the room and sat weeping for what seemed like hours. Joseph was certain he would hang.

*One corpse in the basement, and now another in the bed,* he thought, *What will I do without you Charles? I am all alone.* Then Joseph began to think. *If I could dispose of Chara's things, I could pack my own and disappear, maybe take a train to Saint Louis. Nobody knows Chara except those who know us. They will think we ran off together They will think that Charles, distraught at being cuckolded by his brother, took his own life! It could work, but I will have to move quickly.*

In Chara's room, Joseph gathered her clothes. He burned them, along with the hall runner in the furnace, as he had his own bloody clothes. Next, he emptied his wardrobe and packed as much as would fit into two leather bags. When he unearthed the letters written years ago by the picture bride, he dropped them in the bottom of her own trunk, added other papers and receipts, and lugged it up to the attic.

Joseph returned to the master bedroom. He took the silver handled cane that Charles carried when they first met from its place by the closet. That closet. The one he slipped through nightly to join his lover, and the one through which Charles witnessed the ultimate betrayal. Then Joseph shut and locked the bedroom door and slipped through the closet for the last time. He couldn't bear to look at Charles as his body had begun to stiffen with rigor mortis.

Joseph worked quickly through the night. He knew he had very little time before someone would notice Charles' absence and come calling. When he thought he had burned all signs of Chara and collected his own belongings, he cleaned up the dining room and kitchen, making sure everything was in its place.

When morning came Joseph sat for a few last minutes scanning the ruins of his life with Charles and then Chara.

*Well*, he thought, *I will survive. After all, as my father told me; I am good at one thing: looking pretty ... and pitiful.*

Joseph locked the door behind him and hurried to catch the Montrose streetcar to the bank, then to Union Station.

# Chapter 26
# Perorate

(per- ϵ- ,rāt—*verb*: to bring a speech to a close with a formal conclusion.)

HAVING OPENED MYSELF to allow the spirits to share their memories with me, I decided to let them speak for themselves. Both Joseph and Chara obliged, but Charles remained aloof.

I have spent hours before my candles inviting Charles to reflect on his life and death. His story revealed itself to me in the context of the story of Joseph and Chara, but not once did Charles himself reveal anything to me about his childhood or family. I met him the day he met Joseph. I think that is when Charles himself would like to think his life actually began.

I think that Charles still exists in a state of denial regarding his own death by suicide. It took many years for that to become clear, and it only did as Chara and Joseph revealed their memories to me. Charles, it seems, remains the only one of the three lovers who still feels tremendous remorse. I sense a good deal of self-blame and self-loathing from Charles. As of this writing, I have not been able to help him. I will remain open to him if ever he recognizes a need for help letting go of his guilt and grief, but as for now he remains in the hell of his own creation.

I cannot shake the feeling that Charles continues to hide something essential in an attempt to protect something, someone, or himself. I understand how he feels, having suffered the same reluctance to view my own childhood with clear eyes. I hope for him that he can someday feel release, much as I have. When we allow ourselves to forgive those we love for their frailties, those who may have disappointed or hurt us, we may at last find peace. There is even more power, I think, when we forgive ourselves for our own frailties, for our terrible mistakes and missteps, for hurting others, including the ones we love. When we accept ourselves, flaws and all, it may be that we not only experience peace, but become it, and share it with those around us, whether on this side of the veil, or one of the many others.

I appeal to Charles' own angels, ancestors, and guides to lead him out of the shadows of that closet in the old Portage Park house. I hope that they can now find their own peace in whatever might come next for them. I ask for love and understanding from all who hear this story for the poor souls who have waited more than a century to have their stories told.

# Chapter 27
# **Joseph**

MY FAILURE OF A FATHER RUINED EVERYTHING. My weakling of a mother ruined everything. My stupid, cruel, and violent brothers ruined everything. The rich man who used me to pleasure himself ruined everything. Charles, in his weakness and jealousy, ruined everything. Chara's innocence and love ruined everything. I have suffered as a victim of my fate from the day I came wailing into this world with only a small chance of survival after ruining my mother's body, nearly killing her and myself in the process. Fate punished me whenever I sought love or pleasure for myself. In the end, God himself ruined everything.

As I locked the door to my home in Chicago for the last time, I knew I would make a clean getaway. Plenty of people suspected that Chara and I hid a secret affair. Even the Polish neighbor lady watched us with disapproving eyes as we gaily walked off arm in arm to do the marketing. She noticed how Chara looked at me adoringly. If anyone had the gumption to dig deeper, they would even find Dr. Moore at the drugstore who could confirm our affair.

All the pieces fell into place perfectly. When someone inevitably discovered Charles dead, they assumed he killed himself in response to Chara, his wife, running away with his brother. I cared nothing for how harshly people would judge us as adulterers. It would serve as gossip in the neighborhood and at City Hall for years to come. As for me ... It would not affect my future possibilities at all. Charles made his own bed. And I would not, under any circumstances, hang for his crime.

I procured a ticket to Saint Louis with enough money in my pocket to stay in a hotel for at least a month. I left the name Joseph Davidson behind the door I locked in Portage Park and took my mother's maiden name. The only remorse I felt was for poor Chara. She had no idea what fate had in store for her when we began corresponding. I loved her as much as I could love anyone. She gave me great joy and great pleasure. It was sad that, doing so, she sealed her own fate. God allowed no happiness in my life. Instead, God chose to punish all around me—to punish me for the sin of being born. For the sin of surviving.

I took a room at The Saint Louis Union Station Hotel. Union Station brought back memories of the first time I laid eyes on Cara, but that no longer mattered. I needed to make plans for the next permutation of my stolen life. I acquired a post office box at the station under my new name, then wrote a letter to my attorney.

Dear Sir,

I am writing to inform you that I have decided to relocate to Saint Louis. Though I never intended it to occur, my brother's wife Chara and I have fallen in love. Chara and Charles both suffered in a loveless marriage. I imagine that, after the initial shock, my brother will find relief in the dissolution of his most unhappy marriage.

Please inform Charles that it is not our intention to hurt him, but that we are hopelessly in love. Send him my regards, but do not reveal my location, nor the name under which I have secured this post box.

Sincerely,

Joseph Davidson

I posted the letter and waited for a response. Several weeks later I received a letter from my attorney. He regretted to inform me that my brother had been found dead in his bedchamber after taking his own life.

～

Dear Sir,

I cannot express the terrible grief your awful news had brought dear sweet Chara and myself. I had no notion that he would react so drastically. Poor Charles never possessed the fortitude of character needed to face disappointment. May God have mercy on his soul.

Chara and I will not return to Chicago. Neither she nor I could endure the scandal that will surely follow us the rest of our days. I trust that you will attend to all our affairs including dissolution of property, and sale of the house. Please forward proceeds from that sale to this post office box.

Sincerely,

Joseph Davidson

Feeling great relief, even glee after posting my request for receipt of the proceeds from the dissolution of Charles' and my property in Portage Park, I nearly skipped down the street on that bright June morning in Saint Louis. I had indeed made a clean getaway once again.

From surviving my violent birth, then my violent family, to the time I dug that rusted can of illicitly gotten money from under the filthy steps of the tenement house, to narrowly avoiding a thumping from self-righteous ruffians disapproving of men loving men, to The Great Conflagration itself providing an opportunity to assume a new identity as a Davidson brother, to acquiring a picture bride as cover for our unnatural love, to hiding that love by creating a secret passage between my room and Charles', to secretly loving Chara, to finding a doctor to rid Chara of the proof of our mutual infidelity to Charles, to concealing Chara's murder, and now escaping culpability for the death of Charles.... My life has been a string of clean getaways.

With that money in hand, I would never have to worry about securing employment or finding someone to keep me ever again in my life. I had earned every single penny for the years I endured a fate I never chose.

I met a wealthy businessman several years younger than myself at the hotel lobby. I found him charming and intriguing, and he, it seemed, thought the same of me. He always picked up the check when we dined together, which I made sure happened more often than not. I hoped to strike up a friendship with him to help tide me over until a check arrived from my attorney in Chicago.

With all this filling my head, I noticed him across the street less than half a block ahead. I called to him trying to get his attention hoping we could have lunch together. He did not hear me but kept walking briskly forward. I picked up my pace with my eyes fixed on him, still calling his name. Realizing he still couldn't hear me I skipped off the curb running to catch him.

Suddenly from out of nowhere I felt a great force throw my body to the ground. I found myself lying in the street as a crowd gathered around my twisted, mangled body crushed by a streetcar.

My lack of emotion surprised me. Everything felt strangely peaceful. I looked up the street to see the young man I pursued turn a corner and disappear.

At last, God got his way. In the end God, himself ruined everything.

# Chapter 28
# Chara

I AWOKE WITH A TERRIBLE ACHE as if someone had punched me in my chest. Opening my eyes, I saw Charles standing over me seething with rage. Then I saw the knife. I didn't focus on his face anymore but fixed my gaze on the blade in his hand. I watched him thrust it toward my body, but before it cut, I found myself standing beside the bed, watching. I noticed how easily the blade pierced my body and thought of how strange it seemed that I had sharpened it myself that very day. Not once, but twice. I experienced no pain, only curiosity as I watched the blood drain from my body. I felt amazed at the sheer amount of blood that my skin had contained only moments before.

I harbored no anger toward Charles as he stumbled backwards into the gentleman's chair by the closet, weeping. I understood his grief as he held his head in his bloody hands. I stood watching him for some time when I heard the voices of Papou, Yaya, and Mitéra calling my name. My heart filled with joy as I turned and saw them calling to me as they did when I was a child. I turned to run to them when Joseph entered the room.

I watched him react to my lifeless body lying in a pool of my own blood on the bed. I loved Joseph so. He loved me. I turned away from the family of my childhood and tried to talk to Joseph. He could not hear me. I left him and Charles to themselves, finding myself running along Lake Kopais when it was full of fish, birds, and life. I watched Papou throw his nets over the water from the shore ahead. I heard laughter and singing in my native tongue. I danced on the green hillsides and twirled among the spring wildflowers.

Suddenly I felt a powerful tug and again stood in the place of my demise. Joseph screamed at Charles, who appeared nearly lifeless himself, as they dragged my body from the bed. I walked behind them watching the terror in Joseph's face as they stumbled backwards down the hallway, past the alcove to Joseph's chamber, and past my own chamber door.

I heard Joseph ask if they could just pick me up, but Charles only shook his head, and so they dragged my limp, empty body down the stairs. For a moment I thought Charles could see me following behind as they dragged my body. He began to weep and say that he didn't deserve to live.

No one *deserves* to live, I mused. All of us, instead, are simply compelled to live. We are born. We suffer. We love. We feel joy and we feel pain. We connect and we feel great loss. We are here and then we are not. No one deserves to live. Life is simply something we each must endure.

I watched them drag me through the downstairs hallway, confused about where they were taking my body. I followed them down the basement stairs, but when I saw the grave Joseph had prepared for me, I resisted.

"NOOO!" I screamed in their faces. "Nooo! Please do not leave me here." But they did not hear me.

I watched Joseph hide my body behind the basement wall. I followed him up the stairs, then surprisingly found myself again in Charles' chamber. I watched him weep as he lifted the very same blade he had used to take my life. I watched as he cut deeply into his wrists. As his body slumped backwards on the bed, I felt him standing next to me. I saw him, but it seemed he could not see me. He stood wringing his hands with a grief wider and deeper than the ocean I had crossed long ago to come to America. I felt nothing but pity for him as I watched his spirit walk into the closet.

I observed Joseph panic when he found Charles' body stretched out on the bed like the crucified Christ. Then I watched him try to erase me. I saw him destroy all traces of my existence. He burned my things and papers bearing my name, save for a few. I felt such love for him when I saw that he didn't destroy the letters I had written to Charles, I now knew that Joseph had courted me from across the sea, not Charles. I knew it was Joseph I had fallen in love with, and Joseph I loved all along. I loved him more when I saw him put those letters in my own trunk along with other papers and receipts including the receipt from Dr. Moore. I took comfort knowing that he loved me. I knew that he could destroy my things, and hide my body, but that he would love me for the rest of his life. I watched him walk away forever, then I made my way up the stairs. Reaching the bedchamber, I turned and walked back down following the last path my body traveled. I walked that path for lifetimes determined to not simply disappear behind a brick wall.

I knew you could see me the first time I saw you. I wanted to talk to you, to tell you my story, but you were only a small child. What would you understand of love, jealousy, betrayal and murder? You were so small, so innocent. I imagined you as the babe I cast from my womb and knew I could not trouble you with my pain.

I troubled your father's dreams though. I saw in him the same gifts that you have but knew that he feared and struggled against his ability to *see*, thinking it evil. I told him my name; the way Joseph spoke it. I showed him the terrible crime committed against me. I did not want to be forgotten as if I had never lived.

I tried to show your mother, but she was protected by powerful spirits. She felt me, I know, but her protectors would never let me into her dreams. I know your siblings saw me, but they have forgotten me. Only you have kept me alive in your stories.

I am grateful that you have finally let fear fall away so you could allow me to tell my story.

I am Chara. Born into troubled times, I survived as best I could. I took great risks, and I found great love. I am worthy of being remembered. My story is worthy of telling.

Now with my words on your page I can listen for the voices of Papou, Yaya, and Mitéra calling me home. I can drift out of the shadows and into the light where perhaps I might even find Joseph.

I ask you to please help Charles escape from the hell he created for himself. I know he will appreciate it if you can. I hold no malice toward him. I wish only for peace for all of us imperfect souls.

Again, thank you for opening your heart and allowing me to share the memories of my life as Chara. May your life be filled with great love and many blessings.

# EPILOGUE

Since my earliest memories, I have been terrified by the ghosts of my childhood. Though I have told the stories thousands of times, I managed to block the spirits themselves from speaking to me. I am not afraid of ghosts, mind you. I encounter them all the time, and actually help them when I can. I try to help people who live with hauntings. I have encountered and faced elemental entities, even moving them with no fear or trepidation, confident in my ability to transverse dimensions in order to bring peace to both the entities and the humans with whom they interact, both alive and in spirit. It is only when I recall the elemental or interdimensional entities that tormented me as a little girl that I cringe and recoil in terror.

I am a storyteller. When I began this book, I intended to simply tell the tales as I had done so many times throughout my life. Everyone who listened loved the spookiness when I read what I had written, until I read one of the stories to my daughter. She wisely advised me to tell about myself, my family, and the circumstances in my life as I experienced these hauntings. She affirmed that this is *my* story; the story of how I became a gatekeeper.

This terrified me even more than the spirits themselves. I, like most humans who grew up in the last century, experienced deep trauma as a child, and still carry the scars that, when triggered, can send me spinning into a full-on PTSD panic attack. I had no desire to exorcise *those* demons. I had managed to exist in a comfortable state of denial for my whole life. Yet, as I wrote the stories, I felt all my demons and ghosts hovering nearby. They waited there for me to muster the courage to complete a journey that *something* set me on, perhaps even before my birth.

Much of my childhood trauma revolved around my gifted, but volatile father, who I adore with my whole heart. I feared that revealing his frailties to the world, when he had spent his life creating a persona of power and accomplishment, would break his heart. And perhaps my own. I did not want to expose him to any manner of disdain but wanted him to still remain the hero I loved forever. I also felt protective of my ancestors, not wishing them to suffer judgment. They deserve only empathy and understanding for their circumstances. My mother and father had told me many stories about my ancestors that—seen in today's moral framework—might seem appalling. Each of our individual identities lies firmly in our history, and our family history. We become the furtherance of their story, as our children and theirs become the furtherance of ours. I wanted to keep our reputation safe. I wanted to keep my father safe from scrutiny. I also did not want him to direct any anger toward me for telling family secrets. This kept me quiet for a lifetime.

Then, early last fall, my father died surrounded by all his loved ones. Even my mother came to his bedside, having been released temporarily and carried by ambulance from ICU suffering from her own life-threatening medical crisis, to visit her dying husband. When my father died, my mother grabbed hold of his shirttail and followed him out a month later. We buried them side by side in a tiny rural cemetery near their beloved summer home.

After their death, I knew the time had come for me to begin. I centered myself, cleared the energy around me, called on my angels and ancestors to protect me, and allowed the gate to open. I found that as I wrote I regained long-repressed memories. I felt amazing release as I told my story intertwined with the hauntings I experienced. Then something happened.

As I wrote about my experiences in all their imperfection, I began to feel spirits in my room. I awoke in the wee hours every night feeling them looming. I pushed them away, commanding them to let me sleep.

But when I awoke after these nightly encounters, I found that I had new memories. Not memories of dreams, but real memories. Memories of a time I didn't know. Memories not of my own experience, but of those who relentlessly disturbed my sleep. I began writing.

As I wrote I found the words falling onto the page without thinking, without planning. None of the stories in Part 2—that I furiously and compulsively wrote—had appeared in my outline or notes. They just happened like a stream of consciousness, sub consciousness, or other-consciousness if you will. I found myself describing places, events, and things I knew nothing about. After writing intricate descriptions I would ask someone to google information about a specific event, time or place. To my great astonishment my descriptions proved uncannily accurate, down to the names of streets, buildings, restaurants, and even people.

At first it freaked me out, as you might imagine. Then, when I realized that the spirits themselves were trying to speak through me, I just relaxed and let the story unfold. After writing for hours I would get up to stretch and walk around for a while to move my stiffened body. Then, after time away, I would return to the text to edit mechanics. When I read the words I had written, it felt as if I was seeing them for the first time. I would find myself so very saddened by the great tragedy that befell those formerly-terrifying spirits. I felt pity, understanding, and deep empathy for those poor, suffering souls.

Initially I searched for empirical evidence to support my revelations, but soon found that proof simply didn't matter. Chara did not need me to solve her murder, or even to give her body a proper burial. She simply wanted to prove to me and everyone that she had existed. She wanted me to remember, and to tell her story.

Joseph as well asked for nothing but understanding, and acknowledgment that he did the best he could, given the circumstances of his remarkable life. He just disappeared after Chara and Charles' death. Nobody ever spoke of him again other than to exclaim that the Davidsons were not good people. He only needed someone to hear his side of the story.

Charles still exists in a fog of guilt, shame, and denial. As far as I can tell, he continues to occupy the space that led to his demise. Charles does not need empirical proof. Charles needs only to forgive himself and acknowledge that he was and is worthy of compassion and love. I will keep myself available to him, and send him unconditional love, hoping that someday he may find peace.

I am grateful for the opportunity to tell this story as I remember it, and as I remember learning the stories of my ancestors. I am grateful for the spirits who terrified me but helped set me on this path.

As for the dark entity that tormented my father, and indeed my whole family, I know it is here still. It knows my name. It has tasted my skin and my soul. I do not fully understand its nature, but I have encountered it, and multiple other similar entities, throughout my life, all of them have recognized me. I think these beings dwell in another reality just outside human perception, a place held fast by an unseen gate. Perhaps extreme emotion such as violence, fear, anger, pain, or even love can crack open that gate, drawing these beings into the places between the worlds, or directly into the human space. I have heard others refer to these beings as demons, djinn, faeries, angels, Orishas, Earth Spirits, or other never-human beings.

I have stood at this gate on many occasions. Sometimes I have peered through with my feet planted firmly in the corporeal, and other times I have entered into a world beyond the mortal sphere. I have moved both spirit and human beings through that gate with love, and without fear. That is why I consider myself a gatekeeper, one of many gatekeepers on multiple sides.

I don't know if my journey began when my family brought me, as a baby, into a place where the gate had swung wide, exposing my developing brain and spirit to its possibilities. Or if it began even before my birth, planting me where I could grow. It really matters not at all. This is the first volume of stories from my life as a gatekeeper—the stories of my vivication, that which brought me to life.